READERS RESPOND TO *STEPHEN LIVES!*

"Your book is wonderful—both you and Stephen are wise, courageous souls. . . . An inspiration to us all."

—Kathy Woolway, Edison, New Jersey

"Your book is an inspiring example to all of us about how our pain can eventually be transformed into strength and wisdom. Whether or not you believe in an afterlife, I wholeheartedly recommend *STEPHEN LIVES!*"

—Colleen Loehr, M.D., Topeka, Kansas

"From the first time I glanced at your book it stayed on my mind until I went out and bought it. . . . I think it's an important book and I appreciate the courage it must have taken to write it. . . . Thank you."

—Bonnie Schmidt, New Berlin, Wisconsin

"Your book is one of the most important teaching tools on the planet at this time. Stephen's work is sure to heal and help all those who read it and absorb the excellent information regarding life on this side and the other. . . . May Stephen's words continue to flow through you with the truth and wisdom he fosters in the lives of others you have yet to meet."

—Rosemary Brown Sanders, Carmel, California

"My mother had no idea how I was feeling; she didn't know I was so unhappy. . . . Your book will really be a sort of guide so parents can be aware of what could happen. . . . I have never read such a special book as yours. It will be such an eye-opener to parents and adults in general."

—Jessica Albieri, age 21, Palm Harbor, Florida

"You have touched my life and helped me understand a little bit more of this journey. . . . You are an amazing woman, Anne."

—Sonia McClintic, Wichita, Kansas

For orders other than by individual consumers, Pocket Books grants a discount on the purchase of **10 or more** copies of single titles for special markets or premium use. For further details, please write to the Vice-President of Special Markets, Pocket Books, 1633 Broadway, New York, NY 10019-6785, 8th Floor.

For information on how individual consumers can place orders, please write to Mail Order Department, Simon & Schuster Inc., 200 Old Tappan Road, Old Tappan, NJ 07675.

STEPHEN LIVES!

My Son Stephen: His Life, Suicide, and Afterlife

ANNE PURYEAR

POCKET BOOKS
New York London Toronto Sydney Tokyo Singapore

POCKET BOOKS, a division of Simon & Schuster Inc.
1230 Avenue of the Americas, New York, NY 10020

Puryear, Anne
Stephen lives! : his life, suicide, and afterlife / Anne Puryear.
p. cm.
Includes bibliographical references.
ISBN: 0-671-53664-8
1. Stephen Christopher, 1958–1974 (Spirit)
2. Stephen Christopher, 1958–1974. 3. Puryear, Anne.
4. Suicide victims—United States—Biography. 5. Mothers—United States—Biography. 6. Teenagers—Suicidal behavior—United States—Case studies. 7. Spirit writings. I. Title.
BF1311.D43P87 1996
133.9'01'3—dc20 95-46023
CIP

First Pocket Books trade paperback printing April 1997

10 9 8 7 6 5 4 3 2 1

POCKET and colophon are registered trademarks of Simon & Schuster Inc.

Cover design by Brigid Pearson, photo courtesy of the author

Printed in the U.S.A.

THIS BOOK IS DEDICATED TO

GOD
For the gift of my life and His abiding love

My husband, Herb . . .
The kindest and most loving man I have ever known
and the love of my life . . . times.

My children, Bob, Andrea, and Debbie . . .
I am grateful to God for letting me be your mother.
"I'll love you forever, I'll like you for always."

My grandchildren, Melissa, Robert, Vanessa, and
Krystalyn . . .
I love being your grandmother. I adore each of you.

My very dear mother . . .
In whom I am well pleased. You have been the very
best mother for me. I love you.

My beloved son, Stephen . . .
Who graced my life with love for fifteen years and out
of whose pain and love came this story.

All the young lives cut short by suicide because for
those moments it hurt more to live than die.

The parents and families who survived the aftermath
of those deaths, or the death of any child. My deepest
admiration for your courage as survivors, and my
heartfelt understanding of your devasting pain.

ACKNOWLEDGMENTS

It is impossible to acknowledge fully my appreciation to all the people in my lifetime who have helped me in so many ways and contributed so much to my growth and understanding, which ultimately helped this book get birthed.

My husband Herb has encouraged, praised, and helped me, never faltering in his belief in me and my work. My children have been among my greatest teachers: Bob, my special first-born, Andrea, my dearest first daughter, and Debbie, my precious youngest, have made this journey that has sometimes been uphill, worthwhile. I am proud of them for the fine and loving souls they have become. My four grandchildren bring me hope for the future with their incredible love and zest for life.

My mother welcomed my birth singing, "Joy to the world, my daughter's come. . . ." This was the kind of love and adoration lavished on me all the days of my life. For that foundation of unconditional love, and for protecting me from having my spirit broken, I am forever thankful. My sister Alwayne, an outstanding professional artist, painted a portrait of Stephen that lifts my spirit each time I walk into my office. I am thankful for such a loving sister. My brother Dean, who is a really nice person, somehow survived childhood with me and deserves great credit for the restraint he used in not pulverizing me as I so deserved. My father joined Stephen in the spirit plane several years ago. He was always kind and loving to me. Thank you, Daddy.

Dennis Linehan is not only our administrative director, but a wonderful friend to me. Without his help and support, it would have been impossible to get this book written. No one works harder, with more caring and a better spirit. Elizabeth, his wife, deserves equal credit for enabling him to do the work he loves.

Bill Roberts has been there when I most needed an understanding and honest friend. He is one of the funniest men I have ever known and he heals me with his humor. He made invaluable suggestions and corrections on the original manuscript of this book.

Virginia Ryder is my treasured friend. She lent us her condo on Oahu, Hawaii, every summer so we could write and play. The major part of this book was written there. I am blessed to have her in my life.

Peg Linehan, who "retired" to Arizona, has been a lifesaver to us. Her energy and organization bring order to the chaos of our lives and offices. She is a jewel.

Don Wilson, a dear friend, has aided and encouraged us every step of the way. I gratefully acknowledge his incredible spirit, and all he has done to take this work forward.

No one could ask for better friends with more dedication and love than Stephanie and John Schroeder.

My love and thanks also to Pat Merrill, Ray and Lou Diekemper, Pat Hughes, Daphne Starr Bush, Bob McIver, Pat Harrison, Helen Mae Alexander, Richard Gerber, M.D., Diane Ladd, Dorothy Drew, Marcia and Don Harrison, Cec Storer, Dr. Terri Baltes, Elizabeth and Joe Chevola, Bill Guggenheim, and Dr. Arlene Puryear.

Our wonderful staff at Logos, the many hard-working volunteers, and all those who are a part of the Logos community, as well as our many friends and supporters around the country, deserve a page of praise and thanks each. But, because there simply isn't space, know that you are in my heart and I am so thankful for each of you.

I also want to acknowledge three special friends—women for whom I have the greatest respect and admiration and who have truly made a difference in the world:

Doris Rapp, M.D., a pediatric allergist, and author of *The Impossible Child* and *Is This Your Child?*, has brought hope and healing to thousands of families whose "impossible children" were simply suffering from severe allergies, which made their lives and the lives of their families miserable.

Ruth Montgomery's book, *Search For The Truth,* awakened me from a deep sleep and forever changed the course of my life. I thank her for the courage to be a true herald for this new age.

Elisabeth Kübler-Ross, through her work and many books, including her latest *Death is of Vital Importance,* brought death and dying into the light and paved the way for all of us to have greater understanding about the endings of this physical life, and the handling of our grief.

Tony Robbins's *Personal Power* audiotapes, videos, and seminars were some of the most empowering and helpful tools in my personal growth. The Gary Smalley *Hidden Keys to Loving Relationships* and *Hidden Keys to Successful Parenting* videos and seminars were responsible for helping me in all my relationships.

The publication of this book occurred in a most fascinating way—Dr. Doris Rapp read the unedited version and gave it to her publicist Phyllis Heller who was excited about the importance of its message. Phyllis showed it to Gail Hochman who became the most enthusiastic and helpful agent a writer could ask for. Gail gave the book to Julie Rubenstein, executive editor at Pocket Books, who shared it with Tom Spain, editorial director and associate publisher, Simon & Schuster Audio and through their efforts, the book found a loving home. Julie hired Catherine Whitney, who now knows this book as well as I do, to edit it. I have continued to be aided by the most helpful and greatest team any author could dream of. To all of you my deepest appreciation for what you have done to get Stephen's story out.

Edgar Cayce, the great Christian mystic, gave spiritual guidance through over 14,000 life readings, and the legacy he left the world is unparalleled. He died in 1945. One day, he introduced himself to me from the spirit plane, and began to talk to me much like Stephen did. We began a friendship that has spanned dimensions. His work remains a constant source of inspiration to me. He tells me he communicates, and tries to communicate, with many others who will listen.

I believe it is our natural birthright to communicate with our Creator, and with the angels, spirit plane helpers, guides, and loved ones who have died that He sends to help us. They wait for us to pause to listen and will aid us with the answers to much of what we seek. I am thankful for their guidance and help.

I mourn with all of you who have had a loved one die. Those who have experienced the death of a child in any way, and especially those who have had a child die of suicide, know a pain few can imagine. I pray that this book will bring you hope and healing, and a greater understanding of yourself, of the people in your life, and of your loved ones who have died.

ANNE PURYEAR

CONTENTS

Life is eternal
and love is immortal
and death is only
a horizon
and a horizon is nothing
save the limit
of our sight

—*author unknown*

INTRODUCTION

◆

IN MY DARKEST HOUR

Do not stand at my grave and weep;
I am not here. I do not sleep.
I am a thousand winds that blow.
I am the diamond glints of snow.
I am the sunlight on ripened grain.
I am the gentle autumn's rain.
Do not stand at my grave and cry,
I am not there. I did not die.

—INDIAN PRAYER IN MEMORY OF A FALLEN TRIBE MEMBER

This is a book about the life, suicide, and afterlife of my son Stephen. He took his life when he was fifteen years, three months, and fifteen days old, because he felt it hurt more to live than to die.

It is a story of death and separation, but also of survival. And most of all, I pray, it is a story of hope, because it tells of my communications with Stephen in the years since he died.

I believe that our loved ones continue on after death no matter how their physical lives end. I believe they have messages they want to bring to us about their survival and their continuing love. There are many stories about the survival of those who die as adults, but very few concerning children. So far, I have found none that pertain to children who commit suicide.

I have written this book as honestly and fully as I could. It was not easy to write because it brought up so much pain and sadness. It bares my soul in my search for the answers to the questions that always haunt the survivors of suicide: *Why?* Why did he do it? Why hadn't I seen signs that Stephen was suicidal? Why did I, his mother, do things that caused him to take his life? Why? Why? . . . The neverending whys.

I have come to ask other, better questions now, such as: What can I learn from this? What gift is there in Stephen's suicide and its aftermath? How can I grow from this experience? How can I use my pain to help others? In this process I have discovered some of the greatest lessons in my life, and I have grown in ways I never would have imagined.

Part of the book was *dictated* to me by Stephen from the plane in which he now resides, often referred to as "the other side." Stephen says it's not "the other side" at all. He explains that the souls in that dimension may occupy the same space with us. Their souls are simply vibrating at a different rate than our physical bodies. I don't know that dimension well yet, but I am learning about it with the help of Stephen and others who have gone ahead of me.

Stephen asked me to help him write this book in the hope that by sharing our story, other children who may be lonely and confused might know where to turn to find a solution besides suicide. Stephen's prayer is that young people will see suicide solves absolutely no problems; instead, it leaves in its wake unbearable pain and sadness—on both sides—that is rarely completely healed.

Stephen wants young people to understand that there is always a better option than to take one's own life. When the choice is suicide, a young person filled with promise is destroyed. Loved ones are left to carry the guilt and pain to their own graves.

You may think, and perhaps rightly so after reading this book, "No wonder Stephen killed himself." Or, you may think, "Things like that or worse happened in our family, and our child didn't kill himself. We were very lucky." On the other hand, it may help you see more clearly the words and actions—or inactions—that often do irreparable damage to our sensitive children. And perhaps it will help you to make changes in your own life—and theirs—so that your child doesn't become one of the heartbreaking statistics, and you do not become a survivor of suicide.

✦

In the United States, a suicide attempt is made every two and one-half minutes. Over the last twenty years, the incidence of suicide by young people has continued to soar. According to some estimates, there may be as many as two million suicide attempts among teenagers each year. At least 6,000 succeed. Suicide has been confirmed as the second cause of death among ten- to twenty-four-year-olds, yet many experts suspect it is actually the first cause. The suicide rate of fifteen- to twenty-four-year-olds has increased 222 percent in the years between 1957 and 1987, and the suicide rate of fifteen- to nineteen-year-olds has increased 312 percent during the same period. Of 195 practicing medical examiners polled recently, 58 percent agreed or strongly agreed that the actual suicide rate is probably two times the reported rate. Statistics increase with the consideration of unreported and covered-up suicides, as well as so-called "accidental deaths" such as car accidents involving only one young driver.

Over 400,000 American youngsters suffer yearly from a newly recognized childhood illness: depression. This is felt by many suicidologists to be one of the reasons for the increase in childhood suicide. Another factor to consider is that teenage obesity has increased by 40 percent in the last two decades. Researchers state that 4.5 million youths between the ages of twelve and seventeen are more than 20 percent overweight. This often leads to teasing and rejection by peers, isolation, depression, and lifelong problems with self-confidence and self-esteem. These are among the signs to watch for to prevent teenage suicide.

A child's suicide leaves devastation in its wake. Statistics show that divorce rates rise as much as 70 percent after the suicide of a child. Grief, guilt, and the inability to go on as before; these are the legacy of suicide for the parents and families of children who choose this road.

Perhaps your child or a relative or a friend has already taken his or her own life and you want to understand why. You may, as I did, play back every incident, searching for clues about what went wrong. You suffer with the pain and guilt of not knowing—and the irreversibility of your child's decision.

When your child dies, especially by his own hand, it is as if someone has reached into your chest and squeezed your heart over and over again and the resulting pain is almost beyond your endurance. It feels as if a part of your body has been severed and will never heal or grow back. You agonize over how you failed as a parent. Your child would rather die than live, would rather leave you than stay with you. Your child didn't give you a chance to help or even let you say good-bye. He has left forever—gone where you can't see or talk to him—and he has taken all your joy with him.

Who but *you* can possibly be to blame? This child was *your* responsibility. While your attention was elsewhere, he died. You failed to notice that something was wrong. You failed to stop him. You failed to be there for him when he needed you. *You* killed him. You might as well have taken a knife and pushed it through his heart. He is dead, and eventually, in your darkest hour, there is no one to blame but yourself. He is dead and gone forever, and there is nothing you can do to change that. There is no way you can ever tell him you are sorry or even that you understand. There is no way to find out how he is or even if there's a place *where* he is. You may even begin to hate God. How could a loving, just God let this happen?

This is the kind of thinking we do when we are in a state of grief and confusion. We often remain in that state and begin to die emotionally and break down physically. I was there. I remember.

I have begun to heal at last. I believe you can, too. We can heal by sharing our grief and fear and by remembering the times of joy. For while our children died, *first* they lived! We can heal by talking about our child and not hiding the facts of his death. We can heal by acknowledging our own role in our child's death, then by forgiving ourselves and getting on with our lives. We can heal most by knowing that although the physical body is not present, the soul whom we love continues, often in our presence.

Stephen made a choice to end his physical life. I believe it was an incorrect choice. He also believes it was an incorrect choice. But the act was irreversible. A lifetime of regrets, guilt, and questioning cannot change the finality of it. With that act, my life and the lives of my three remaining children would never be the same.

But in my darkest hour, a marvelous thing began to happen. I was given a gift beyond imagining. I could feel Stephen's presence and hear his voice—not only I, but others. An electric, thick energy would fill the room when Stephen entered, and my heartbeat would speed up. Sometimes I could hardly breathe and my whole body and brain reacted. It was the way you feel when you see someone you really love who you haven't seen for a while. It was somewhat the way I always felt when Stephen was alive and walked into a room. The feeling of Stephen's presence was so powerful that without thinking I would say, "Stephen. Stephen, you're here!" I couldn't see him or touch him, but I could feel his presence.

Shortly after these feelings began, I heard a voice inside my head, talking to me: "Hi, Mom. It's me, Steve." The sentences and expressions were phrased exactly like Stephen talked. The information he gave me was often verifiable. Even though at first I thought it must be my imagination, Stephen's words were so comforting and the information he wanted to share so fascinating, that I soon relaxed and just listened. Then I began a dialogue with him.

I spoke to him out loud; he usually spoke to me telepathically. Occasionally, he spoke out loud so clearly that I turned in the direction of the voice. On those occasions when someone else was in the room as he spoke "aloud," they usually could not hear him. However, there were several friends who could hear him just as I did. Sometimes they wrote down what they heard and shared it with all of us. When he finished, he would say good-bye, and the feeling of his presence left the room.

I am thankful to be able to hear him and to communicate with Stephen from the spirit realm. But I wish he were here beside me so I could give him a hug and fix his favorite meal and check his homework. I would much prefer to see his loving smile and blue eyes and watch his face light up with laughter as he leaned forward to talk to me. I miss hearing his barbell bump against the floor in his room as he did his workouts to keep in shape. I miss seeing the man he would have become and having the house filled with the sound of his children.

What I have with Stephen now will have to do until the day we are together again in the same dimension. I don't hurry toward that time; it will come in good measure. Although there isn't a day I don't miss him after all these years, I find myself feeling stronger as the healing continues.

As Stephen spoke, month after month, about his new life and provided clearer advice about my own, I, too, began to live again.

ONE

STEPHEN

"I'll lend you for a little time
a child of mine," he said.
"For you to love the while he lives,
and mourn for when he's dead.
It may be six or seven years, or
twenty-two or three;
But will you, till I call him back
take care of him for me?"

—EDGAR A. GUEST

The note from Stephen was sitting on the kitchen table when I arrived home from work.

Mom,

I had to get away and think because I don't know if life is worth living. I'm going to sleep overnight in the woods. Don't try to find me. You won't.

Steve

I couldn't believe it. I couldn't comprehend my son's words. How could life not be worth living for him *now?* We had been through a long, painful period together, but things were different—better. I thought the pain was over, the wounds were healing. For years we'd endured hardship and abuse, but no longer. We were making a new start.

Our story wasn't that different from thousands of others, although it always feels different when it's you. For years, I had been married to a man who was mean, abusive, and controlling. Richard tormented me and our four children every day of our lives. He called it love. He called it being a responsible father. It took many years and a great deal of strength to reject his cruelty, but I had finally walked away. I met Tom when I was in the deepest crisis, and now, in the fall of 1973, we were together. Tom was as different from Richard as night from day. With Tom, I thought we were beginning to heal. And now this.

Stephen was only fourteen, and he'd been afraid of the dark since he was a small child. It was starting to rain. How could he spend the night in the woods instead of home in his warm bed?

I was frantic. I insisted on driving to the woods and bringing him home. Despite what he said in his note, I was sure we would find him.

Our split-level home in Alexandria, Virginia, was a mile away from a dense forest that covered many acres. Stephen often went there during the day, but at night it seemed ominous and cold. Tom and I walked to the edge of the woods. The rain was heavier now, and the wind felt icy. My voice high with panic, I yelled Stephen's name. I didn't know if he could hear me. I screamed his name and pleaded with him to come home. He still didn't answer and it was too dark to go into the woods. I called again and again, and the silence was like a judgment against me. How could I have been so insensitive? I'd had no idea Stephen was so unhappy.

Tom finally said we should leave, that Stephen would come home in the morning. I wanted to stay and keep calling him, but I realized it was doing no good. I shouted Stephen's name a few more times, but he did not reply. Sobbing, I rode home and cried myself to sleep. My baby, alone in the dark woods.

I woke up with a shudder in the middle of the night, remembering that Stephen was gone. I prayed for him and tried to understand his hurt. I replayed the last few months in my mind, searching for clues.

Perhaps it was the fact that several weeks before, he had asked not to have to go to his dad's, but I had insisted. Richard maintained visiting rights with the children, but he had been so cruel to them when we were together that the children dreaded those visits—especially Stephen. Stephen had returned from his most recent visit and cried for two days, his confidence utterly shattered. Richard had been on him about not folding up his sleeping bag, about getting urine on the toilet, about his hair length, about almost everything he did. When Stephen came home, he was very upset. He cried, "I hate him! I hate him!" We talked for a long time, and he stopped crying but he told me with a hurt, choking voice, "I love Dad but I don't like him. He makes me feel like shit." These were harsh words from a child who had always possessed such a sweet and gentle disposition. I told him I understood. I said the children were all Richard had, and I asked Stephen if he couldn't try to tell him what he had told me about how he felt. In retrospect, I realized it was a ridiculous idea. Honesty only made Richard angry. Did I fail to support Stephen enough in his struggles with his dad? Was that why he ran away?

I also had to face the fact that while *I* was feeling so much more peaceful and content since Tom had come into our lives, Stephen hadn't really taken to Tom. One night, while Tom was taking his children home, Stephen said, "Mom, you're different around Tom from the way you are with us." He confessed that Tom made him feel uncomfortable, and that I seemed to be too busy trying to please Tom and his children. I gently explained that we were in a period of transition and that he must be patient. I was sure he would come to love and accept Tom as I did. But maybe I was expecting too much, too soon.

Stephen was also coping with a new school where he hadn't made friends yet. He thought he was too fat, so he wore loose clothes and an overcoat to hide his body. He didn't see himself the way I did. I tried to convince him that he wasn't fat, but maybe I should have taken him to a doctor anyway to help him lose a few pounds. Did the pressure make him want to leave school and run away? What could I have done?

All night I thought about Stephen and agonized about what I had done and what I could do when he came back. I thought about how things could be changed. I prayed for him and asked God to help him. Maybe he was dead and I'd never see him again. Maybe he'd had an accident in the woods and needed help. My imagination tormented me. I would die if something happened to him. "Oh, Stephen, *know* how much I love you and come home," I prayed. At last, I fell into a troubled sleep.

Morning came and no Stephen. I stayed home from work and watched the clock, my fear growing with the passage of every minute. At noon, just as I was ready to call the police, Stephen sheepishly wandered in, looking damp and exhausted. I ran to him and wrapped my arms around him. "Oh, Stephen, you had me so worried," I cried, holding him to me like he was a baby.

"I'm sorry, Mom. I'm really sorry," he said tearfully. "I didn't want to leave, but I just couldn't take it anymore. I had to get away by myself."

I wanted to understand. We talked for hours, and Stephen promised he wouldn't do it again. I prayed he was okay, but I felt uneasy. Was this just a typical teenage crisis, or was it something more?

Later, I would see that Stephen's night in the woods was a cry for help that I didn't hear. I didn't hear it because I wanted so much to believe that things were getting better. We had been down such a long, painful road together, the children and I.

✦

I can't say for sure when that road began. It's hard to look back. I have searched my heart many times over the years, trying to face the truth—to find out why our journey went one way instead of another.

I never planned for our lives to take the turn they did. But then, I never planned to be married and a mother at age seventeen. Maybe that was the beginning.

We had moved from Kentucky, where I was born, to Ohio when I was fifteen. I met Bill, and fell madly in love with him, when I was sixteen. Handsome, blond, and charming, he was the most popular boy in school and I felt lucky because he had chosen me. I know I suffered the usual pains of teenage angst, but in general life was good. I was a straight A student, loved by my teachers, energetic and creative. I never thought I was particularly beautiful with my short blond curly hair and blue eyes, but I knew I had a good personality. Having a boyfriend like Bill made me feel very special. Then, my family moved from Ohio to Tennessee and I left Bill behind. I missed him! At Thanksgiving, he came for a visit and it was wonderful to be close to him again. But soon after, I realized I might be pregnant.

Pregnant! In 1955, abortions were out of the question. They were illegal, and those done were performed in dirty back rooms by questionable "doctors." Besides, we had no money to even consider that. I called to tell Bill.

"We'll get married," Bill said honorably, and I started to cry. I didn't want to marry him, even though I loved him, and I doubt that he wanted to marry me. But it's just the way things were then; it seemed like the only choice. We were married in March by a justice of the peace, across the Tennessee border in Georgia.

We went home to tell my mother, and I saw her cry for the first time in my life. That night, we stopped at a motel on our way back to Bill's home in Ohio. After Bill fell asleep, I sat by the window and cried and cried. I didn't want to be away from my family. I wanted my mother. I didn't know anything about babies. This was not what I had planned for my life. I wanted to finish high school and go to college. All of my life I had dreamed of becoming a teacher, of doing something to help people. I had planned on having a different life than my parents had—one rich in culture and art and excitement. How could I have let it all slip away?

We moved back to Cincinnati, where my first son, William Robert or Bobby, as we called him until he got older, was born on August 10. The moment I saw him, I adored him. His angelic face gave me confidence that everything would be fine.

I loved being a mother, but as the years went by, Bill and I didn't fare so well. I worked as a secretary during the day, leaving Bobby with a sitter. At night, I studied for my high school equivalency test. Bill worked hard in the mailroom at General Electric and went to school at night. We had little time for each other, and we were growing in different directions. I felt bored and longed for more, and I'm sure Bill did, too. We separated a couple of times, but got back together because of Bobby. We didn't plan to have another child, but on one of our reunions I became pregnant again. I was only twenty, and Bobby was barely three years old.

Different from the first one, this was a very difficult pregnancy. Almost from the beginning, I suffered morning sickness that lasted all day and all night. I would nibble on anything to keep from being so nauseated, and my doctor prescribed a different medication every week, but nothing worked.

I had never felt this awful in my life. To make matters worse, I gained fifty pounds and looked like a butterball. I was a wreck—depressed, sick, and feeling ugly.

There was no one to talk to about my fears and questions. Because of that, my fears intensified and I began to think that I was going to die during delivery. The idea grew and took hold until I became convinced that neither my baby nor I would live. Frightened and confused, I began to prepare for my death.

In the evenings, while Bill was at school and Bobby was asleep, I sat in my room and wrote letters and cried. I wrote to my family telling them how much I loved them. I asked them to take care of Bobby after I died and to tell him how much his mother had loved him. I sealed the letters and put them in a place where they would be found after my death.

My time was running out. The new baby was due around December 6 and I had to make each moment with Bobby count. Often, I would tiptoe into his room and watch him sleep, his thumb in his mouth and his curled finger resting on his little upturned nose. He always perspired and his golden hair would be damp. Little drops of moisture would be on his nose. I'd gently touch his face and whisper that I loved him. The thought of not being around to see him grow up was so painful I could hardly bear it.

I didn't share my fears with anyone—neither my family in Tennessee nor Bill. It was my private vow to spare the people I loved from pain until it was time. But I was haunted by the story my mother had told me about her own mother's death when she was only two. She had no memory of it, but she said her father later described to her the scene at the graveside. As they were lowering her mother's body into the earth, she screamed, "Don't let them put my mommy in that dark hole!" I cried every time I thought about that story, imagining Bobby experiencing the same heartbreak. I knew, too, that my mother had no memory of her mother—only some pieces of unfinished quilt her mother had been working on just before she died. That's how it would be with Bobby, except for the notes I was leaving.

Although this wasn't my first pregnancy, I was still pretty ignorant about what was happening to my body. The few older women with whom I tried to discuss it would only laugh and say, "Honey, it's all just natural and God will handle it just like he has for thousands of years." So, when I went into labor, I headed for the delivery room with the same lack of knowledge I had the first time.

In the labor room, the nurse had me undress, put on a white gown, and lie on the bed. She raised the rails and locked them, then shaved me, gave me a shot in the hip, and left. No one explained anything, nor did I ask. As I began to lose consciousness, I thought, "This must be what death is like." I saw only darkness, and everything became a point of light. The points sounded a "ping" to communicate with other points. I didn't know this language, but they continued to move and touch each other, and I continued to hear their "pings." I felt very left out, even though I knew I was one of them.

When I opened my eyes, I was in a large room. Three women whom I didn't recognize were lying in beds in different corners. I guessed we were all dead and in heaven or somewhere. I became vaguely aware of a nurse hovering over me, taking my blood pressure. She was talking to me, saying what a rough labor and delivery I'd had. "You have a boy," she added. Still partly sedated, I mumbled, "What kind?" She laughed, and Bill was there smiling as I slipped back into my "ping" world.

When I awoke a few hours later, I remembered it was December 3, 1958, and I had given birth to another son. I was alive—and so was the baby. Soon, a nurse brought him in. He was sweet looking, his face a soft dusty pink color. His eyes were blue and he had light brown hair. I unwrapped him from the blanket and saw that everything was perfect. He was strong and healthy looking at seven pounds, fifteen and a half ounces. He wasn't as beautiful as Bobby had been, but he was cute and very quiet and peaceful.

It seemed impossible that I could love another child as much as I loved Bobby, but it took no time at all for me to fall in love with this quiet, hungry little boy with his chubby pink cheeks and sweet disposition. In the afterglow of giving birth, I forgot all about my earlier fears. It wasn't until weeks later when I found the bundle of letters that I remembered I was supposed to be dead.

We decided to name the baby Stephen Christopher, after my dad, Stephen. I wanted to please him and it did. My dad always had a soft spot for "little Stephen," as my family would call him the rest of his life. Later, I discovered that

Stephen meant "crowned with glory," and Christopher, "the Christ bearer." I always loved his names.

When Stephen was eight months old, we moved from our small, two-bedroom apartment into a larger, four-family building. We had our own washer and dryer, and shared a basement. There was a big yard where the boys could have a swing set and be outside more. As boxes and furniture were moved in, I picked Stephen up again and again from his crib to hug and kiss him. He wore a pale blue sleeper and he looked like an angel with his golden hair framing his face. He rarely ever cried, and when I kissed him under his neck on his "sweet spot" he would chuckle delightedly.

Bobby ran in and out around the boxes, bubbling with excitement. At four, Bobby was filled with total enthusiasm and joy for life. He raced his bike up and down the sidewalk, so utterly charming that the new neighbors all stopped to talk to him. He became instant friends with everyone.

Stephen was quieter. He had a special quality that made you want to touch him and squeeze him. Everyone around him commented that they couldn't keep their hands off him. For years we heard, "I could raise that one like my own," and, "I have never held a child who *feels* so good."

Even as Bill and I focused on the boys, our own relationship continued to deteriorate. When Stephen was still less than a year old, Bill and I separated for the last time. Amid tears and much sadness at things we couldn't reconcile, Bill moved back home with his parents. I kept the apartment and the children. He visited the boys regularly and sometimes kept them overnight or for weekends. I didn't have a car, so Bill lent me his when I needed to shop.

Our separation meant that I had to go back to work. Bill paid twenty-five dollars a week, which covered a babysitter, and I earned the rest to meet our needs. I found a secretarial job that paid barely enough to make ends meet.

It was a difficult period in my life. Like most working

mothers, I felt guilty about being away from my children. And I missed them desperately. It didn't seem right that I was not there to see them growing, to observe every moment of their lives. I finally decided to look for a job that would give me more flexibility to be with them. I found a job as a secretary-receptionist at a small family-run business near where I lived. I was thrilled to have work only ten minutes from home, even though the salary was lower.

My new boss was president of the company, as well as a minister in a church that believed in *The Book of Mormon*. I made it clear to him that this was only a job for me; I wasn't the least bit interested in joining his church. He didn't pressure me, and I developed a genial relationship with the people in the company. Everyone was quite solicitous about my children, and they didn't object to giving me time off to be with them when it was necessary. Life settled into a manageable, even peaceful, routine.

That summer, the company hired a young engineer named Richard who was a member of their church. He was single and four years older than me—a tall, thin, serious man whom I did not personally find very attractive. But I began to see Richard in a new way at the company Christmas party. Richard made a point of sitting with me and playing with the children all evening. He hoisted them on his shoulders, and they all laughed wildly. It made me feel very good to see my boys having such a wonderful time.

After the party, we began to date and were together almost daily. Richard was attentive to me and the boys and he took us to the "company church"—the Reorganized Church of Jesus Christ of Latter Day Saints. In fact, most of our dates involved the church. Richard explained to me that he was a priest—a lay minister called by God. He and his family had belonged to the church all of their lives.

I enjoyed being part of a church that made it seem that God was alive, that a caring God was speaking to his children. The people there were so warm and welcoming, and seemed nonjudgmental. The services were interesting and often inspiring. The boys loved Sunday school. I felt embraced by the church. There was a sense of security I had missed desperately for many years. It felt good to belong to something—and to someone—again.

TWO

✦

BROKEN SPIRITS

We are in the monsoons and we must weather it out—the way of wisdom is, instead of pining for calmer days, to learn to live wisely and well in the midst of continuous strain.

—Elton Trueblood

If I had known how to listen to my heart, I would never have married Richard. But I was young and lonely. I mistook Richard's control for love. He always knew exactly what to do. He wanted to take charge of everything, and I let him. I was attracted to his certainty about life, his confidence at a time when I was weary of responsibility and very uncertain. When he asked me to marry him, I said yes, burying my doubts about it being too soon.

While Richard was courting me, I ignored the signs that perhaps this wasn't a good match—that he was too dogmatic and controlling—too tough on the children. My indecision haunted me: Was this the right decision? I needed to know that Richard would be there for us, that he would be as dedicated to the boys as I was.

Then, a dramatic event happened that sealed my decision to marry Richard. One evening, with snow covering the ground, we attended our usual Wednesday night prayer service at the church. After the service, members of the congregation milled around in the upper sanctuary, talking. Stephen had turned two in December, and had begun to speak in short sentences. People stopped to talk to him as they went by; he looked adorable in a little navy blue suit, white shirt, and red bow tie. Bobby was dressed the same.

Suddenly, a woman began screaming hysterically. I swung around and saw that Richard was not holding Stephen's hand. Each of us thought the other had Stephen. But Stephen had toddled away and begun to climb down the steps. He slipped through the metal rail and fell a story and a half onto the concrete floor below.

Choking with dread, I ran to the top of the stairs. Stephen's little body was lying awkwardly below, one leg bent to the side, absolutely motionless. Richard and I ran down the stairs to where people were beginning to gather around Stephen. Someone yelled not to touch him or move him in case his back was broken. Someone else went to call an ambulance.

There was nothing I could do. I bent to touch him but was afraid because everyone was screaming, "Don't touch him!" I felt like an actor trapped in a terrible scene. I was fully aware of everyone around me, their eyes piercing me. But I couldn't speak. I couldn't cry. My face ached, and I couldn't force out tears.

After what seemed like forever, an ambulance finally arrived. The attendants carefully loaded Stephen into the back, and let me sit in the front. As we drove to the hospital, I was separated from my child by a glass window. I couldn't touch him or learn what the white-coated technician was doing. During the half hour it took to get to the hospital, I couldn't be sure whether Stephen was dead or alive. He wasn't moving.

When we finally pulled up to the emergency door at the

hospital, I watched as they carried Stephen inside on a stretcher. His eyes were open but his head was firmly strapped down to prevent movement. I followed the stretcher inside, talking to Stephen all the way. He wasn't crying, but occasionally he moaned.

"Please, God, don't let him die!" I silently implored. I promised God anything if only he would let Stephen be okay. I made a hundred pacts with God during those long hours.

Richard and two of the ministers at the church arrived shortly afterward. I told them the doctors had taken Stephen into an examining room and wouldn't let me go with them. One of the ministers asked the admitting clerk if they could go in and do laying-on-of-hands healing for Stephen. They explained that they were members of a church that believed in this type of healing. They then let us all into the room. I could see Stephen now and touch and comfort him.

He cried when he saw me. I would always bless the ministers for getting us in. They anointed Stephen's head with oil that had been blessed, laid their hands on him, and prayed for him. I prayed, too, but I kept my eyes open, and Stephen never took his eyes off me. He was frightened and in pain.

The doctors made us leave after only a few minutes. We waited for hours and were not allowed to see him again. Finally, a doctor came out to us. He said they would have to keep Stephen in the hospital for several days. The X rays showed a fracture from the top of his head down the left side. There was no bleeding or swelling, and he would probably be all right, but he had to be watched constantly. The doctor assured us that Stephen had no broken bones and was in very little pain. They had given him something to help him sleep. He said it was a miracle he wasn't dead or more seriously injured. A miracle! "Thank you, God," I murmured over and over.

Stephen's accident endeared him to the church members even more. They felt God had spared him for some special reason. Richard was very caring and helpful; his support and kindness during Stephen's accident pushed away my remaining doubts about him and the marriage.

Our wedding was scheduled for the middle of February. The whole church prepared for the event. Richard's parents came from Pennsylvania and my parents from Tennessee. Stephen was adorable at the ceremony and many photos were taken of people holding and loving him. My mother and dad took the boys to Tennessee after the ceremony to keep them while we went on our honeymoon. Stephen and Bobby loved their Nanny and Poppy and were excited about going, so I had no worries about leaving them.

But the honeymoon was a disaster. A side of Richard surfaced that I had never seen before—or, at least, one I had not been consciously aware of. First, Richard had refused to tell me where we were going. Nor did he give me any hints. It turned out to be Niagara Falls. Since I hadn't known, I didn't bring snow boots or any of the right clothing. I got so cold climbing a snow-covered mountain where we stopped to hike on the way that I cried from the pain. Richard was irritated and angry at me because I couldn't make it to the top. But with snow in my shoes, my feet were freezing.

I longed for Richard to pamper me and treat me like his lover. It was our honeymoon—a very special occasion. Instead, he was rigid about every penny we spent. He wanted to skip meals to save money; I was hungry. He brought along a grill to cook in the room. I reminded him there was a "No Cooking" sign, and worried that if the management smelled food, we would be kicked out. Nevertheless, we cooked every breakfast and some dinners in our room.

On the way back home, late at night, Richard stopped the car at a gas station on top of a mountain. He said we were going to sleep there overnight until the station opened. I asked if we didn't have enough gas to make it to a motel.

He said we probably did, but to think of what we would save in a motel bill—at least thirty dollars. I almost froze. Richard slept in the back, I in front. We had no blankets, just our coats. With the cold, the steering wheel, and the narrow seats in his 1953 Ford, I couldn't sleep all night.

It was an awful experience. I came home five pounds heavier from the stress. I was disillusioned, insecure, and irritable. I hardly recognized the man I had married. There was a cruel streak in him and a lack of compassion and understanding that I had never seen before. We picked up the boys in Tennessee, and the honeymoon fiasco was buried for the time being.

But Richard's rigidity continued. On the entire trip back to Cincinnati, Richard corrected and disciplined the children, yelling at Stephen and Bobby over the slightest little thing. He refused to stop to let them go to the bathroom or to get a drink until he found the "right place," which was sometimes over an hour after they expressed a need. The boys cried, "Mommy, we have to potty. We can't hold it." I begged Richard to please stop. He said they were sissies. I was confused and upset. I had never seen Richard like that. Or had I?

Grimly, I faced the fact that the signs had been there from the beginning, as sharp and clear as a ringing bell, but either I did not see them or I convinced myself that I was overreacting. Now, it was too late. I would have to try to live with Richard, and I was determined to find a way to make this marriage last.

When Richard told me that he wanted to adopt the boys and make them his own, I resisted the idea until he finally wore me down. I said yes reluctantly, although I didn't expect Bill to agree. He did, however, and Richard officially became the boys' father.

It was my fervent hope that the great stores of warmth and love that flowed from the boys would infect Richard—soften and change him. When Richard spoke harshly to the boys, or disciplined them over a minor infraction, I cringed, but shook off my worries because I believed that Richard loved the boys very much. I was determined to teach him how to express his love more gently, but instead, we fought daily in the early part of our marriage about the discipline of the children. At first, if I challenged him or stood up for the boys, Richard would storm out of the house. When he returned, he would be cold and silent, withdrawing from me until I apologized. It was impossible to resolve anything that way. I would finally apologize because I couldn't bear his silence. As the weeks passed, Richard would no longer storm out, but stay and fight. Our raised voices shook the house on many nights, and I now realize how frightened Bobby and Stephen must have been, huddled in their beds behind a closed door. It's foolish to think that children don't hear and aren't aware of what's going on with their parents, but I actually convinced myself that they didn't hear.

Richard sent out feelers for a new job, and was offered one in Washington, D.C. He and I drove there without the children to check it out, and I loved the whole area. It was the most exciting place I had ever been. A dusting of snow covered the ground, and the monuments glistened in the moonlight when we arrived.

Richard thought the job was ideal, the salary was bigger, and the setting was perfect. He assured me that things had a chance to get better here, away from Cincinnati. It would be a new start. Bobby and Stephen could visit Bill and stay in touch, and we could get on with our lives. I thought, maybe Richard was right. Maybe it *would* help. Maybe everything would get better.

It didn't happen that way. Bill never wrote or called the boys. I wrote to his mother and sent photos and a letter every Christmas, but there was no response from Bill. I later learned that he thought it was better for the boys if he stayed out of their lives.

Of course, Richard was quite pleased that the boys didn't see Bill. After all, he said, *he* was their father now. Whenever I mentioned Bill and showed the boys pictures of him, Richard became annoyed and reprimanded me for not letting them get on with their lives. Richard nagged me to destroy most of the pictures of the children with Bill, and to keep the peace, I finally did so.

Soon Bill was rarely ever mentioned. Bobby asked me about him occasionally, but Stephen, barely three and a half, soon forgot—or seemed to forget—his real father. He acted like he loved and looked up to Richard as much as he had Bill.

Our life in the Springfield, Virginia, suburb of Washington, D.C., was again centered around the church. It was located not far from our home, and the members were as warm and supportive as those in our old congregation back in Cincinnati. We didn't mention that Richard wasn't the boys' real father, although a few people knew. Richard was very intent on people believing that Bobby and Stephen were his real sons. The deception was stressful for me. I wanted to be more honest, but few people in the church were divorced, and divorce wasn't approved of except when adultery was the reason—not the case with Bill and me. So, I reluctantly went along with the ruse—living a lie with some while being honest with others.

I loved staying home with the boys. But while we appeared to be a happy family to outsiders and people at the church, behind closed doors our life was one of constant fighting. Richard sometimes got so enraged at something I said or did (or didn't do) that he would slam his fist through the wall. Occasionally, in desperation, pain, and anger, I would strike back by throwing things at Richard, but my aim wasn't very good and I always missed. I didn't want to hit him anyway. I wanted him to stop being so mean to us.

We attended church on Sundays, Wednesdays, and whenever the doors were open—dressed up and smiling, holding Bobby and Stephen's hands. No one knew how bad things were at home. I was embarrassed to tell anyone, and I kept thinking that our situation would get better. The boys were fine—or so I fooled myself into thinking. It seemed as if I was the only one who was feeling the stress. Once again, I blamed myself.

Several times we drove to Missouri to visit Richard's parents, and these trips were tense and unpleasant. If the boys played outside so they didn't mess up their grandparent's trailer home, making little rock piles in the gravel, they were reprimanded immediately by Richard's mother for disturbing the yard. They weren't allowed to dig; they were allowed only to sit and play games. It was easy to see where Richard got his rigidity and his need to control every situation.

I know Richard believed he was a good father, but often his behavior toward the boys chilled me to the bone. I remember one occasion when we stayed at a motel for a night on our way to Missouri. Stephen was only four. There was a swimming pool, and we were enjoying ourselves splashing around in the water when Richard ordered the boys to the side at the deep end. He told them to jump in, and they both protested because neither one could swim. But Richard urged them on, promising to pull them out of the water when they went down. Bobby took the plunge and emerged laughing, but Stephen was terrified.

"It's okay," I called to him from across the pool. "You don't have to jump." But Richard eventually shamed him into it, and with panic-stricken eyes, Stephen jumped. When Richard pulled him out of the water, he was shivering with cold and fear. It broke my heart to see how far this little child would go to please his father—and how cruelly Richard took advantage of that desire.

The situation and our relationship continued to crumble, yet Richard wanted a baby. I agreed because I thought having his own child might make him more mellow and less strict with the boys. I tried for months to get pregnant, but nothing happened. We finally went to the doctor for tests and discovered that Richard was sterile. I hurt for him, knowing how much he wanted his own child. But I also thought that maybe since he could not have children of his own, Bobby and Stephen would mean even more to him. Instead, he became increasingly demanding and critical of them. I finally suggested that he might be taking out his anger on them for not being able to biologically father a child. My remark enraged him. We could not talk about it. I hated for Richard to hurt so badly, and I hated the pain he caused the boys.

In 1962, television news reports told of the dire state of foster child care in our area. Hundreds of children were being housed in crowded conditions in Washington, D.C.—sometimes two to a bunk bed, twenty-five or more to a room. My heart went out to these children. I began to think that since I had discovered I could love two boys as much as one, there might be room in my heart to love another child—at least until a permanent home was found.

Richard and I discussed becoming foster parents, and he agreed since all of the expenses would be paid. He even calculated that we might make some money doing it. I doubted that, and besides, we weren't in it for the money—at least, *I* wasn't.

After extensive interviews, we were cleared to become foster parents, and soon after we received a fifteen-month-old girl, Andrea. She was a little doll, but it was clear she had been neglected. When the boys helped me change her diaper, they pointed with alarm to her little bottom, which was covered with fluid-filled blisters from lying unchanged for days. They gently helped me put salve on her. The boys adored Andrea from the first moment they saw her, and we were all thrilled when we received permission to adopt her.

Stephen wasn't in school yet, and he and Andrea became buddies, spending long hours together. Bobby and Stephen helped bathe her, and taught her to walk, holding tightly to her hands so she wouldn't fall. In response to their love, Andrea blossomed. She began to walk and talk and smile.

It was fun to have a daughter to shop for, and I bought Andrea dolls and little girl toys. The boys would play house with her and pretend they were the daddies to her dolls.

Richard was sarcastic about the boys playing with dolls—even the G.I. Joe dolls that Bobby loved.

Stephen had a natural inclination to cuddle animals and even Andrea's dolls, but he was reluctant to do so when his dad was around. Several times, I found him sleeping with his arms around his metal robot. It was cold and hard. This was ridiculous! I went to the store and bought him Beany and Cecil dolls. Cecil was a dragon and Beany was his friend. Stephen loved them. Although Richard teased him, he was able to endure it, and he slept with Beany for years. When I went into his room to tuck him in at night after he was asleep, Beany was always snuggled under his arm and covered up with his blanket.

There was a housing development in downtown Washington where welfare mothers and their children lived. I organized a group of women at the church to go there twice a week. We taught classes on arts and crafts, took the families on field trips, and volunteered at the community day care center held at a nearby church. Since he wasn't yet in school, Stephen went with me each time, while Andrea stayed with a neighbor.

Stephen took the plight of these families to heart. He worried that they didn't have much, and he would often go through his own toys and clothes and give away things he really loved. He let the smelly old lady with the pale face, ragged clothes, and stringy gray hair hug him whenever she wanted. He was as friendly and loving with the unwashed, runny-nosed little children as with his many well-dressed and clean friends in our neighborhood. With the turmoil in our life, this volunteer work was a blessing to Stephen and me. We enjoyed our time there. When we returned home, we gathered toys, clothes, food, and books to take for the next visit.

✦

Stephen was delightful to raise. He brought such joy into my life—into all of our lives. He was so affectionate and loving, and he was very kind and considerate of everyone and everything. He entered the first grade at six and fell in love with school. He knew Andrea missed him at home, and he brought her his drawings and special papers, trying to teach her what he was learning. He made friends so easily—the house was always filled with his various playmates. He seemed to be especially aware of the good qualities of his friends and was rarely critical of them. I doubt that he was ever aware of how different he was in this respect from the rest of his friends. The others fought constantly among themselves and were always angry at one another for some imagined thing or another. Stephen tried to help them make up. He was our little peacemaker, and I often thought of the Scripture, "Blessed are the peacemakers," when I watched him play.

He loved "Superman" on television and heroes with swords and capes who always won over the "bad guys." I made him a Superman cape and he flew around the yard rescuing the cat, the dog, and other imagined victims. On his sixth birthday, I surprised him with a black cape inset with a large golden eagle covering the back. It had taken hours for me to design and sew this gift. I bought him a gladiator sword and helmet to wear with it. These were his prized possessions for years. With sword extended and cape flying, he spent hours preparing his "army" to fight to save the world. He needed little attention, playing alone quietly for hours. He also enjoyed being with his friends. They played cowboys and Indians and all the wonderful games of the imagination in which children of that age excel. His years were filled with celebrations of birthdays, Halloweens, Christmases, and Easters.

I loved buying presents for Stephen, because he appreciated them so much. I loved doing things for him because he didn't expect them. It was a rare day that he didn't come up to me several times, unasked, to give me a hug and kiss and say, "I love you, Mom." How could one not respond to a child like that?

He often called me outside to show me something, saying, "You've gotta see this, Mom," as he leaned down and pointed to a ladybug crawling up his metal robot or to the cat sleeping peacefully against the dog's belly. He always saw things we didn't notice, and they became special to him and to us when he pointed them out. I loved him so much that, when my mother visited, she said, "When Stephen walks into a room, you light up."

It was true, although I also adored the other children. And Bobby and Andrea needed far more attention than Stephen did. Bobby was often going through some crisis with friends or at school. As the youngest, Andrea needed more physical attention. Stephen seemed to have far fewer needs and wants than either his brother or sister, or his friends. Despite all the criticism from Richard, Stephen remained loving and caring with him.

As the children grew, Richard spent a lot of time with the boys, but there was always a cutting edge in his manner. Games that should have been fun were filled with biting criticism that stressed winning, not the joy of playing. The children and I began to get nervous several hours before Richard was due home, because we knew the faultfinding would soon begin.

Bobby began to rebel. Stephen gained weight and began to look a little chunky. I gained back my pregnancy weight. There were so many rules. We loved mayonnaise, for instance, but Richard liked only mustard, so we were not allowed to put anything except mustard on hamburgers. Only two pieces of ice were allowed in a glass. If Richard saw more, they were removed and thrown away. We had to eat every bite on our plates, no matter how full we were. Richard usually served the children, so they couldn't put smaller helpings on their own plates. If the boys cried, Richard told them not to be sissies—to be men. He told me I hadn't had enough discipline when I was a child, and he was going to correct that.

Richard and I battled almost daily. I tried to get him to

ease up on the children, while he told me we all needed more discipline. It seemed none of us could do anything right. He drove us crazy. One minute he told us how much he loved us, and in the next breath he berated us for some imagined wrongdoing. If Bobby and Stephen were playing with building blocks, he had a better way. Whatever any of us did, *his* way was better. We either changed quickly to his way, or he withdrew from us until we complied.

A crazy thing started to happen to me. I began to feel that I was alive only to please Richard. If I didn't please him, any happiness I might have from doing things my way was wrong. It was very subtle at first; I wasn't even aware of it. I had both the compulsion to try to please him and an instinctive rebellion against his control. I felt as though I was losing my mind. Sometimes I fantasized about hanging myself over the bedroom door with a note pinned to my chest stating, "Look what you did to me!"

My mother once told me that during the years my grandmother lived with us it sometimes became so unbearable, she would think of killing herself. But when she thought of her children, suicide was no longer an option. That's how I felt. I couldn't leave my children or hurt my children that way. Lots of women I knew said that they sometimes wished they were dead or felt like killing themselves. We all understood that it was just talk. No one ever did it, no matter how bad things were.

I didn't let myself realize at the time just how bad the home situation was becoming and how traumatizing it was for the children. I kept thinking that Richard would mellow, that we would stop fighting. I felt that somehow, whatever I was doing wrong, I could correct it so he wouldn't be so angry all the time.

I began to do everything I could to keep the peace. Unless something was of earthshaking importance, I tried not to fight with Richard. I let him do things his way. We all tried to get him to love us, to gain his approval. We agreed with him, we complimented him, we tried to meet his every wish. Nothing worked. Something was always wrong. If he came home and the house was immaculate, a home-cooked meal was on the table, the children and I were dressed up, and we greeted him with hugs and kisses, it still wasn't good enough. He'd begin to interrogate us: "Did you boys read your Bible today?" Or, "I bet your mother didn't work on the budget. You didn't, did you?" When we answered, "No," he began his lengthy lectures about why we shouldn't neglect the Scriptures and how we had to get our priorities straight.

In spite of the constant turmoil in our household, Stephen's sweet disposition made him a pleasure to be around. He was very kind, often bringing home kids that no one else liked or who were dirty and obviously neglected. He possessed a pure acceptance of people just as they were. He didn't experience that at home. It was a rare day when Richard didn't find fault with something Stephen or Bobby did. Because of this, I began a very destructive pattern of my own. It made sense at the time, but now I look back on my actions with shame and disbelief. I began disciplining the children before Richard walked through the door, because I knew that my yelling and punishment wouldn't be as bad as his. Often, I discovered if I was yelling at them or punishing them when Richard came in the door, he would leave them alone. It was my foolish way of trying to make things easier on the boys. But nothing I did made things better. I felt helpless, confused, and frustrated as the situation at home continued to deteriorate.

Then, in the midst of all this trouble, Richard decided he wanted to adopt another baby. He complained that he'd never had the experience of raising a child, his own child, from infancy. I tried to believe that deep down Richard really loved the children and that he would change once he had a baby to call his own. I finally convinced myself this was true, and agreed to apply to adopt a child. The thought of a new baby appealed to me; the thought of a new Richard appealed to me more. I loved children, and although I was overwhelmed by the family situation and the arguing, I rationalized that it would be healing to have a baby.

We applied through the Child Welfare Division of the welfare department in Washington, D.C., where we had adopted Andrea. In 1965, there were hundreds of children waiting to be adopted. With military and transient government personnel moving in and out all of the time, the institutions were filled with children of all ages needing homes. We applied for a girl or a boy of any nationality, but specified that it be a very young baby. The same caseworker who had helped us adopt Andrea came out to interview us. The rules were somewhat more strict for the adoption of an infant.

She interviewed Richard and me together, then separately, and interviewed all three children. I coached the children to say only good things yet be as honest as possible. That was actually an impossible task.

A few days after the interview, the caseworker called saying she didn't think she could recommend us to adopt a baby. She explained that when she interviewed Richard alone, she found him to be overly strict, unbending, and dogmatic. I was so easygoing that she wondered how in the world we ever got along. Didn't we fight? Wasn't there great difficulty in our different ways of dealing with children? She also noted that the children were fearful of Richard, even though they seemed to love him. They loved me, she said, but they felt I wasn't able to protect them from their father.

Richard would have been furious if he had known what the caseworker said, and I was in a state of denial. Instead of listening to the truth of her words, I lied. I told her that yes, Richard and I had different styles, but Richard's ways were good for the children, and for me, who had lacked discipline as a child. Actually, I neither believed that nor was it true. I had been loved as a child and didn't feel any lack of discipline.

I must have lied convincingly, pleading Richard's case well. I felt in my heart that this was my only hope of saving my marriage and my children. To mellow Richard out, to give him a baby to love so he wouldn't hurt the children so much, seemed to be the answer. Either my assurances changed the caseworker's mind or she figured that the children were so desperately in need of homes that ours would be better than nothing. I will never know for sure, but shortly thereafter, she gave us the okay to adopt a child when one became available.

On February 27, 1966, we received a call from our social worker. She said a baby girl had been born on February 22, and we could come down in two days to see her. If we approved, she could go home with us. We rushed out to get diapers, clothes, and last-minute items for a baby girl. We fixed her crib with new sheets and blankets. Stephen placed toys in the crib. Bobby and Andrea rearranged the room. We were as excited as if I were about to give birth.

At the welfare department in Washington, D.C., we were ushered into a room to wait. Our social worker was a lovely middle-aged woman whose kindness and smile were so genuinely warm that you couldn't help but like her. She walked in carrying a very tiny bundle wrapped in a pink blanket with blue satin trim. She removed the corner of the blanket to let us see the baby. We both fell in love with her on the spot. She was so very tiny—only six pounds, twelve ounces at birth and slightly smaller now. She had the tiniest little face and head, dark hair, blue-gray eyes, and hands so small they could barely reach around our fingers. I would have fought an army if they had tried to take her away, such was the immediate love I felt for her. I thought she was beautiful beyond description.

When we arrived home and Stephen and Bobby saw her, they passed her from one to the other. They said over and over how cute she was, how beautiful, how adorable. Andrea was allowed to hold her, too. She was nearly five and held her lovingly, like a mother. Together, we chose the name Deborah, although she would always be called Debbie.

Stephen held her as she slept. He bent his head to kiss the top of her nose and did anything to wake her up so she would look at him. She would grin at him the moment she saw him and laugh out loud. He could always get her to make noises and cute expressions. As she got older, he played outside in the snow with her, pulling her up and down the sidewalk on the small hill in front of our home—Debbie never tiring, Stephen never complaining.

He would rush home from school to watch her sleep, to play with her, to feed her, to cuddle her. He adored her. Bobby did the same. Debbie was racing down the hill in his bike basket when most babies would be lying in their playpens. It was a love affair with their little sister throughout their childhood. They included Andrea in everything they did, and the four of them played together by the hour.

I had naively placed all my hopes in Debbie—that her presence would make a difference, that Richard would soften and become more gentle and loving. But it never happened. Eventually, I had to face the fact that both Bobby and Stephen were being affected at school by the constant turmoil at home. I realized that our family needed help, but I didn't have a clue where to look. Fearful and desperate, I took a chance and called a counselor whose name I found in the Yellow Pages. She suggested that Richard and I come to see her together. When I related this to Richard, he ranted and raved. He thought counseling was a waste of money, especially since *I* was the one who obviously needed help, not him.

"Okay," I said bravely, "I'll go alone." He didn't like that idea, either, because he claimed I'd only tell my side. Therefore, we went together for counseling, first to one, then to another. Each counselor, when pointing out something Richard might change or see more clearly, was met with denial and anger. He wouldn't go back to that particular counselor, and I'd be forced to find another.

Finally, one very tender and loving woman said, "Richard, you want a master/slave relationship and you want your wife and children to be your slaves." Richard became violently angry, saying I'd never had any discipline and neither did the children, and he was going to see to it that we had it.

He wouldn't go back, so I sneaked out alone for another session. The counselor asked me if I was going to put up with that kind of treatment. I, also into denial, told her that Richard was a good man and he really loved us. I said he didn't mean to hurt us and couldn't help how he was. I began to tell her all the things I did wrong, trying to take the blame. I asked her what I could do, what I could change so Richard wasn't so angry all the time, so faultfinding with us.

She looked at me sadly. "The only solution I can see is to leave him," she told me gently. I rebelled. I wasn't ready to hear that. I found yet another counselor, and another. I only received the same advice over and over: Leave him! Most counselors asked me why I tolerated living this way and why I didn't leave. They did not feel Richard was willing to make any changes. No one suggested bringing the children in, nor did I think of counseling for them at that time. I had never heard of children getting counseling. There was so much I didn't know.

Nothing helped. I guess I wanted a counselor to say, "It's *you,*" and give me some quick solution so I could be healed. But it didn't happen, and things became even worse after the counseling. I suggested to Richard that we go to see one of our ministers, but he refused, saying we didn't need to drag the church into our private affairs. But in another act of courage, I secretly went to see one of our ministers. He was kind and loving, did not suggest separation, and tried to help me see what I was doing wrong so I could correct it. He asked to see Richard, and since the secret was out, Richard had little choice. We both went in for several sessions that turned into yelling matches. On our last visit, the minister said, "I don't usually recommend this, but I don't see how you two can possibly stay married. I suggest a divorce."

That was unheard of in the church. I should have felt justified, happy, and vindicated, but I simply never went back.

I didn't want a divorce. I prayed daily that I could change enough to help heal our relationship. I prayed for God to give me another chance and that we wouldn't divorce. I prayed that Richard would be kinder and love us. I prayed with all my heart, but it didn't seem like there were any answers.

While I still tried to fool myself that what was happening in our family was no worse than most, every day it seemed we were losing ground. The children began having more and more difficulties—not sleeping well, experiencing problems in school, fighting with each other. They were beginning to lose their childhood enthusiasm and joy. I felt as if I was losing my mind.

✦

One day, I found Bobby's two gerbils dead in their cage. My heart sank to my feet when I learned that Stephen had killed his brother's animals. It was an inconceivable act of violence for a boy who cherished living things so much. I knew something was terribly wrong, but I felt helpless to stop it.

In a way, I had seen it coming for a while. Bobby, who was reaching his teenage years and hurting badly, took out all his aggression on Stephen. I realized this displacement of anger was a fairly normal response to the sick situation in the family. Richard took his anger out on us, I took mine out on the children, Bobby took his out on Stephen. And Stephen, always so sweet and sensitive, was finally pushed to take out his anger on Bobby's helpless animals.

Stephen confessed that he killed the gerbils because Bobby had been particularly mean to him. Bobby was furious and rightly so. He demanded that I punish Stephen. I tried to tell him that he had pushed Stephen beyond his limits by constantly picking on him. But Bobby was not in a mood to be compassionate. He only saw my explanation as my way of taking Stephen's side. In retrospect, I can see that Bobby was stretched beyond his own limits with Richard's cruel disciplines and my criticism of his behavior toward the other children. He must have felt totally unsupported despite my love for him.

When he fully realized what he had done, Stephen was grief stricken. He cried over the dead animals and apologized profusely. He loved animals. To have killed the gerbils was like murder to him. I tried to comfort him, but disturbing thoughts were running through my mind. What Stephen had done was a warning to me. I must stop the damage Richard was doing to the children before something even worse happened.

But as time passed, I did not take any action. Stephen never again hurt a living thing, but there were other signs I was too weary to see or take seriously. Both Stephen and Bobby began to bite their fingernails down to the cuticles, which I should have noted with more concern. They fought constantly. Bobby deliberately tormented Stephen. I tried to reason with Bobby, but it made him more angry. I couldn't punish Stephen because Bobby usually started the fights and made Stephen's life miserable. While I understood Bobby's pain, I couldn't let him constantly hurt his brother.

Now, standing on the battlegrounds, were Richard and me, Bobby and Richard, Bobby and Stephen, and Bobby and me. Stephen seemed to survive with his usual good disposition, but he became more quiet and subdued. Andrea began to have trouble in school. She, too, developed some aggressive behavior with teachers and classmates, although, like Stephen, she was pretty easygoing at home.

During these dark days, just before Christmas of 1971, I did something that made them even darker. Money was missing from the house and, of course, no one would admit that they had taken it. On a previous occasion, Stephen had admitted to taking some money, and Richard had punished him severely. I could hardly stand the pain he suffered.

There was still a question that he actually took it. He might have confessed just to get Richard off everyone's back. Now there was a can of money missing. I was sure I remembered putting it in a certain place, and it wasn't there. Things had been particularly stressful for days, and I was tense, irritable, and distraught. I went down to Stephen's room and asked him about it. Richard followed me and said, "We've got to do something about this. He's got a problem. I'll handle this. When I get through with him, he won't steal anything again." I asked Stephen if he had taken the money, but he swore he hadn't. I asked him again and again. He became more frantic in his denial. I thought he must be lying, and I knew Richard would really hurt him if he admitted it.

Something snapped in me. I began to slap Stephen. I hit him on the arms and on the face. I went crazy. I had never done such a thing to him. I wasn't hitting him that hard, but the terrible thing was that I was hitting him at all. He cried and I screamed at him. In the back of my mind, I thought that this wouldn't hurt him as bad as Richard would if he hit him. That was no excuse. Stephen was crying and pleading with me to stop. Finally I did, and walked out of the room, shaking and crying.

What had I done? I had beaten my little son, my beloved Stephen. Richard went upstairs, assuring me Stephen had deserved the punishment for stealing. I stayed downstairs on the couch in the family room crying, feeling as bad as I ever had in my life.

In truth, I didn't really believe Stephen would steal money. It just wasn't like him. He knew I would give him money whenever he needed it. I felt sick at my stomach. I started to vaguely remember something. I walked into another room and found the can of money. I had put it in a special place so I would be able to find it.

I ran back into Stephen's room. He was lying on the bed, still sobbing. I told him I had found the money, that I was wrong, and how sorry I was. I held him, stroking his damp hair, and patting his back as I cried and apologized. I promised I would never hit him again. I told him I loved him and promised him this hell we lived in was going to end. I apologized again and again. My heart ached for what I had done to this tender soul.

My son, my son!

THREE

✦

THE VOICE FROM NOWHERE

I firmly believe in the continuation of life after what we call death takes place. I believe there are two sides to the phenomenon known as death; this side where we live, and the other side where we shall continue to live. Eternity does not start with death. We are in eternity now. We merely change the form of the experience called life—and that change, I am persuaded, is for the better.

—Norman Vincent Peale

To this day, I believe that God saved me because I was too weak to save myself. A trip to the grocery store is rarely a life-changing experience. But for me, on the afternoon of January 10, 1972, it was.

I welcomed the opportunity to get out of the house for a few moments of peace. I even drove to Giant Food, a grocery store farther from the house, because they carried clothes, books, and items that were not in most food stores then. All I really needed was milk and bread. I was disappointed when I discovered that I had forgotten my checkbook and had very little money with me. Shopping was sometimes therapeutic, and I needed that with all the turmoil.

I walked past the book section and was drawn to a small paperback with a blue cover. As I was reading the title on the front, *Search for the Truth*, by Ruth Montgomery, a loud voice right behind me said, "Buy that book!"

I turned around to see who had made such a suggestion.

There was no one there! No one! I was the only person in the entire department. I even looked in back of the bookshelves to see if someone was hiding and playing a joke on me. No one was there. My heart began to race. Something unusual had happened. I didn't even know the word "paranormal" at the time, but had I, it would have been appropriate to describe my experience.

I bought the book, climbed into the car, and headed for home. I was still shaken by the voice, wondering what it meant. I reasoned that if a voice out of nowhere told me to read a book, at least I'd consider reading it. I didn't tell Richard about the voice. He would have thought I was crazy—crazier than he already thought I was. I couldn't wait to read the book. I felt as if something wonderful was about to happen, but I had no idea what.

The book was fascinating. Ruth Montgomery, a former political writer during several presidential administrations, wrote convincingly about her experiences with her guides and helpers from the spirit plane. People who had died spoke to her. They dictated books from the "other side." I was intrigued by her story—even more so when she revealed that everyone had such guides.

Ruth Montgomery's guides told her that people lived after they died, discarding their physical bodies. They worked and learned on the spirit plane, and they were able to communicate with us on the physical plane.

Ruth Montgomery wrote that a man named Edgar Cayce had been able to lie down, go to sleep, and travel into the spirit realm. He then began speaking and bringing information from that realm. It was dramatically clear that it was accurate information that was completely unknown to him when he was awake. These "life readings," as they were called, had brought help and healing to many people.

The book read like sacred scripture to me. It filled in all the places I had always thought were missing. It spoke to my soul, my heart, my mind. I felt as if I'd been asleep most of my life and had just awakened. I was so excited I couldn't sleep or eat.

I felt intuitively that the truths this book contained could change people's lives because no one ever had to fear death. People who died could still communicate if we learned how to listen. A few of them were even assigned as guides, for periods of time, to help those of us who were still living. How wonderful!

The next morning, after a sleepless night, I rose early and sat alone in the living room in the blue reclining chair. I often sat there to relax and think when all the children were asleep or at school. My thoughts were filled with the revelations in Ruth Montgomery's book. As I tried to make sense of what I had read, I looked at the wall. Something moved! There were pictures on the wall, moving pictures! Some were of people I knew; some were of me. It was like a movie, and somehow I knew the scenes I was viewing were yet to happen. This was the future. I was amazed and blinked my eyes. I discovered I could still see the pictures with my eyes closed. I relaxed and allowed it to happen.

Besides future happenings, I saw what seemed to be visions from the past. A battlefield with soldiers appeared, as if I was viewing it from a hill. Men in armor with swords and spears were fighting one another. It reminded me of Roman soldiers from a movie, but a movie I hadn't seen. I could see the maneuvers in a 360-degree circle from atop a hill, yet I was watching from my chair. How was that possible? I watched for a long time. No one seemed to be winning, although men were falling down and dying in battle. Then the "movie" stopped.

I was amazed. But as if that weren't enough, a voice began to speak to me, then another voice, then another. There were three distinct voices. They identified themselves as my guides. I couldn't see them, but I could hear them just as if they were speaking out loud, only the voices were inside my head. I wondered if I was going crazy. The voices assured me I wasn't crazy at all, just finally able to hear them. They told me they had once been alive in physical bodies but were now assigned as my guides and had been waiting to communicate with me when I was ready to listen. They said that they were assigned to me for the next few years, would never interfere with my free will, and that I could stop their voices at any time, just by asking. They further said they didn't have all the answers, but if I asked them things they didn't know, they would try to find the answers from those with more wisdom.

My mind was racing with confusion and disbelief, but my guides were patient and understanding. They suggested that the next day at 2:00 P.M., before the children came home from school, I sit at my typewriter. They would talk to me, and I could type what they said so I wouldn't forget it. It didn't dawn on me to say no. They told me they could see the pathway only somewhat more clearly in all directions than I could. Further, one of the guides told me that I had been meditating all my life, not even realizing it, during the times I sat silently and reflected about my life. Another said that I should never be afraid because my prayers had created an aura of protection around me. They said I should always pray before receiving guidance, and I would continue to have that protection. If anything was ever revealed that made me uncomfortable, I could challenge it until I felt at ease with the information. If I still felt doubtful, I could refuse to listen or accept it. In that way, I would not be misled. I didn't tell anyone of the experiences. People would have thought I had lost my mind, even if my guides assured me I hadn't.

Shortly before 2:00 P.M. the next day, I pulled out my manual typewriter, set it on the dining-room table, and placed a clean sheet of paper through the roller. I was a fast typist and this was an easy mode of expression for me. Still, I was somewhat embarrassed. It felt kind of silly. Perhaps I had imagined the voices. Maybe I would sit there at my typewriter and nothing would happen. I began to pray.

Promptly at 2:00 P.M., one of the voices began to speak. I

looked around to see its source. It seemed to be coming into my head from outside to the left but, again, I was hearing it inside my head. Then another voice spoke from behind me, and another to my right.

The voices said to breathe deeply and relax, not to be afraid, and to begin my meditation with a prayer. I repeated the prayer they gave me: "I ask for the very highest spiritual guidance to come through. I ask to be protected by the white Christ light and to be a clear, pure channel of truth. May all things I receive be helpful and hopeful."

Then the voices instructed me to wait until I saw a white cross. That would be the sign from the Spirit that only the highest and purest guidance would come. I did so, and when I saw the cross I prepared to begin.

"Listen, so your own thoughts won't intrude, and type what you hear," the guides instructed. I listened, and began to type the words I was given. Often, I stopped typing and questioned them. They instructed me as if I were a child just learning to read or write. Sometimes they gave me one letter at a time until I got it correct and then a word at a time when my thoughts wandered. They explained that they were communicating with me at a soul level, telepathically, putting their words into my thoughts. Their thoughts could enter my head if I would allow them to.

I discovered years later when using biofeedback equipment, that the act of "listening" would alter my consciousness to an alpha or theta brain wave pattern. At the time, I knew only that when they said "Listen," something happened and then I heard them clearly. I often described it as "clicking down" to hear. The information given to me ranged through many subjects such as how the world was created, life after death, the work I was to do, and my children. There was also information about other lifetimes, other incarnations. They spoke about a God of love, about Jesus, about wars and man's inhumanity to man. True to their promise, when I questioned something, they carefully explained and let me ask as many questions as I wished.

Nothing was ever given that didn't make sense. When they didn't know an answer, they told me they would try to find out before our next session, and they usually did. The guidance continued for an hour.

When I asked them who they were, they asked me to just use their initials, J and M and G. One said he had been a writer and that I would know his name. It was not important who he was; instead, I needed to concentrate on receiving the information he had to share. Another said I wouldn't know who he was but others might, and he didn't want to detract from the guidance by revealing his identity. The other said I didn't know him but had known him in another place at another time.

The pictures on the wall continued, but by now I knew I was seeing them inside my head, without my physical eyes, and I could turn them on and off. They were not always significant things, but they were evidential in that I saw them before they happened, and I continued to see things that seemed to be from the past. All the while, as I continued to listen, the ability to communicate with my guides became stronger and clearer.

Later, filled with joy and hope at what was happening to me, I thought this might help to heal my marriage, too. I begged Richard to read Ruth Montgomery's book, but he wasn't interested in it. I talked to Stephen and the children about some of what was happening, but I didn't want them to get in trouble with their dad until I saw where all of this was leading.

✦

I was growing and gaining faith and confidence, but in the beginning things changed very little. Richard refused to listen to my gentle urging that he share in my discoveries. More and more, the children and I formed a bond that did not include Richard, but did include a growing faith in a loving God and a hope for a better future.

We bought an old piano for the family. The evening before had been one of the terrible times when Richard over-disciplined the children, I intervened, and we quarreled long into the night. The next afternoon after school, the children and I talked about what had happened. I tried to bring them some hope that things would get better. I reminded them of how much I loved them, and told them that God loved them even more. I assured them that God was trying to help us. We were all exhausted from the previous night, and we laid around the family room, resting and talking.

Stephen then sat down at the piano and began to pick out a tune. I sat beside him to watch him play. I couldn't read music or sing very well, but we began to compose a song together. We wrote several verses, both of us adding lines and words. Stephen picked out the notes as I hummed a tune. It went like this:

Cast your burdens on the Lord,
And He will give you peace.
Let Him gather all your cares and woes,
His loving arms beneath.

Let Him know you trust and love Him.
Never doubt His loving care,
When the days are dark and gloomy,
You will always find Him there.

Let no doubts and torments hold you.
Put your faith and trust in Him,
And He will lift and bless you
Through golden days and dim.

Oh, praise be to my Savior.
For His patience, love, and care.
I will always trust and seek Him,
For He said he would be there.

Thank you, God, and thank you, Jesus,
For a place to turn and rest.
When the burdens of the world
Weigh too hard upon my breast.

We were very proud of our creation. We played and sang our song so often that Andrea and Debbie learned the words and joined us. We never sang it in front of Richard.

When Stephen was almost nine, he woke up every morning and told me about his dreams. Often, these dreams involved conversations with Jesus. For months, he reported that Jesus visited him almost every night. In the mornings when he woke up, Stephen's face was glowing with joy as he related his experiences. Even Richard was touched. There was no denying that something very special was happening to our child.

The years from age eight to ten, Stephen seemed very happy. The school had skipped him from first to third grade, but he was doing well in school (both Bobby and Stephen scored very high on their IQ tests and were ranked in the upper 5 percent of their age group), and was making lots of new friends. But as he turned eleven, I could see that Stephen was struggling. I thought he was growing into a very handsome young man, but Stephen was worried that he was getting fat. This worried him all the time.

There were also problems at school. At one point I was called in for a conference with Stephen's teachers. They said that with his high IQ he should be making straight A's, but he wasn't applying himself.

"Is Stephen a problem in class?" I asked. They assured me that he wasn't.

"With his mind, Stephen should be getting much better grades," one of the teachers said.

"But isn't he happy and well adjusted?" I asked.

"Oh, yes," the teachers agreed. I told them I wasn't going to force Stephen to do better just for grades. He was a happy child and I wanted him to stay that way. But his teachers were very annoyed at my attitude, which they translated as lack of support for my child. Richard agreed with the teachers and started putting extra pressure on Stephen about his grades.

The summer of 1971, we took our camper on a trip to

Algonquin Park in Canada. Stephen was twelve and a half. Some friends met us there with their son and his friend. These boys and Bob, all several years older than Stephen, were going to hike and camp overnight by themselves. Stephen didn't have a backpack but he wanted to go so badly that Richard made him a makeshift one. It was bigger than Santa Claus's pack, and he trudged off with the older boys, barely able to stand upright. The straps were already cutting into his shoulders before he left. I knew he couldn't possibly make it up and down the mountain trails, and he would feel so bad when he had to turn around and come back. Richard insisted it would make a man of him and he would be fine. But I knew how discouraged he would be.

He returned six hours later, totally downhearted, feeling like a failure because he couldn't keep up with the older boys and carry the weight of the pack. I knew I couldn't protect him forever, but I felt somehow I had let him down terribly.

It was time for a change, but I felt isolated. I asked my guides to give me direction, but there was no adult with whom I could really talk. Then, at church one Sunday, Tom, a minister who had counseled Bob and then Richard and I, came up to talk to me after the service. He noted how different I looked and acted, and asked what was happening to me. Were Richard and I doing better? I decided to take a chance and hint at what was occurring in my spiritual life. He seemed interested, and I found myself telling him even more. Tom told me it sounded fascinating and he wanted to read Ruth Montgomery's book. I gave him a copy and he promised to let me know what he thought.

The following Sunday at church, Tom said he had read the book and he believed it was true. He felt, as I did, that it filled in much that was missing in Scripture. He bought several copies and gave them to friends; I bought thirty more copies and gave them to others. Some of my friends were enthralled and excited, others said it was the work of the devil.

One day, another minister to whom I had given a book told me that he seriously feared I was being misled by the devil. His doubt planted some doubt in me. That night, after everyone else was in bed, I sat on the couch and prayed. I asked God to give me a sign that this was from Him and not the devil.

Within moments, across the room, there appeared a sphere of white light in front of the wall, about eight or ten feet away. It was a glowing, brilliant light. I started to sit up, but I couldn't move. Although I was propped on the arm of the couch, with my head tilted to the left side, I could see the form as if I was sitting up straight. Try as I might, I could move no part of my body. A peaceful feeling came over me. The being of light did not communicate with words or even thoughts, but I felt totally at peace and at one with it. It stayed almost fifteen minutes and then disappeared. I could move my body again and I sat up. I questioned in my mind what had happened, and I could not deny the incredible peace I felt. I knew that God was answering my prayers.

Only a few minutes later, the being of light appeared again! As before, I could not move, but this time I was sitting up. The being stayed about ten minutes before disappearing. More of God's healing, peace, love, and light filled my whole body. When He left, I knew that Jesus had been with me. At first, I was reluctant to tell others it was Jesus. I thought myself unworthy to say that He had appeared to me. I would refer to Him only as a "being of light." Years later, when He spoke and appeared to me again, He confirmed that He had come that night as I prayed, and I finally acknowledged the truth publicly.

From that night on, everything became much clearer. Deep within me was a knowing of what I must do with my children, my personal life, and my spiritual life. I would have to leave Richard. He couldn't or wouldn't change during this lifetime. I knew I was unable to be strong enough to handle him, nor need I live in such misery. I could see that my children were already damaged and would continue to be until I got them away from his influence. Most of all, I knew that what I had received and continued to receive was not the work of the devil but a gift from God. With a certainty, I was aware of some mission or work I had to do, but I had no idea of exactly what. I wanted Stephen and the children to be part of that. I needed to prepare myself first.

Where before there had been fear and indecisiveness about the relationship, now there was confidence and determination to do what was best for all of us. Where there had been timidity and lack of self-love, now I was filled with power from on high and the return of a deep inner strength.

The answers to my questions fell into place. They were not easy but they were clear. My guides said my life was going to change completely. I welcomed the news with open arms. Never before had I felt so alive. When I told one of our ministers of the spiritual experience, he actually said, "I could understand this happening to you if you were a man, one of the priesthood, but you're a *woman.*" I knew then that my life with the church I had so loved was ending.

My guides directed me to an organization of ministers and people from all faiths who explored the esoteric and metaphysical teachings, yet were encouraged to remain in their churches, helping to expand the consciousness within their own organizations. Since I had shared my experiences with our minister, Tom, I told him about the meetings. He wanted to go. I explained that I was leaving Richard. He agreed that it was for the best, and said he would help us both in every way he could. He also said he had realized months before that there was little chance that Richard and I could work things out, but he hadn't wanted to discourage me further.

As our search and friendship continued, Tom began to confide in me, telling me of the great difficulties he had been experiencing for years in his own marriage. He loved his children and couldn't bring himself to leave them. But sadly, he said, he had never been in love with Sue. They had met when he was in the military, stationed in Alaska where there were very few women. She got pregnant the first time they were together, and like Bill and me, they felt they had to get married.

We commiserated with each other. We both had four children. His daughter and three sons were about the ages of my three youngest. I liked Tom, although I didn't find him physically appealing. He was two years younger than me, short and stocky—a real contrast to Richard who was tall and thin. What attracted me to Tom was his caring and apparent sincerity. He was, like me, a searcher. We were drawn together by our common interest in the metaphysical and spiritual field. Tom seemed to have a trust and complete faith in these teachings from the beginning.

Finally, I was strong enough to ask Richard for a divorce. I wanted to keep the house so that the children could continue in their schools, but he refused to move and told me to get a court order. Even then, he warned me, the police would have to drag him out. I pleaded with him to think about the children. I told him I would get a job and pay the bills and mortgage, and when it came time to sell the house, we could split the proceeds. He would not bend. He told me he was going out of town for three weeks on business and if I wanted a divorce, the children and I would have to move out.

I went to an attorney. She said not to move or Richard might sue me for desertion and try to get the children. She explained about getting a court order, but I couldn't bring myself to have the police come in and bodily remove Richard in front of the children.

My guides worked with me daily, helping me become clearer and sharing their knowledge with me. I studied, read, and prayed, always asking what God would have me do. I knew that when Richard returned, if he again refused to move, I would have to move out with the children. We couldn't continue in the house with him. I began to look for a job.

Tom had reached a decision to end his own marriage, and told Sue he was leaving. She reacted hysterically, screaming and threatening to kill herself. Tom talked with his children to help them understand. He knew he had to leave.

When Richard returned from his trip, he was adamant about not moving out. "You want the divorce, *you* move out." I had no choice. It was a very difficult time for the children. None of them complained about the divorce or encouraged me to stay. Despite his abuse, they cared for their dad but were happy with the "new" me who wouldn't put up with his treatment of them any longer. They didn't mind living without him in the house, but they didn't want to move or leave their school and friends. It was a time of tears and pain and happiness all mixed together. There were no apartment buildings within miles of their school and the suburb where we lived. I could not afford to rent a house like ours in the neighborhood.

Then, Tom threw me a lifeline. Besides being a minister, Tom was the warehousing manager of a large company, and his secretary was leaving to have a baby. He offered to hire me to work for him and I grabbed the opportunity. Now, I had some hope for the next step.

I found a two-story town house halfway between my new job location and the children's old neighborhood. It was all I could afford. It had three bedrooms, a living room, and a kitchen, with a tiny yard. It was in a nice complex that would have to do until we could move to bigger quarters.

Despite the problems, I felt as though we had been let out of prison. No one criticized me or yelled at me. No one yelled at the children. No one said degrading and humiliating things to them or to me. We were finally safe and free.

But it was almost too late. Things didn't change right away for the children. Bob was difficult to communicate with and always rebellious. While I understood his suffering, I felt helpless as I watched him go through such pain and unhappiness.

Stephen was at loose ends. His friends were miles away, and he was alone with the girls much of the time. He wasn't old enough to drive and, besides, my Rambler station wagon wasn't working well, only shifting into forward gear. I couldn't back it up, and I didn't have enough money to fix it. I was working every day while Stephen watched Andrea and Debbie after school.

I held on to the knowledge that this period of change was only temporary; soon, everything would fall into place. I promised the children that life would get better. They must be patient.

During this period, my guides directed me to a school and church in Washington that taught parapsychology, religion, philosophy, psychology, metaphysics, and much more. They offered a two-year and a four-year school, like a seminary or university, which culminated in certification and ordination. The directors, Reverend Diane Nagorka, and her husband, Henry, immediately struck us as sincere and well educated. Diane gave us individual readings, and what she said to me had a ring of truth, some of it evidential. I liked her and felt an instant trust. We decided to enroll in her school.

Classes at the School of Spiritual Science were to begin in September. In the meantime, Tom and I attended services and began to understand Spiritual Science teachings. It seemed a place was being opened for us to "belong" again. My guides confirmed our decision to participate and to graduate from the school. This was a next step, they said. They encouraged us not to be limited by just these teachings, but to explore further in many directions.

People at the school accepted us fully. We explained about our background and the church situation. There was only friendship and unconditional love. No judgment! They understood. Many of them had experienced very similar things in their own churches, relationships, and lives when they had the courage to change and grow.

Stephen, meanwhile, was pursuing new interests of his own in which we joined him. During the summer, Stephen had discovered karate, so Tom and I enrolled with him in a weekly karate class. Our instructor, a man dressed in a white karate gi and black belt, was a hard taskmaster. Before we began our instruction, we had to do a series of warm-ups, jumping jacks, push-ups, and other aerobics to get us ready. I hardly made it through ten push-ups, while many of the men in the class could do a hundred or more. I was out of my league. Stephen not only kept up, he loved outdoing us. He performed the exercises and practiced the kicks for hours on end. We bought him a white gi and a matching white belt. It became his uniform. He always wore it before and after school and on weekends.

As I prepared dinner in the kitchen at night, Stephen would come up beside me, do his karate yell, and practice high kicks so I could watch him. He became quite good at it and bought books on karate, read Chinese philosophy, watched every "Kung Fu" program on television, was devoted to Bruce Lee, and practiced to get his next color belt. He taught all the children the karate kicks. The house was alive with their yells, kicks in the air, and makeshift karate outfits. Stephen loved the outfit so much that I bought him a short bathrobe in the same style, which he wore whenever he didn't have on his gi.

✦

My divorce was now final, but Tom's wife would not give him a divorce. In 1972, Maryland had a law on the books that prevented couples from getting divorced if either person contested it. Tom was impatient to be free and have closure on his marriage. Virginia had an easier divorce law at the time—residency for a year in the state, then a divorce could be granted even if it was contested. Tom knew he might never get his freedom if he continued to live in Maryland, so he decided to move to Virginia. Our relationship had evolved past friendship, so we agreed to move there together and share a large split-level home in Alexandria. My children could live with us and there was room for his children to visit. It was a long drive back and forth to work each day. I explained to Stephen and the children why we would be moving there. They understood and were cooperative and good-natured about it.

The children loved the house. Everyone had a room again and there was a large family room where we could put a pool table. The yard was big and grassy with a tree they could climb. Schools were within walking distance. We settled in for the year.

I felt good for the first time in many years. It was heaven to be free and out from under the constant fighting and criticism. My children would be fine. Richard couldn't hurt them anymore, and I could love them and try to make up for what they had gone through. I was delighted to find that Tom loved the very things Richard found in me as faults. I would have done anything for Tom, I was so appreciative of his treatment. It was a blessing for me and for the children.

Then, Stephen ran away and spent the night in the dark, frigid woods, and nothing was ever quite the same.

FOUR

STEPHEN'S PAIN

If while you are a child, just one someone loves you uncritically, then you will have love to give the rest of your life.

—FLAVIA

From the very first time I had communicated with my guides, I knew that their guidance depended on my having a clear and receptive mind and spirit. If I turned away from them and did not listen, I would hear nothing.

I know now that this is the reason my guides never warned me about Stephen. For a period of time, I immersed myself in my new life with Tom and the excitement of my new learning, and I simply closed off to their messages. Now, in the evenings, I was too busy or exhausted to sit quietly and ask for guidance. Ironically, at the same time I was discovering a new universe of spirituality all around me, I was neglecting my own.

Maybe subconsciously I was afraid of hearing a truth that would challenge my belief that we were finally on the right path, that Tom was the man I would marry, that the children would be fine.

But it wasn't just Stephen who was suffering. Bob, now

eighteen, was going through his own hell. He had joined the Air Force at his uncle's suggestion. His uncle thought it would cure Bob of his rebellious streak and keep him away from drugs. But Bob hated the military. So he told someone at boot camp that he was going to run away and kill himself, and the entire fort was put on alert to find him. They called us, and in desperation, I called a general's wife whom I knew. She called her husband who knew the general in command at the fort where Bob was stationed. He personally sent out special troops to find Bob. They found him, called me, and sent him home with an honorable discharge. The general said he understood the problems some of the very young kids had, being away for the first time. He was so compassionate about Bob's well-being that I still carry a warm spot in my heart for him.

Bob came home. He had nowhere else to go, and besides, I wanted him home. It was more peaceful when he was gone, but I missed him so. I wanted my son living with me where he belonged for a time yet. I wanted to make up for all the years of hell before he moved out on his own. I loved him and wanted to help, but I couldn't undo those years of what Richard and I had done to him.

Bob turned the house upside down. He picked on Stephen, he wouldn't follow any rules, he made the children's lives miserable—except for Debbie who brought out the best in him. With her, he was gentle and loving just like when he was a little boy. We couldn't handle him, and after a short time, he moved out on his own.

Finally, Tom and I decided to get married, and we scheduled the ceremony for November 1973. We were married in our home in Alexandria with our teachers, the Nagorkas, presiding. The house was filled with our new friends and fellow students. All eight of our children were there. During the ceremony, I presented each of them with one of eight different flowers from my bouquet, to celebrate their individuality and specialness. As my eyes met Stephen's, I could not fail to notice his unhappiness. He still did not like Tom. But I knew in my heart that it was only a matter of time.

The year's lease on the house in Virginia was almost over, and we could now move back near our jobs and not have to travel back and forth so much. What a relief! Stephen had made some friends as had the girls, but there was no way we could stay; the driving was killing us. Besides, I rationalized, their friends were only months' old, this would be our last move, and they could settle down and make new and lasting friends.

This was our third move in less than two years, and I was determined that it would be our last. We decided to buy a new house that was just under construction. As the house was being built, we supervised it weekly. Each child had a room, the upstairs unfinished second floor would be Stephen's room and a classroom. Stephen was to have his longed-for privacy to lift weights, practice karate, and play his music with no one to bother him.

At last, we could begin again. The children were enrolled in schools where they would be able to remain until graduation. New friends wouldn't have to be left behind in another move. It was only a fifteen-minute drive to pick up Tom's daughter and three sons twice weekly. We felt that we belonged there in the brand new house, with rooms planned for each child and a huge yard. It was on a corner with a wooded hill in back that provided privacy, and there was a vast woods across the bridge from our street.

We moved into the house at the end of November. On December 3, Stephen celebrated his fifteenth birthday there among the unopened boxes. We had a cake and gifts for him, including a padded blue weight bench with weights. No one can remember his other gifts, and no pictures were taken since we were so busy unpacking, working, and going to school.

We placed Stephen's things into the large, attic-like room. It became his private retreat. Stephen was delighted to have his own room. We could hear him recording music and typing by the hour. Often the house would shake when he dropped the end of a barbell or a weight. He continued to practice his karate, and we could hear the noise of his movements and cries echoing throughout the house.

I prayed that this would be a new beginning for Stephen—that he would finally relax and find the normal joys of youth. It was hard for him, though. He was making a few acquaintances at Largo High School, but it was very slow. He was fifteen and cliques had been formed from grade school that didn't allow penetration by a new kid during the middle of a school term. The subjects were different, and he found himself behind the other students in some of his classes. The teachers were new to him, and they didn't have much time to help a new student.

Stephen was given extra assignments to bring him up to the level of the class. He worked diligently on them, but he wasn't happy. He often said that he didn't want to go to school. I understood what he was going through. I remembered having had the same experience myself when I changed schools twice at his age. I told him if he'd just hang in there it would get better and he'd begin to fit in just as I had done. Some days I talked to him and encouraged him to go to school. Other days, I gave in to his plea to stay home. He had various complaints to confirm not feeling well enough to go. We both knew without saying it that he wasn't sick. I tried to sense when he could handle going and when he couldn't.

I thought Stephen would soon overcome feeling like an outsider, settle down in school, and enjoy it as he had before. We often drove him to school on our way to work, although it wasn't a long walk. The three of us sat together in the front seat. Tom drove, and I rested my hand on Stephen's knee, squeezed it, told him I loved him, and encouraged him to have a good day.

One cold and windy afternoon, we picked Stephen up near the shopping mall after school. He had taken a shortcut; we watched him walk to the car. His shoulders were stooped, his raincoat blowing in the breeze. I saw him in a different way. How lonely he looked. How very alone. I was aware for a brief moment that some of his spirit was gone.

Afternoons after school, Stephen worked in his room on his weight bench, making lengthy schedules about the number of leg lifts, biceps exercises, push-ups, and conditioning exercises to do daily. We heard the weights bump as he diligently worked out, trying to discipline himself to his schedule. He wanted a body like Billy Jack or the Karate Kid. He thought his body was flabby and not strong enough. His hair hung across his face as perspiration dripped from his body after his workouts, but he was pleased to have completed what he had set out to do.

He still loved karate and wore his white gi most days. He wanted to enroll in a karate class but there wasn't one near us. He couldn't get a driver's permit yet, and with both of us at work it meant driving him back and forth a long distance for a class. We procrastinated about finding a class for him since there were so many other obligations.

Stephen was now about five feet, eleven inches tall. He didn't discuss his weight except to say he was "fat, fat, fat." I found a notation on his calendar that he weighed 183 pounds. I assured him that he wasn't fat. If he wanted to lose a couple of pounds—or even ten—to feel that he looked better, fine. But he wasn't fat. I thought he was so good-looking that his worry about being fat seemed more funny than a concern. I remembered being obsessed with looking in the mirror when I was fifteen, thinking I was fat and ugly, but in my rational moments knowing it wasn't true. He'd get over it. I did. All kids go through that, I reasoned. He had a clean-cut face and hair below his ears but not down his back like so many young men of the early 1970s. Our friends thought he was handsome and had a wonderful personality. Everyone we knew liked him.

I took comfort in recalling my own insecurities and fears as a teenager. When I was about thirteen and had developed and matured so quickly, with large breasts and baby fat, I was kidded at school. That was part of life. It hurt, but it had made me stronger and less judgmental about how people looked. My parents couldn't convince me that I wasn't fat and ugly. I was sure no boy would ever look at me. Remembering my feelings, I praised and encouraged Stephen about how good he looked, but my words didn't help much. I understood and thought he would get through these emotionally painful times as we all did.

He swore off food, then ate and berated himself. During one of his most unhappy times, complaining that he couldn't stop eating, I gave him two or three old diet pills I had used years before. He took them, with my warning that they weren't good for him, but probably wouldn't hurt for a day or two to help him get his appetite under control. He didn't like the way they made him feel, but he lost a pound or two. I was glad he didn't ask for any more or want to go to the doctor for a prescription. Our doctor believed in diet pills and would have prescribed them, and I intuitively sensed that they were dangerous.

Every week when Tom's children came, Stephen played football with them and took them into the woods to build forts. They learned to tie knots, as he had, and to build fires outdoors. The younger children must have irritated Stephen on many occasions, but he was always patient, played games with them by the hour, taught them his karate kicks, and shared the weight lifting knowledge he had. As their leader, we never saw him become angry with them or shout at them. He had the energy to tackle almost anything they wanted to do. He was never overbearing or bossy. The weekends or holidays were his happiest times. Monday mornings brought the pain of another week of school. My heart ached for him. Stephen had always loved school, excelled, and had usually been something of a teacher's pet. He had never before lacked for friends.

Now, here was a Stephen who said the teachers didn't care. They probably didn't, actually. Stephen had never been critical of his teachers before, but he insisted over and over that no one wanted to listen to him or to help him. Ordinarily, I would have gone in to see his teachers because Stephen's perceptions had always been so accurate, and bent over backward to be fair. But I continued to rationalize that these were just the normal adjustment problems that would resolve themselves in time. If they didn't, I could do something later.

Stephen often complained that the kids at school ignored him. I suggested he pick out some who looked lonely and be friends with them, which seemed good motherly advice at the time. He said he had tried. I suggested he get involved in some activities. He said the clubs were already full or too far along in their projects for him to join. I told him many times that I had felt the same way when I changed schools and was away from my friends. I assured him that it would get better. I should have known that kids don't want to hear such platitudes. Who cares what Mom and Dad experienced in the "old days?" He would nod and go up to his room.

When I came to pick Stephen up after school one day, he was sitting on a bench talking to a boy about his age who overflowed the bench, weighing at least 300 pounds. Later, Stephen told me that the boy was very nice and they'd had a good talk. I don't feel proud of what I said next: "But, Stephen, wouldn't it be better if you found someone else to be friends with, too? This boy can't even play sports with you. He may not be the best person for you to hang around with." As I said it, I felt like a heel, but Stephen had been so unhappy recently. I was fearful that if he were to be friends with this poor soul, obviously an outcast because of his being so grossly overweight, it would make things even worse for him. Stephen said that no one else would even talk to the boy. I apologized. I was being judgmental and very wrong. Nevertheless, in my concern for Stephen I had said some very unfair things that couldn't be unsaid.

During the week, Tom mostly ignored Stephen, speaking to him occasionally but with no particular interest or genuine concern. I tried to talk with Stephen every day and ask him how things were going. Sometimes he shared the way he felt; usually he was not very happy. Other times he would just say, "Okay," or "Fine," or "It's all right, Mom." I was honestly relieved when he at least pretended things were all right since so much else was going on in our lives. How I fooled myself!

Stephen had developed a cautious, then growing interest in the whole field of parapsychology. We told him more about what we were learning, and he would listen to the weekly discussions and meditations that we held in our living room, often joining in at the breaks to ask questions. Some things he thought kind of crazy, as did we. Other things stimulated question after question. Much of it was in conflict with his former church teachings, which we discussed. There was less dogma, more openness, more acceptance than we had experienced in our old churches.

Stephen told us he tried to talk to his dad about it, but his dad ridiculed everything we were doing. This planted occasional doubt in him. We talked it over, trying to help him see different perspectives, sharing our personal feelings but letting him make up his own mind. He seemed enthusiastic and happy talking and hearing about everything. Then, when he visited his dad, he came home depressed and confused. This was not always because of what he told his dad we were studying, but because, as he would say, "He makes me feel like shit."

Despite all the stress, December brought the anticipation of Christmas and lifted all of our spirits with renewed hope. Tom was his most friendly, outgoing self, and he arranged the lights on the tree. The children and I added most of the ornaments. When we finished, there was the sense of pride that perhaps our tree was the most beautiful in all of Maryland.

The days were filled with the children playing football outside except when the melting snow and rain halted their fun. When they had to stay inside, they baked Christmas cookies and cakes, which they devoured almost as soon as they came out of the oven. If ever the happy family was in evidence, it was that December. Any worries, problems, and fighting were put on hold. It was the time to love everyone and everything, to give thanks for this new life, this new chance we had to begin again.

I had placed eight small candles, each a different color and one for each child in each of eight windowpanes in the living room. As we lit them, I told the children it was to celebrate how special each one of them was to us. Each child knew one of the candles to be his or her own, but we hadn't assigned anyone a particular color. The little candles glowed in a brilliant rainbow.

No expense was spared at Christmas. It was both Tom's and my own favorite time of the year. Christmas of 1973 was celebrated on the day before Christmas since Tom's ex-wife insisted she have the children every Christmas. The day of our Christmas began before dawn with the younger children waking up the older ones.

It was almost lunchtime before the gift orgy was finished. The living room looked as if a tornado had whipped through it. Stephen got lots of toys and presents that year, as did the others. One gift was a belt, which he opened, smiled, and thanked us for appreciatively, but I could tell he was a little disappointed. There was enough of the kid in him that games, toys, and fun things outweighed the more practical items. He helped the younger kids open gifts that were tied too tightly, and played with them with their games and toys the rest of the day. He wore his bathrobe over shorts and a T-shirt. None of the children had combed their hair or dressed in anticipation of Christmas pictures.

Taking Christmas pictures reminded me of an incident that had happened several weeks before at school. We were being taught to develop our intuition in a weekly class and our teacher, Billie, giving me an intuitive message said, "Be sure to take plenty of pictures this Christmas. Things will never be the same and you will want to take more than the usual number of pictures." I didn't think that was very profound. In our household, things were never the same from one day to the next, much less from one Christmas to the other. Nevertheless, as I watched Stephen and the children open presents, I remembered this strange prediction and had the camera out, trying to remember to photograph everyone. Stephen kept avoiding the camera because he said he looked awful and asked me to wait until he combed his hair and got cleaned up.

Stephen gave us a *Jonathan Livingston Seagull* record album because he knew how much we had loved the book. It was a great gift; we were surprised and delighted, and Stephen was pleased.

It was a perfect day: laid-back, peaceful, and relaxed. Children found corners of the house where they stacked their gifts, going back to them again and again. Stephen took his presents upstairs to his room. Everyone played—alone, in small groups, and together.

Stephen and the girls were out of school until January. They kept themselves occupied with reading, bicycling, and retreating into their own inner worlds. They did not have baby-sitters, but, instead, took care of one another. Stephen, fifteen, was in charge, and Andrea, twelve, was second in command. Debbie was almost eight. Stephen and Andrea had temperaments much alike and even looked alike. Both were more kind, loving, and quiet, more well behaved than the child on each end. Bob had always needed attention and demanded attention, with one crisis after another, even after he moved out on his own. As the youngest, Debbie also demanded much attention, partly from age, partly from her personality. She was bossy, charming, loving, and irritating, often within the same five minutes. Sometimes, when Stephen didn't do what she wanted, Debbie called him "a fat slob." When I heard her, I told her how much it hurt him and made her apologize.

Stephen's worries seemed rather normal alongside Debbie's, Andrea's, and Bob's. Bob hated his too curly hair, Andrea thought nobody liked her. Added to that, my remembrances of my own insecurities, although twenty years in the past, convinced me that Stephen was going through a childhood rite of passage.

◆

Stephen was not happy when school began, but he talked about being really determined to make a new start with friends and teachers. He went back to school with renewed optimism. Almost immediately, the same pattern reappeared. He was ignored and left out and even the teachers had no time for him. Why I didn't go to the school cannot be excused by Tom's insisting that Stephen had to learn to handle his own problems, or by my feeling that perhaps I wasn't cutting the apron strings sufficiently and letting him grow up. The end result was the same: I didn't talk to his teachers and they didn't ask to talk to me when his grades dropped and his assignments weren't finished. I kept hoping that time would solve the problem.

As the weather got a little bit warmer, Stephen continued to wear his navy blue raincoat, even though some days it seemed he didn't need it. He felt it kept him from looking so fat. He seemed relaxed and happy on weekends, and while at home he was his old smiling and joking self. Every Monday his face changed, his shoulders sagged, as he forced himself to go to school, reluctantly putting his arms into his raincoat just before he left.

We talked about Stephen's friends a lot during February and in early March. He had a crush on a girl from our former church, and we had a long discussion about it seated on the couch in the living room one evening. She had kept in telephone contact, and he saw her when his dad insisted on taking him to church. This was mostly a distant, unrequited love on Stephen's part. She was in love with someone else, which Stephen seemed to understand with little jealousy, but a bit of sadness. Now she thought she was pregnant. She couldn't tell her parents who were pillars of the church, and there was no one in whom to confide but Stephen. I doubt that she knew how much he cared for her. He told me he didn't know what to tell her, and he asked me to talk to her. He assured her that I wouldn't tell her parents or anyone. When she and I finished talking, he hugged me and said, "Thanks, Mom. I knew you would understand and help her."

We discussed many things that night: his worries, fears, hopes, his philosophies, karate, girls, life. Afterward, I felt so good. He had always talked with me about his feelings, but this time it was like two adults talking. I was pleased with his concern for his friends, his maturity in dealing with his thoughts and desires, and his confidence in me. Also, I was pleased that he was so affectionate. Most of his friends would not let their mothers hug them much less return the hug with a kiss and say, "I love you." I felt very proud of him. My young son was becoming a thoughtful and caring person. I had no worries about the man he would become. After all the difficulties with Bob, Stephen made me feel that perhaps I had some redeeming qualities as a mother.

He was becoming quite handsome, losing the little boy chubbiness of body and face. His eyebrows were growing darker and somewhat bushy, and his blue eyes radiated kindness and warmth and mischief. Plainly and simply, I adored him. Perhaps he acted and looked like a thousand other boys his age. I saw him through the "mother glow" of love. To me, he was very, very special, not only in looks, but in spirit.

But his loneliness continued to break my heart. One Friday night late in February, Richard had already picked up the girls before Tom and I arrived home, exhausted from a long, hard week. We did not have Tom's children, and the house was quiet—a most unusual occurrence.

Stephen was sitting in the lounge chair, watching television, and eating. He had on his favorite blue slacks and navy blue, long-sleeved shirt, rolled up to the elbows, his bare feet hanging over the end of the footrest of the chair. Tom and I decided to go to a movie, and I asked Tom about inviting Stephen to go with us—feeling guilty because I knew we didn't have a lot of time alone. He agreed but wasn't very enthusiastic about it. I knew he'd prefer that we go alone. I said I wanted to ask Stephen anyway, so he didn't have to be by himself. When I invited him, Stephen's eyes lit up. Then, hesitating a moment, he said he didn't want to go.

I tried to talk him into coming with us, but it was one of those conversations where the main communicating was being done nonverbally. I really wanted him to go and he knew it, but also I didn't want to disappoint Tom. I realized if we were to maintain our relationship with eight kids, we needed time alone. I think that Stephen knew that, too, and that was why he declined to go. My heart ached when I couldn't convince him because I could feel his loneliness. I let him decide, and his decision was for *me*. He knew this, and I knew that he knew. The whole thing made me sad all evening.

With Stephen's growing maturity, he felt good enough about himself not to subject himself to further browbeating by Richard, so he seldom went to Richard's anymore. He said he hated being there because his dad was always finding fault with him. He would, however, sometimes go when Richard's new girlfriend had her fifteen-year-old daughter along. Then he would come home and say he had a wonderful time, and that he really liked the daughter. He hoped her mother and his dad would marry. Richard had a series of short relationships after we divorced, but none of them lasted long.

Stephen said that every time he didn't go with his dad, he felt guilty—guilty that he didn't want to be with him because he loved Richard but didn't like him, guilty that somehow he was hurting his dad each time he didn't go. Richard would call him and amplify the guilt, but Stephen generally stood firm and made excuses about other commitments. The times he gave in when he didn't want to, he would be in a deep depression for days after he came home.

The girls, not as strong, acquiesced most of the time, and even when I told them they could stay home, they often went anyway so their dad wouldn't get upset. While he did not treat Debbie as badly, even she made sarcastic comments about how he treated the other two.

Stephen had a gym bag he carried back and forth to school. It became his security blanket and his purse. Everything went into it—books, socks, clothes, and all the mysterious things a fifteen-year-old boy carries. Once in his room, I saw several new things from the drugstore. I asked him where he got them. He said that he had bought them. I questioned if he had enough money, asking if he had just taken the items without paying for them. He denied it.

I wondered about this because a year earlier, I had picked up an extension phone by accident while he was talking, and heard his friend mention shoplifting. Curious, I listened further and heard Stephen say he had shoplifted the ring he was wearing. I confronted him and told him I had listened. He said he really hadn't stolen his ring, he had bought it, but all the other kids were shoplifting and he felt left out, so he had bragged that he had done it, too. He was always honest with me, so I had no reason to doubt him. He also knew I had never snooped in his room or listened in on his conversations. My mother had honored my privacy, and I did the same with my children. I never went in his room or read his writings even when he wasn't home. Knowing that, he and the other children left personal things out and were usually honest with me. I respected the fact that sometimes they simply didn't want their mother to know everything. I honored this as a sign of their growing up. So, while there was a tiny seed of concern that maybe Stephen had shoplifted the items, my past experience with him overrode these suspicions and it was soon forgotten.

My heart would ache each time we drove him to school. He looked so lonely and vulnerable—his shoulders stooped, blue raincoat unbelted and flapping around his body as he walked slowly into the building for classes.

Every day without fail, when he got home in the afternoon before the girls arrived, Stephen telephoned me at about 3:15 P.M., at work. When I answered, a familiar voice would always say, "Hi, Mom, it's me." Or sometimes, "Hi, Mom, it's me—Steve." He always called himself Steve, I always called him Stephen. He never said, "Don't call me Stephen," but he liked to refer to himself as Steve with everyone else. I would ask him about his day or he would ask me about something. If there was time, we visited awhile, and I played "mother" by phone. If we were very busy, the conversation was short—just Stephen checking in that he was okay and that I was there. I often dictated a few things for him to write down that I wanted the children to do before I came home—such as turning on the stove to cook the meat, or cleaning up their rooms, or emptying the trash. The conversations usually ended with "Bye, honey. I love you." And he responded with, "Bye, Mom. I love you, too." After Stephen's call, there were often others from each of the girls. Working for Tom as his assistant and secretary in a private office gave me a chance to keep in touch with the children until we went home at five o'clock. The three of them got along reasonably well, with Debbie the most difficult to handle and discipline. They sometimes reported on one another when I got home. I scolded, laughed, disciplined, or smoothed things over, depending upon the situation.

I wasn't always consistent. For some things that probably needed correcting, I laughed and hugged them. For others that might have really been minor, I reprimanded them. I didn't like to punish them physically or emotionally—they'd had too many years of that. Mostly, I fussed at them or hugged them or talked to them. I was not a very consistent disciplinarian.

The mistakes that I made with them, which were many, were based partly on my absolute ignorance of child-rearing.

There was, no doubt, a kind of self-centeredness in being in school and working, consequently becoming overly tired. Nevertheless, everything I did was overshadowed by the incredible love and pride I had for each of my children. They seemed to be exceptionally good kids—very, very special. And I felt that nothing very bad could ever happen to us again now that we were away from the hell we had endured for so long.

In many ways, their childhood seemed so much richer and fuller than mine. They had all the material things I had always wanted. I had never lacked emotional support and love; and, I thought I was giving them what I had received and more plus all the material things. I had my work and my education, my life separate yet a part of theirs. I let them have a degree of freedom to make some of their own decisions as they matured. I took joy in their accomplishments and they in mine. I didn't feel I had much trouble letting them break free of me to grow up. Basically, I doubt that I was as good a mother as I aspired to be or thought I was, nor was I as bad as I could have been. Time, the great healer, may have dimmed my memories of my shortcomings and magnified the memories of my strengths.

✦

Stephen continued to be ambivalent about school most mornings. One morning I found a note on our bedroom door, "I can't force myself to go in. Please let me stay home and sleep today." I let him sleep, not even going upstairs to talk to him. His note was so boldly written, so intense. He called me later at work, thanking me, and explaining how he felt.

One afternoon in early March, he came home from school carrying a yellow belt for his karate gi. He said his biology teacher had let him demonstrate karate in class. The teacher was a black belt so he was able to test Stephen and graduate him to the next level—a yellow belt. Stephen was beaming with pride. He intensified his practice of the karate kicks, yellow belt tied firmly around his white gi, which was getting a little short in the legs due to his added height. The outfit was now a year-and-a-half old and despite numerous washings, looked somewhat dingy. The dirty and much-used white belt, which was never washed, was hung over the back of the door, having served its purpose. Stephen was preparing for all the next stages of colored belts, from brown to the coveted black. He loved karate and practiced, not to hurt anyone as he said, but to stay in good physical shape, able to defend himself, and to be strong. He continued to watch "Kung Fu," cheering the good guys winning over the bad with their soft words and martial art movements. Stephen checked books out of the library about weight lifting, Chinese philosophy, karate, and the martial arts. He read, practiced, and set up disciplines and sets of exercises to follow. Few kids could have kept up such a regimen, but he tried and was hard on himself when he faltered. His heroes did not falter. They could jump tall buildings, take on half the Chinese army, and stop wild animals and criminals with a soft-spoken word and a cool look in the eye.

Stephen had finally made a friend at school and invited him over to practice karate in his bedroom. While trying a kick, the friend broke his finger. Stephen rushed to the neighbor's house across the street and they drove him to the emergency room. Stephen called me at work, concerned, but feeling he had handled the crisis pretty well. The neighbors were very helpful. The boy was going to be fine. It was no big deal. Still, the boy's parents never allowed him to come back, and I'm sure Stephen was crushed.

I had no idea of the depths of Stephen's loneliness and pain. When weekends came, he was his old self—playing with the kids, teaching and helping them with homework, cooking, watching TV, practicing his karate. He was full of life and laughter, and I thought maybe things were getting better for him. But the situation at school was wearing down Stephen's gentle spirit little by little. It was only in looking back that I became so painfully aware of that.

FIVE

✦

RAINY DAYS AND MONDAYS

Good night, sweet prince,
May bands of angels sing thee to thy rest.
—Shakespeare, *Hamlet*

Monday afternoon, March 18, I came home from work and Stephen wasn't there. He hadn't called me as he usually did, and I had been so busy I hadn't called home.

I asked where he was, and Andrea said he had gone camping in the woods. Camping on a school night? The girls told me they had come home from school and found him packing his gym bag and getting a sleeping bag ready. When they questioned him, he told them he needed to get away and to tell me not to try to find him—he wanted to be alone. He was going across the bridge into the woods for the night and would be okay.

I sighed. What was I going to do? That morning he had once again not wanted to go to school, but I insisted. A half hour went by and there was no noise from upstairs to indicate that he was dressing. I was losing patience and beginning to feel very annoyed with Stephen. Something had to be done. Refusing to go to school was bad enough, but I had also seen some items from the drugsstore on his bed the day before. I was pretty sure he hadn't bought them, but I hadn't taken or found time to talk with him. I was in a hurry getting dressed and felt agitated. I just didn't know how to handle the situation regarding Stephen's unhappiness in school. Quite unlike myself, I asked Tom to go to Stephen's room and tell him that I insisted he go to school. I also asked him to tell Stephen to leave his gym bag at home since I didn't want him taking any more things from the store.

This was out of character for me. I seldom asked Tom to talk to Stephen about *anything*. I normally handled my children and their problems and needs myself. Tom usually paid little attention to Stephen. But perhaps I also asked Tom to go to Stephen's room because a few nights before Tom and Stephen had had a long talk—they seemed close for once. They discussed life after death and reincarnation, and Stephen had asked many questions with great interest. He wanted to know more about all we were learning and studying. I hoped this was a sign that Stephen was coming out of his shell and that Tom and Stephen were growing closer.

Tom came back down from Stephen's bedroom after a few minutes, saying he had talked to him and told him to leave his bag home from now on and that he was to get dressed for school. I asked him what Stephen had said. We were interrupted by one of the girls, and I didn't learn any more about their conversation.

When we were ready to leave, Stephen yelled downstairs that he'd walk to school and for us to go ahead. He had recently admitted to riding to school with us, then coming back home, skipping school. This had to stop. I told him we'd wait, that I wanted him to come with us. When he slowly climbed into the car, I asked him to promise to stay in school until it was out. I assured him that when we got home that night we would talk and work things out. I decided I had put off talking with his teachers at school too long. It had been over three months and things weren't improving.

We were sandwiched in the front seat of the car. Tom was driving, Stephen was on my right next to the door, and I sat in the middle. As usual, I squeezed his knee and thought how good he still felt, just like when he was little. His head was down and he didn't say anything. I told him he *must not* shoplift things, that if he needed something we would buy it for him or give him the money. When he climbed out of the car, I said we'd see him when we all got home. We would talk further then. He agreed. He walked toward the school without looking back, his shoulders slumped, blue raincoat blowing in the March breeze. I couldn't bear for him to hurt so much. This just wasn't like him. A few days before, he had even given the other kids all of his karate equipment and knives. He had loved his karate gear so much, I was surprised he had given it away.

Now he was gone for the night. Boy, was I irritated with him. He knew we were going to talk that afternoon. I had made special plans to be with him and here he had gone camping in the woods just as he had when we lived in Alexandria. This time, I wasn't going to try and find him. He wouldn't answer anyway. He would either come home tonight when it got dark or tomorrow. When he did, I would be tougher on him. Maybe I was babying him too much. I was definitely going to the school tomorrow and get things straightened out. The school was falling down on its job, and I would let his teachers know in no uncertain terms.

Stephen didn't come home that night and I was more irritated than worried. How insensitive of him to do this, knowing how I'd agonized the first time he ran away for the night. I couldn't believe he was this uncaring. It wasn't like him.

After we went to bed that evening, I fell asleep but awoke in the middle of the night to the sound of rain beating down on the roof. I felt such overpowering sadness, I burst into tears. My son was outside by himself in the dark and pouring rain. Stephen must be cold, wet, and feeling scared and unloved. I wanted to go out in the dark to find him and bring him home and just hold him. I loved him so. If he would spend the night in the dark and cold and rain, things were pretty bad. When he came home, I would talk to him and then go to the school right away. I swore it as I prayed for him and fell asleep again.

In the morning, I decided to stay home from work. I had been awake off and on all night. I couldn't go to the office and worry until I heard from him. I waited and waited. It was noon and he still hadn't returned. I talked to Tom, who said he was picking up his children after school. He would come home early and we'd go get Stephen or send the children to the woods to find him and tell him to come home. He could tell how upset I was and assured me that we would find Stephen.

Tom and the children arrived home around four o'clock that afternoon. While they were getting a snack, we discussed going to find Stephen and what to do about how miserable he was in school. There was a knock on the door. Andrea answered and brought two men in dark suits into the living room. They showed me their badges, asked me my name, and said they were there about Stephen.

Oh, no! I thought anxiously. What on earth had Stephen done to get him in trouble with the police?

One of the policemen kindly asked us to sit down and motioned us to the couch. The two men pulled up chairs and sat across from us. The children hovered in the doorway.

One man spoke quietly and said, "Your son is dead. Two men gathering firewood found him in the woods."

I felt as if someone had hit me in the stomach with a sledgehammer. The pain was so intense that I gasped for breath. I couldn't exhale or breathe. Finally I asked, "What? *What?*" He said that two men gathering firewood in the woods across from us had found him hanging from a tree, called them, and they had come and cut his body down.

This couldn't be possible. There must be some mistake. I didn't cry. The pain was so bad in my stomach that I couldn't cry. I heard gasps from the children and cries, but my pain blocked out everything else. I needed to question the men, but I couldn't speak. Shock and pain had knocked the breath out of me.

The policemen told me that Stephen had left a notebook containing messages to us. I could read it if I wanted, but they would have to take it for a few days. They handed it to me. As I read each page, it sounded so much like Stephen, I smiled through my pain. He had written every one of us some words of caring and comfort. He had even made some jokes about it all. It was so like him, yet the notes were also heartbreaking. The words confirmed that Stephen was no longer alive. My body heard and felt the words, but my mind didn't register them fully. I think I expected Stephen to walk through the door at any moment and say, "Just a joke, Mom. Fooled you, didn't I?"

The policemen gently told me that Stephen's body was just outside in an ambulance. Did we want to identify it there? We would have to identify it there or in the morgue. His body? I had seen only one dead body in my life and it almost made me throw up. His body? My baby's body! Stephen had been hanging on a tree with a rope around his neck. How could I look at his precious body with a rope around his throat? How could I see him dead? I didn't want to see my baby dead. I couldn't bring myself to look at him. All my life I had stayed away from funerals and dead bodies. I couldn't stand to *think* of dead bodies. How could I possibly look at my own son's body?

I thought about the neighbors, none of whom we knew. I couldn't face going outside and seeing them watching Stephen and me and our family in our pain and grief as they pulled back the sheet to show us his body. I couldn't think clearly. I was frightened. I was so sick. I clung to the feeling that if I didn't see him dead, Stephen would still be alive.

I didn't know what to do. I wanted to see him, but I was frightened and in pain. I asked Tom to identify him. He went outside with one of the detectives and came back in the house with tears in his eyes. In the years to come, I repeatedly asked him if Stephen's eyes had popped out. I had read an account of someone who had hanged himself and was found with his eyes popped out. He assured me they weren't. To this day I don't know if they were or not. The policemen took his notebook with them. I wanted so much to keep it, but they wouldn't let me. They promised to return it later.

The ambulance pulled away without sirens. The children were crying and heartbroken. I hugged Andrea and Debbie. Andrea sobbed and sobbed. She and Stephen were the closest of the four. Debbie had no real awareness that this meant Stephen wouldn't come back home again, ever.

I looked down at my lap after the men left. I was wearing a blue-and-red-patterned flannel caftan. It was my favorite warm and comfortable outfit to lounge around in. In a fury, I pulled it over my head and stuffed it deep into the garbage can. It had covered my body on the worst day of my entire life. I felt an overwhelming desire to bathe all over or to claw the skin from my body. I wanted to die myself.

People had to be called—my parents and sister, Richard, our ministers, whoever loved and knew Stephen. One call melted into another. Everyone cried. I cried.

I tried to comfort the girls, feeling waves of pain flow in and out of me like sharp razors. I put the girls to bed, held them, and tried to tell them Stephen was okay, for them not to be afraid. Then I fell across my bed and cried until I couldn't breathe or sit up, I was so weak. I would stop, blow my nose, and start again. My life was over, my son was dead. I wanted to die, too. "Oh, Stephen, Stephen, I love you, I love you." I moaned the cry heard throughout the ages from parents who have lost a child. The pain was as searing as if a torch were being shoved into my heart and stomach.

I cried and moaned and sobbed all night trying to cover the sounds in my pillow, not realizing the girls were probably doing the same in their rooms. Tom held me as I rambled on and on about Stephen, how I should have gone to the woods to find him, how he must have been hurting more than I knew, how I wanted to die.

I blamed everyone. Richard had killed him with his faultfinding. The judgmental people at church had driven him to this. The cruel, uncaring students and teachers at school had made it happen. Most of all, I had killed him. I didn't know he had hurt so much he would rather be dead. Tom held me, comforted me, and listened. I kept us awake all night, crying.

Just before daybreak, I fell into exhausted sleep for an hour. I awakened to the sun on my face. I looked around and felt so happy. I looked over at Tom sleeping. Then I remembered! Pain hit my heart and stomach and head, and I moaned in agony. I cried and cried and cried. Tom woke up and held me and tried to comfort me. I was immobilized. I could barely walk to the bathroom. I wanted to lie back down and sleep and never wake up. Stephen was dead. My son, my beloved son. He had everything to live for, things couldn't have been that bad. They *must* have been that bad or he wouldn't have preferred dying to living.

I tried to remember his notes. He had assured me he would communicate with me, saying to keep the channel open. His notes were hopeful, almost funny. He had said he was writing the last ones with the rope around his neck. I had told my mother that while he was hanging there dying he had continued to write. How long did it take him to strangle, hanging there? I learned later, of course, that he had written them with the rope around his neck before he jumped to his death, not as he was hanging. But for several days, I pictured him hanging, gradually suffocating as he grasped his pen to write his final words.

The morning after we learned of Stephen's death, we had to drive to Bob's and tell him in person. On top of everything else Bob was going through, he would have to deal with the death of his brother. The day before Stephen's death, the two boys had gone to the movies and seemed to have a good time. It was the first time they had acted like buddies in a long while. They seemed like loving brothers and friends again, really enjoying themselves. The next day Stephen had killed himself. How would Bob handle it?

When we arrived at Bob's, I hugged him and told him his brother was dead. He sobbed uncontrollably as I held him and tried to comfort him. With my limited knowledge at that time, I even said some stupid things about it being Stephen's right to kill himself and we had to understand. Later I learned that, of course it *had* been his right, it was his life, but perhaps we could have done something to stop him until he was thinking more clearly and could make a more rational decision. It was especially difficult for Bob during the next weeks; the rest of the family had one another, but he was by himself. I had always loved him. Now he was the only son I had left, and I wanted to do anything, *anything* to make things better for him.

When we returned home, I called the number on the card the detectives had left. The police had Stephen's belongings, everything they had found on and around him when they cut his body down. I could come to the station and claim them the next day. They asked what I would like to have done with the body. I got off the phone, and discussed it with Tom.

Stephen had said in his notes to cremate him. I couldn't bear to have his body burned, but I didn't want his precious body buried in the ground, alone. I had read only a few months before how few bodies of children were donated to the hospitals for research. Physicians in the article were expressing how important it was for them to have young cadavers to study to help save other children's lives. My naive picture of this at the time was that they would open his mouth, check his throat, eyes and ears, and examine his body, just like his doctor did for his checkups. I was so distraught, I falsely assumed that they would write what they found on a chart and then save his body forever in a drawer. Autopsy was just a word; it had no visual or intellectual meaning to me then. Feeling so unbearably sad and not thinking clearly, I decided that my act of love for Stephen and the children of the future would be to donate his body to science. In fact, I told myself, it could be Stephen's gift to the world, too. It was too late to donate any of his organs. His body hadn't been found until some twenty hours or more after he died. Donating his body would be all that he and I could do to help others.

I called and told the police what I wanted to do, and they agreed to make the arrangements. When we arrived to pick up Stephen's belongings, they told us the name of a hospital where I had to go to sign papers for the donation of his body.

In the car, I cradled the plastic bag that held Stephen's things; his sleeping bag and clothes were in the back seat. The bag contained his favorite silver ring, along with his watch, which wasn't running. His billfold was there, with only his social security card, but he had signed his name and I held that to my cheek and cried. The rope had been wound and was also placed in the bag. I unrolled it to see where it had been around his neck and realized he had been cut down, and, of course, they wouldn't send that part of the rope.

I removed the book in which Stephen had written his final words. It began, "Give this book to my mom, please . . ." Oh, Stephen!

STEVE
NEW ORCHARD
DRIVE.
RIGHT ACROSS
BRIDGE.
GIVE THIS
BOOK TO MY
MOM, PLEASE
DEAR WORLD
BEING OF
UNSOUND
MIND + BODY
I LEAVE MY
LAST WILL
AND TESTEMANT.
THE WORLD
IS IN BAD
SHAPE + I
DID NOTHING
TO HELP IT
CHANGE

AND THERE-
FORE AM
NOT FIT TO
LIVE IN IT!!
I LEAVE
FINAL INSTRUCT-
IONS TO MY
LOVED ONES

MOM - I'LL
BE IN TOUCH
(YOU NO WHAT I
MEAN) I LOVE
YOU

DAD - TRY TO
TAKE KARATE
KEEP DOING
THINGS YOU
ALWAYS WANTED.
IF THERE IS
LIFE AFTER
DEATH ILL
LET YOU
KNOW SOMEHOW!
I LOVE YOU
IN A SPECIAL
WAY.

MRS. H[redacted]-
YOU ARE A
LADY OF POISE
GRACE + LOVE
YOU ARE A
TRULY REMARK-
ABLE WOMAN
YOUR BUEATY
WIT + CHARM
ARE ENDLESS
PEACE BE
WITH YOU FAIR
LADY + I LOVE
YOU

LYNN H[redacted]

YOU ARE ONE
OF A KIND YOU
ARE BUITIFULLY
STUNNING, KIND +
GRACEFUL + I
FOUND MYSELF
IN LOVE WITH
YOU. IF WE
LIVED IN
MID EVEL DAYS
I WOULD BE
YOUR NIGHT AND
YOU A BUITIFUL
PRINCESS. LOVE ALWAYS!

MARK R

IF REINCARNATION
IS TRUE
ILL BE IN
TOUCH OR
IF THEIRS
LIFE AFTER
DEATH!
HANG LOOSE

LOVE,
STEVE

TOM—

SMILE AND
TAKE CARE
OF MOM!

THE
KARMIC
KID

KATHY

I LOVED
YOU IN A
SPECIAL WAY!
AND WILL
FOLLOW MY
PLEDGE TO
BE THERE IF
YOU NEED ME
EVEN AFTER
DEATH! YOU
WERE TRULY
BUITIFUL
—LOVE
Steve

TO ALL
WHOM I
LOVED,
I
SHALL
RETURN!!

MOM - TAKE
CARE OF
KATHY E.'s
PROBLEM IF
SHE NEEDS
HELP -

DAD -
ENJOY LIFE
TAKE CARE
OF
MRS. H
&
LYNN

SHOW THESE
TO
WHOM THEY
WERE
ADDRESSED!

EVEN IN
THE END
I FELT
NO REMORSE
WHAT I
COULDNT DO
IN LIFE
I WILL
DO IN
DEATH!!

I
WILL USE
MY SPIRITS
WILL TO
HELP OTHERS
THRU TROUBLES

DO NOT
SPEND $
ON A
BIG FUNERAL
CREMATE
ME I
GUESS

I NEED TO WRITE SOME BOOKS SO KEEP THE CHANNEL OPEN

I WILL LET YOU KNOW THE TRUTH

HOPE
BOB
GETS
BETTER

I
LOVE
HIM

DONT
SPOIL
DEBBIE
(HA) (HA)
I
LOVE
HER

IM
GOING TO
BE A
SUPER
HERO
AND
YA'ALL KNOW
IT

IF
THERES
ANYTHING
YOU
NEED TO
KNOW
CALL TOLL
FREE
HA HA

I
LOVE
DEB
+
ANDREA

TAKE
CARE
!

I

LOVE...

LOVE

Steve

I HOPE

I

BROUGHT

SOME

HAPPINESS

TO

SOMEONE

I
KEPT MY
WARPED
SENSE OF
HUMOR
EVEN IN
THE
END!

YES
I
DID
SHOPLIFT

I
LOVE
KATHY
+
LYNN

PEOPLE
WHO
MAKE
FUN
OF
PEOPLE
ARE
FULL
OF
SHOOT

I
ALMOST
DIDNT
DO IT
BECAUSE
I
WANTED TO
LOVE
KATHY
+
LYNN

IF PEOPLE
WOULD
JUST
BE REAL
PEOPLE
COULD
JUST
BE LOVED
(QUITE PROFOUND
DONT YOU THINK)

MY STUFF
IS
RIGHT
BY
THE FIELD!

JOANNE
HAS
GOT A
NICE
BODY
BUT SHE
WAS TO
OLD
HA HA

MR + MRS
2[illegible]
YOU WILL
LOSE WEIGHT

PEACE
LOVE
HAPPINESS
+
A CHICKEN
IN EVERY
POT TO
ALL

LAST WORDS:

THE FINAL VICTORY WILL BE MINE !!

LOVE STEVE CHRISTOPHER DENNIS

MONDAY

DUS

IM WRITING THIS

IM WRITING
THIS FINAL
NOTE WITH
THE ROPE
AROUND
MY NECK
I LIVED
I LOVED
I LOST
←

ON THE TREE
I AM
SORRY
FOR ALL
THE
PAIN
I
CAUSED

ON THE TREE

I LIVED LIKE A FOOL

I DIE LIKE A MAN

I TOLD GOD TO STOP ME IF I SHOULDN'T DO IT

I rode to the hospital to sign the forms with a mixture of pain and fear. At the desk, an overly cheerful nurse gave me the papers to sign for release of Stephen's body. But just as I was ready to write my name, I suddenly decided I wanted Stephen's body back. I didn't want to donate his precious body to any place, ever! I wanted to go find his body, pick him up, and take him home, climb in bed with him, cover us up and protect him always.

Panic rose within me, but I tried to stay calm. "I want to see my son's body," I said to the nurse. My secret plan was to grab it and run away with it, but I didn't want the nurse to suspect anything.

"You *can't* see the body, I'm sorry," she said quietly.

"Oh, please. I want to see his body for just a minute. *Right now,*" I insisted.

My heart sank when she answered, "I'm very sorry, but it isn't here. It's been moved to the Baltimore morgue. Then it will be taken to the teaching hospital."

I wanted to scream, to cry, to yell, to break down the doors and find him and to steal his body back. But I knew she was telling the truth. There was nothing I could do. If I called the morgue in Baltimore and told them they couldn't have Stephen's body after all, that I wanted it back, they would think I was a fool. What would I do with his body? I couldn't stand to bury it or burn it. I couldn't leave it in the house.

Again I rationalized that many children could be helped by doctors studying Stephen's body, which he could no longer use. I still had no idea what happened during a research autopsy and how a body was disposed of afterward. A part of me felt guilty that I had let them have it, while another part tried to remember it might help some child or maybe many children. No one told me until years later that I could have requested his ashes when they were finished working with him. No one even told me that the body would eventually be cremated. Somehow it seemed the act of donating Stephen's body would keep him alive for all time.

We decided on a memorial service instead of a funeral. Where would we hold it? Most of his friends were from the old church or neighborhood where he had spent so many years. He hadn't attended the church where Tom and I went, although they were willing to have the service there. I talked to Richard and together we decided that for the good of all, and for Stephen, the old church might be the better place for his service, despite all that had happened. However, I told him that since Tom and I were to be ordained the next year, we wanted to conduct the service, and he could assist us. The ministers at the old church could not possibly conduct it with the love and caring we could. He reluctantly agreed and had one of the ministers call us to set it up.

The minister, a friend of Richard's from years past, and supposedly a friend of mine, said they would be glad to have the service in the church, but Tom and I could not possibly participate in conducting the service. I told him that Richard, Tom, and I had talked and agreed that this might heal the chasm between all of us. Despite our new directions, we cared for the people at church and thought many of them cared for us. Stephen was, after all, *my* son, and as his mother and a ministerial candidate, no one could conduct the service with more caring than I. He insisted the church would not allow it and that Richard did not want it. We never spoke again.

Richard decided to hold the service without us. I protested, to no avail. Richard said Stephen had been mentally ill, that I was trying to pretend he had been normal. I argued that he was depressed but certainly not mentally ill. Richard told me it was my fault Stephen was dead. With great cruelty he stated that if I hadn't left him, Stephen would be alive. He also told this to the girls at every opportunity.

I tried to keep my perspective, to remind myself that Stephen was *not* his child. He had done nothing but bring misery into his life—into all our lives. He had no right to pretend this great interest and love now. His church had treated Stephen like an outcast because of me. None of them had the right to conduct this last rite for him and pretend great concern about him. When he was living they didn't care, except to confuse him. Now he was dead and it was too late to be concerned. I was angry, hurt, and felt helpless. They had no right to do this without my approval. Richard had no right to do this, but there was no way I could stop him.

We had no choice but to make other plans ourselves. We decided to have the memorial service in our home, instead of at our new church. We would invite only our close friends and those who loved Stephen. Richard was not invited. We would read the things Stephen wrote, express our love for him, and celebrate both his short life and his death in the way we felt appropriate.

✦

The memorial service would be held on March 23. We asked that no flowers be sent for the service. When friends wondered what they could do, we suggested they donate to some favorite organization in Stephen's name. Tom and I went to the grocery store the day before the service. As I walked the aisles buying food and drink for after the service, the pain at Stephen's loss was so severe I felt weak. I held on to the grocery cart to help me remain upright. People were smiling and walking around as if nothing had happened. I wanted to scream, "Don't you *know? My son is dead!* Stop smiling! My child is dead! Stop acting happy! Stop smiling!" Why couldn't I just die right there and make it stop hurting? How could they be happy when I hurt so much?

We passed by the refrigerated cases containing flower arrangements. I needed to buy him some flowers in spite of what I had requested of others. There was a beautiful arrangement of pink roses with baby's breath and greenery. I reached for them and held them close.

The girls were at home and my mother was coming shortly. Our friend, Cathie, had stayed to clean up the house for us. Stephen had especially liked her and her husband and had left a funny note to them about their weight. As we drove in, Cathie rushed up to us. She said, "While you were gone, I heard footsteps from up in Stephen's room, but when I went up no one was there. I came back down to finish dusting, and I heard them again. Then I heard a voice. It was Stephen! He said he wanted me to give a message to his mother."

She began to read what she had hurriedly written down. It sounded like Stephen, but I wondered if Cathie was only trying to make me feel better. Or maybe she had wanted to hear a voice and think it was Stephen. I couldn't be sure. Though I was skeptical, I hoped it was true. This was a gift I could accept only years later.

I thanked Cathie, but she could read the doubt in my eyes. "It's all true," she cried. "No one dies. He's alive. Stephen is alive." I wished *I* could have been that positive. If all the things about life after death were true, why hadn't he spoken to *me?* I was his mother. I needed to hear his voice. Why not me? Jealousy, sadness, and hope fought against each other. We told everyone what Cathie had experienced, but somehow it was neither very comforting nor could I be sure it was true. I went in my room and pleaded with Stephen to talk to *me* and I cried and pleaded some more. I didn't hear anything.

I took the roses and placed them on the mantel over the fireplace with a card that said, "In Memory of Stephen." On the day of the service, a minister friend crossed out *Memory* and wrote in *Awareness.* "In Awareness of Stephen."

Cards, telegrams, and letters arrived each day as people heard the news. Some people came by to console us. Others tentatively hinted that Stephen must have been mentally ill. I was defensive. I didn't think he was mentally ill, and I wasn't even sure what people meant by that, but I didn't have any other explanation as to why he killed himself.

Many people were so uncomfortable about suicide that they didn't know how to act. I wanted to choke the people who said, "God wanted Stephen to be with Him." Or those who assured me, "God saw the pain and suffering in his future and called him home." Their words didn't ring true.

One dear person wrote, "We're with you in your grief. We love you. We're here if you need us." I knew she meant it. The mother of a friend sent a card that said, "The caged bird is free," which I found comforting.

One friend wrote, "I'm sure that the future holds the answers to his questions. Anyone so sensitive is destined to glory in the next life."

These communications would comfort me for a few moments. One of the most helpful and delightful letters was from a woman in our old church who had known and loved Stephen. She reminded me how Stephen and I had sat at church with her family one Sunday, and he had proposed to her daughter. He was about nine, she was about sixteen. He asked her to wait and marry him when he grew up. The memory lifted my spirits. It was as if someone had given me a special gift, because it enabled me to remember something that I would have forgotten and might never have recalled again. Such memories were like precious jewels.

Another friend, Joanne, to whom one of Stephen's notes was directed, wrote, "How can a person take another's pain away? I can only say I share your sorrow. You must remember that he was God's child also. He was young in years, but years mean nothing as far as Stephen was concerned. He was a truly beautiful soul. He has touched the lives of all who knew him. None of us will ever be the same from this time on. Each of us has learned a new awareness of life. We all pain with you and we all struggle to understand what is not always easy—death. But he's not dead and that's your joy. To know, when the raw pain is over and the channels are open, you may communicate at will. Stephen will be with you always and God is with you. He feels your pain. Look to him for the relief you need and the knowledge that death is not the end, only the beginning. Peace to you and all my love."

Several people wrote poems or expressed feelings they had about Stephen's life and death. Others brought uplifting messages they felt were from the other side about what was happening to him. These were helpful, even though I doubted their authenticity. I showed Stephen's notes to all our friends. They cried, laughed, and smiled along with us.

I prayed that someone from the old church, from anywhere, would send me photos they had taken of Stephen. No one ever did. That would have been such a gift. Since then, whenever anyone dies, I try to find photos I have taken of the person and send them to the remaining family members.

It helped when friends who visited shared their memories of Stephen and then let me talk about him. It helped when they openly discussed how he died, asked questions, and didn't act embarrassed. It made me angry when someone who had treated us badly wrote and bragged that they had made a contribution to their favorite charity in Stephen's name. I was very touched when a big company we were associated with sent a gift to Children's Hospital in his name. My emotions were raw. I veered between anger and gratitude, but no feeling could cover my emptiness.

On Saturday afternoon, March 23, we began Stephen's memorial service with the help of Diane and Henry. The four of us who would conduct the service sat in chairs up front. Our friends sat on borrowed folding chairs that filled the living room, entry, and hall.

I turned and looked out the window. Such crazy thoughts ran through my head. I remembered that as I was packing decorations after last Christmas and putting the children's special candles in a box, I had accidentally dropped and broken one. One child would be without a candle. I had looked for matching holders since but could find none. I should have seen that as a sign. Only seven candles. One child would die. One child died.

In order to be able to conduct the service and not cry, I programmed myself to believe that, in a short time, Stephen and I would be conversing daily. I forced any doubts I had about that communication out of my mind. I intended to show by my strength, courage, and belief that anyone who died continued on and lived fully aware in another dimension. If I could be this confident, when my beloved Stephen had killed himself, had hung himself in a tree just across the street, then surely this would comfort people who had lost loved ones themselves.

As we waited for everyone to be seated so that we could begin, I heard a voice inside my head: "Go into your bedroom. In the seventh pile from the bathroom door, against the wall with the window, pick the seventeenth book from the top and open it."

How did that voice get inside my head? It wasn't Stephen. In fact, I couldn't tell if it was a man or a woman. It wasn't any of my three guides. I had forgotten all about them for weeks. I whispered to Tom what I had heard, excused myself, and went down the hall into the bedroom to do as instructed.

Books were piled along every wall, some stacked halfway to the ceiling. I counted across and down. I pulled out the seventeenth book. It was *The Wisdom of Gibran,* by Kahlil Gibran, author of *The Prophet.* I had read *The Prophet,* but this book was one I didn't remember ever seeing. It looked new and was stiff like it had never been opened.

I opened it at random to a page marked "D . . . Death" and began to read:

> The Reality of Life is Life itself, whose beginning is not in the womb, and whose ending is not in the grave. For the years that pass are naught but a moment in eternal

life; and the world of matter and all in it is but a dream compared to the awakening which we call the terror of Death.

The soul is an embryo in the body of Man, and the day of death is the Day of awakening, for it is the Great era of labour and the rich Hour of creation. Death is an ending to the son of the earth, but to the soul it is the start, the triumph of life.

Death removes but the touch, and not the awareness of all good. And he who has lived one spring or more possesses the spiritual life of one who has lived a score of springs.

Again, I felt impressed to open the book, and this time I turned to "Immortality":

Death on earth, to the son of earth
    Is final, but to him who is
Ethereal, it is but the start
    Of triumph certain to be his . . .

If I did not covet immortality, I would never have learned the song which has been sung through all time.

Rather, I would have been a suicide, nothing remaining of me except my ashes hidden within the tomb.

Life is a darkness that ends as in the sunburst of day. The yearning of my heart tells me there is peace in the grave.

If some fool tells you the soul perishes like the body and that which dies never returns, tell him the flower perishes but the seed remains and lies before us as the secret of life everlasting.

I couldn't believe it! My heart beat so loudly I could hear it in my head. Goose bumps were all over my body, tears flooded my eyes. I turned the page down, and held the book against my heart, crying. I was deeply moved and grateful. I knew I had never read this book before, certainly I had never heard these passages. How beautiful. Someone *was* up there helping me. It was true, then—Stephen lives! Soon he would be talking to me, just like the voice I heard that led me to these comforting words.

I dried my eyes, and went back and sat down, holding the book. The service began. Tom and I each shared things about Stephen. He read things we found in Stephen's room among his writings. Although the following seems mature beyond his years, it was apparently Stephen's own composition. His own editing work was apparent from the words crossed out and corrections made. It began:

> It was whispered in the wind, it was screamed across the plains, it fell in hushed silence on the tops of great mountains, even the deep vastness of the ocean seemed to know this dreaded message, and as the mighty waves crashed in the foaming surf, they fell with a scream of terror for the prophets spoke of the deaths of the fiery sun and the gentle moon.
>
> And this time, as in no other time since the dawn of man, peace was restored to this lowly planet called Earth. As each man paused to observe his fate, another hand reached out for the comfort that is only found in the solace of being not alone. Whether black or white, rich or poor, all men were joined in mourning for the sun and grieving for the moon.
>
> And in the courtyard of the fire temple, standing shrouded in black with hands upraised, chanting a fearful song to a god who was hidden far away, stood a feeble, graying, religious man who lived in a time when religion was nonexistent and God was thought dead. And when this man's mission was completed, he smiled, lowered his arms and departed. And as he paused at the gates, a faint sunrise could be seen beginning over the horizon.

When my turn came, I told everyone about the voice and read the passages from the book I had been instructed to find. People gasped in amazement and many eyes filled with tears. When I finished, a friend of ours—another Steve—

stood up and asked if *he* could speak. He said that someone had called to tell him that Stephen had killed himself and nothing more. He knew Stephen, and with two children of his own, his heart ached for us. He got in his car, drove out of the city, and parked. He sat for hours sharing our pain, crying and thinking. He explained that he was an agnostic but had heard the words to the poem that he now wanted to read to all of us, as it was given to him.

Stephen

Some will say you flamed a brilliant day
and died just once forever;
But we will say your flame is brighter now
than all the stars,
for how you went
and what you left.
Some will say your life was cut far short
and should have blossomed longer;
But we will say your life is fuller now
than all the fields,
for what you sowed
that now we reap.
And some will say that place is haunted now,
haunted by a tragic death;
But we will say that once upon a wooded choir,
a young man took his soul in hand,
and raising eyes to all unknown,
he took a step we all must take,
but took it bravely,
took it gladly,
and thus gave strength to every
step we ever take,
with courage, peace
and love.

—Aaron Hastie Robertson

We all cried. With my knowledge at the time, it was a most beautiful gift to me. Then, Cathie and others stood up and read or shared their feelings, and the service ended.

Everyone stayed afterward to join us for cookies and coffee. I felt it had been a happy memorial for a child in pain, who had taken matters into his own hands, and left earlier than we had hoped, in a way we had not expected. Everyone said they felt hopeful and comforted.

My mother cried during the service, during the socializing afterward, and for most of her visit. She took Stephen's death very hard and all my upbeat statements about our beliefs in life after death didn't console her one bit.

I wished she wouldn't cry. Stephen wouldn't want her to be sad. The fact that I was crying myself to sleep each night and every time the bedroom door closed didn't seem the same. As long as everyone else was happy, I could pretend that I was.

Mother's coming was a godsend for the children and for me. We basked in her love and caring. When she left to go back home, it was much worse for all of us. The real grief set in. I was a walking zombie.

Nothing had any joy, nothing would ever be the same again. How could I go on?

SIX

✦

GRIEF—THE CONSTANT COMPANION

> *Grief fills the room with my absent child, lies in his bed, walks up and down with me. Puts on his pretty looks, repeats his words, remembers me of all his gracious parts. Stuffs out his vacant garment with his form.*
>
> —SHAKESPEARE, *King John*

> *On hearing of the death of his son, King David wept and cried out, "O my son Absalom! My son, my son Absalom! If only I had died instead of you—O Absalom, my son, my son!"*
>
> —2 SAMUEL 18:33

Night after night I went up to Stephen's room. I would begin to cry on the way up the stairs. I needed to be in his room by myself, alone. I wanted to sit on his bed and breathe his special smell that filled the room, and cry where no one could hear me. I begged Stephen to speak to me. I pleaded with God to bring him back.

His bed was still unmade as he had left it. I laid on his bed and held the bedding to my nose. I moaned and cried and rocked back and forth, screaming his name into the pillow. Dirty clothes lay around the room. I held his shirts to my nose and inhaled his faint scent, then inhaled deeply at the underarms where his odor was stronger. I even held his underwear to my face and breathed the soiled smell.

After a few days, I sealed the underwear and clothing that still had any slight odor in plastic bags so the smell wouldn't be lost. I opened the bags daily to keep Stephen's essence in my memory. I didn't judge anything I did. I couldn't hold back in my grief.

I went over the room, section by section, day after day. Stephen's maple chest was filled with clothes, papers, and an assortment of his things. I opened and searched each item of clothing. I turned each paper over, searching for something he had written—anything. I felt for impressions on blank paper. His room was filled with books, some from the library, some ours, some his. I went through each book thinking perhaps there was some note or something underlined to give me a fuller answer as to why he had killed himself. Perhaps some message might be found, another piece to the puzzle, another part of him. I found poems he had written and sayings he had copied. I searched with the intensity of a cat burglar hunting for jewels.

I smiled through my tears when I read the notes he had written:

> What makes one instrument sacred and another secular? Is an organ really more holy than a guitar? What if there were no pipe organs in heaven, and angels played guitars, drums and tambourines? What if God danced instead of walked? What if angels told jokes and Saint Peter laughed a lot? What if finger painting was required and Heaven's board meetings were held on a merry-go-round?
>
> Let them hear music blasting from the sanctuary and dare to believe that God is not turned off by jeans. If you dress up so much on the outside, don't you tend to dress up on the inside too and bring to God a presentable self—instead of the real you?

And later:

> If God doesn't fizz, how come I feel all these bubbles? May the Holy Spirit zap you!

On his calendar Stephen had made a concerned notation for Sunday, February 24:

> Weighed 186 today. Got to start cracking down on myself! Keep Kool!

I also discovered a list of his goals that read:

> 1) Lose all excess fat. 2) To be very well built. 3) To be very strong. 4) To run fast without tiring. 5) To have fast reflexes. 6) To be very good at karate. 7) Have conditioned hands.

I made a pile of each paper that had his name or even the tiniest drawing or mark. His wastebasket was filled with papers, wrappers, trash. I went through every piece. I found treasures: a picture Stephen had created on the typewriter, a half-finished school assignment, the wrapper to a beef jerky stick that he had eaten, gum he had chewed that still bore his teeth prints.

In typewritten pages that spoke eloquently of his loving and gentle spirit, and how he felt for the girl to whom he could not express these words, Stephen had written:

> In the silence of dreams I have felt your tears and seen a gentle beauty in your eyes. I have reached to touch your hand and feel you near, and tell you of the secrets that I feel in the wind and the majesty that I find on a starlit night. I have seen the wind playing through your hair and the sparkle that is found deep within your eyes. I have seen you move with the grace of a panther and the sleekness of a tiger and I imagine you floating high above the world, mystic and lovely, carried by the wind that swirls about your beauty. And as I observe you there, I feel a closeness that radiates from your soul and I try to speak, for I want to tell you that I know of life and love and living. But most important, I know what it means to love you. You listen quietly and speak softly, reminding that love is not promises that are soon passed by, but a re-

> membered kiss or a touch or sigh that is shared in a time of happiness between two people. I look at you silently. You smile and then my dream begins to fade and you turn to leave. I want to follow to call your name but all that I could say was, "Take care, my love."

I searched through each drawer of his desk, finding pencils, sketches, little bits of his life. I was glad that he was so messy, that he hadn't emptied his trash, that he was a pack rat. I pulled up the corners of the rug, searching as far back as I could lift it, disappointed to find nothing but paper clips and coins.

Occasionally, I would find a note, which I read ravenously. Often, his words were like a stab of pain in my heart. Stephen wrote:

> Lord, forgive me for my efforts to serve you only when convenient to do so and only when it is safe to do so. Father, forgive me. Renew me and send me out as a usable person that I may take more truthfully the meaning of your love.

And then, words which I feared were written shortly before his death:

> Nurture strength of spirit to guide you in sudden misfortune. Do not clutch at pain and it will not linger.

I searched every pocket of every item of clothing. My eyes raced from one thing to another. I was like a squirrel, scurrying from place to place, reaching, grabbing, hoarding anything I saw. In between searching, I would lie on Stephen's bed and cry into his pillow until my eyes were bloodshot and swollen shut, until my ears rang and my throat was raw. I felt no physical pain. The pain in my mind and heart were so severe that I felt neither thirst nor hunger for days.

In his tape recorder on the desk, I found two tapes Stephen had made. One, dated April 10, 1973, concerned his insecurities and the things that he was feeling. It was about how he didn't like to be fat and was self-conscious around girls. The other contained songs he listened to on the radio, and part of a *Kung Fu* movie we had watched together. I played them over and over to catch the sound of Stephen's voice. Each word, each phrase, was like a gift.

✦

I felt totally alone in my sorrow and agony. Surely no one in the world had ever felt like this. People would say they knew how I felt. They had no idea. Had any of them had a *child* die? I had forgotten about the grieving woman with whom I worked whose daughter had been murdered a few months before. I had forgotten that Richard's mother had lost twins at eight and twelve months of age. I had forgotten that children were killed in accidents, murdered, raped, and kidnapped. I was so consumed by my own pain and grief, I completely forgot that other people had lost their own children and loved ones.

I read that many parents put all the pictures away when a child died. I could not! I searched for every picture ever taken of Stephen. I looked at them over and over again. I tried to find all the old negatives in the house. With a magnifying glass, I went through them, putting aside any of Stephen, even if there was just a partial side view of him, or if only his arm or leg showed. I had them developed, copied, enlarged. Some rolls from Christmas hadn't been developed. I put them in the camera shop on a rush order. Since I left Richard, I had taken so few photos. The only ones of Stephen were almost two years old. The Christmas rolls were current and I couldn't wait until they came back.

When I picked up the developed film, I ripped the packages open. There were only two side view photos of Stephen. At Christmas, he had asked me not to take any pictures of him until he got cleaned up. He assured me he would dress up for better pictures after we opened the gifts, but he never had. I wept, heartbroken. I remembered Billie's intuitive message: "Be sure and take plenty of pictures this Christmas, things will never be the same. . ."

No one could console me. My friends tried, and their smiles, conversations, and assurances that Stephen was fine helped for the brief moments they were there. When they left, I went into Stephen's room again and again. I dropped my pretenses, and let down my guard. How could I admit to everyone that it was I—I had killed him? The real truth must be that I had killed him. I had driven him to his death. I had insisted he go to school that last day. I had instructed Tom to tell him to leave his gym bag home. I had accused him of shoplifting. I insisted on finishing my education and had little time left over for his needs. I had foolishly thought things would get better at his school without my intervention. All my life I would know, everyone would know, what a failure I was as a mother, as a person. I had killed my own son. I said I loved him, then I had driven him to kill himself.

When I tried to tell this to close friends and family, they interrupted me and assured me I wasn't responsible. Stephen had made that decision himself and I needed to stop blaming myself. That was not what I needed to hear. I needed to express my guilt, but no one would let me. I carried the guilt hourly in my heart and mind. Stephen would still be alive if it weren't for me. Richard, still self-righteous, confirmed that on several visits. "If you hadn't left me . . ." he would start in.

Sometimes I imagined turning back the clock and going back with Richard. I'd do it if Stephen could still be alive. I fantasized about it many times. Other times, when thinking about the hell of our lives during those years, I couldn't bear the thought of living like that again, even to keep Stephen alive. That caused me more guilt. What kind of mother was I that I couldn't have made that sacrifice to save him? In rational moments, I knew that I could not have stayed in the marriage any longer, nor would it necessarily have spared Stephen if I had.

I thought about Stephen all the time. He was so good, so

loving, so tender. It hadn't been *that* bad for him. He rarely complained. He was so well adjusted, so normal, so okay—so able to cope no matter how bad things were.

How ridiculous. He *wasn't* okay. He had been stretched and pushed beyond any reasonable limits. He was dead by his own hand. It must have been a living hell for him. We had all killed him.

In those months there were many dreams about Stephen. Stephen going north. Stephen talking with us. Stephen still alive. Stephen dead. In most of the dreams, Stephen was about twelve or thirteen; in some he was much younger. Each dream was like a gift, no matter what the content, because I *saw* him, I talked to him, sometimes I embraced him. For that moment he was *alive.* When I woke up, filled with joy at our encounters, I remembered he was *dead,* and I began those mornings by crying into my pillow.

The remaining three children became even more precious to me after Stephen died. It had never entered my mind that any of my children would die before I did. They somehow seemed invulnerable. *We* seemed invulnerable. Death, accidents, suicide only happened to *other* people. Never again would Tom's children demand and get all the attention; I would see that my children's rights were attended to. I'd like to think this was accomplished from then on, but, actually, things didn't change much.

Debbie became frightened to stay home alone for the half hour after we left for work and before she went to school. She was equally afraid to be by herself the few minutes after school, before Andrea got home. We enrolled Debbie in a day care center for the short time before and after school. I assured her constantly that she was safe and there was nothing to fear. Andrea seemed to handle it better, although her pain must have been deeper. She and Stephen were so close and loved each other so much. I had called her school and Debbie's to tell them about Stephen's death and both schools were caring and considerate, making this period somewhat easier for the girls. We couldn't help but see the difference in caring between their schools and Largo High School where Stephen had attended. Not one teacher nor the principal ever called about Stephen's death.

Sometimes I wanted to die, too. I thought of killing myself to stop the pain, and I begged God to let me die as I lay crying in Stephen's room. But I was responsible for three other children, and no matter how much I might want to join Stephen, I could not and would not ever take my own life.

Even though there were those awful times of such sadness, I mostly asked God to please *not* let me die and have the children be raised by Richard. Each month that I stayed alive, I believed it was only through the grace of God.

I was in such pain; I hadn't even made time to listen to my guides for weeks. Then I read a book by a father whose grown son had also killed himself, and who communicated with his father from the other side—bending safety pins and speaking through "mediums." Here was a ray of hope. If these people could speak from the "beyond," surely Stephen could get through. Even if he didn't have a body anymore, at least we could talk to each other again. I needed to find out about all the things Stephen had been feeling and thinking. I needed to tell him I loved him. I needed to hear his voice.

With this sense of purpose, I took five large safety pins and placed them in a certain pattern, open, on top of the high armoire in our bedroom, and noted it in my journal. I wanted to place them on an end table or somewhere easier to reach and to see, but with all the children touching them, I wouldn't know for sure whether Stephen moved them.

By standing on the bed, I could just barely reach and see the pins where I placed them. I didn't tell anyone except Tom, just in case the children investigated. Day after day I checked the pins, but they stayed the same. They never moved. I closed the pins and rearranged them and noted that in my journal. Nothing happened. I was getting discouraged. So much I had read made communicating with the dead sound so easy. I wasn't finding it to be easy at all.

Ready to give up, but still checking each day, I stepped up on the bed one evening to look at the pins. This time, the pins were all moved around. They were still closed but they had been moved. I was so excited. Then my rational mind took over. Something didn't feel right. Maybe there was a logical explanation. I asked each child if they had touched them. Each one said they hadn't. Bob was visiting that weekend and I asked him. He said, "Oh yeah, Mom, I was looking for something and found all those pins on top and picked them up to look at them." Disappointed, I rearranged them, but the pins were never moved.

Since I had heard the voice at Stephen's service, I expected to hear it again or talk to Stephen or to receive some sign from him. There had been nothing.

Since the pins were not getting moved, I had to do something. I had to know how Stephen really was, what he was doing, if he was okay. I realized I could ask my guides these questions. They had always given me correct guidance, always answered my questions or searched for the answers elsewhere to help me. They were "dead" just like Stephen. They had no bodies either but talked to me as if they still did. *They* could help me locate Stephen. They could show me how to talk to him and to find out what had happened to him. I could hardly wait to sit and listen and to make contact with them.

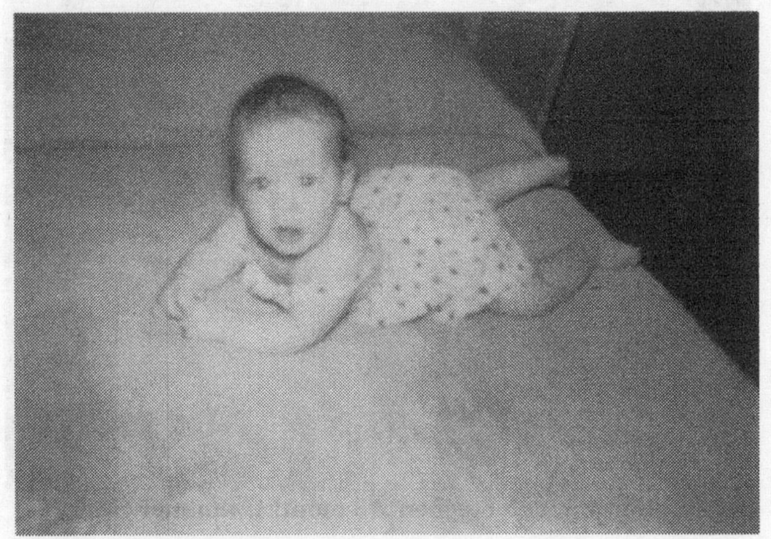

Stephen, 4 months old, April 1959.

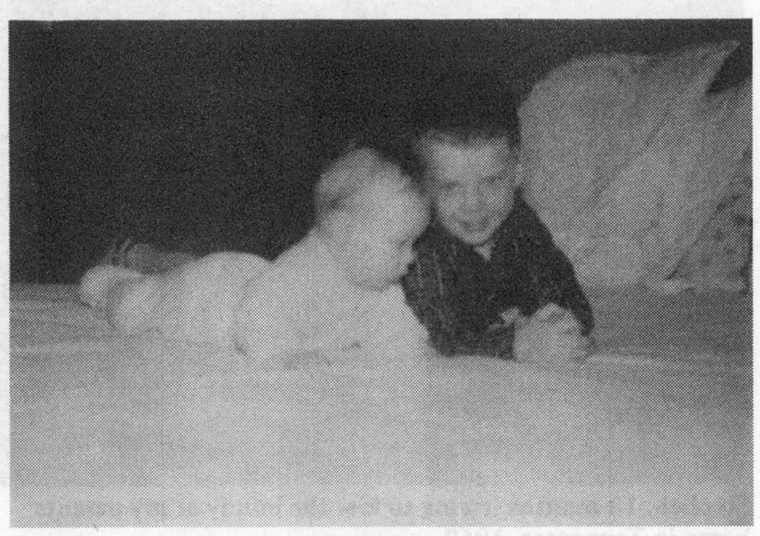

Stephen, 5 months old, and Bobby, 3½, 1959.

Bobby, almost 5, and Stephen, 18 months, summer 1960.

Stephen, 18 months, trying to kiss the bunny at my parents' home in Tennessee, 1960.

Bobby, 5½, and Stephen, 2, December 1960, before my marriage to Richard.

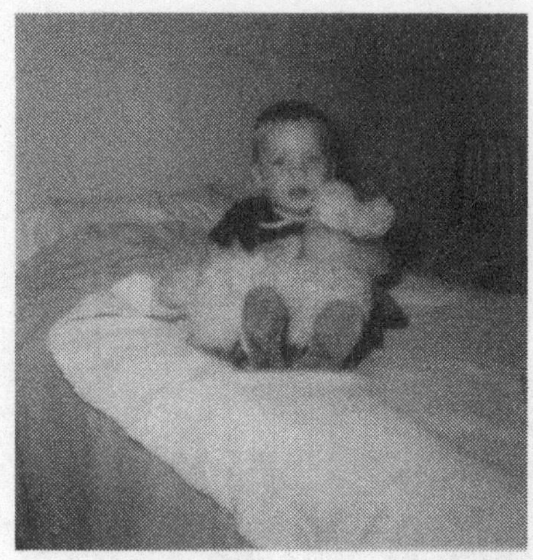

Stephen, 2, home from the hospital after his fall, 1961.

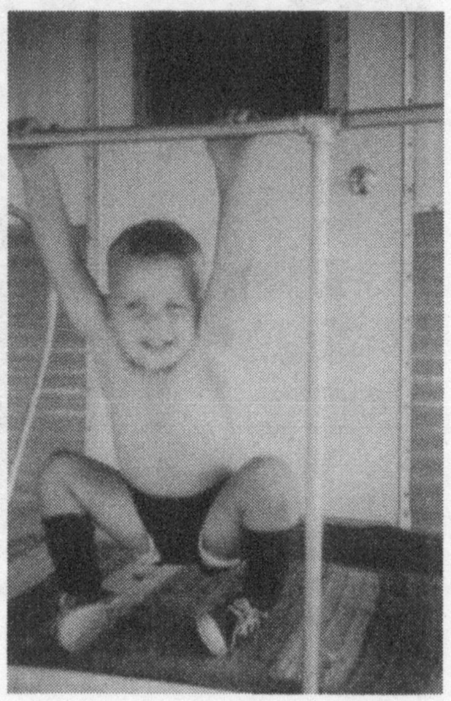

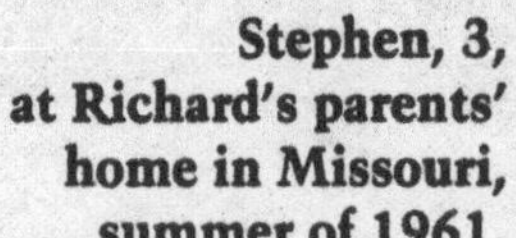

Stephen, 3, at Richard's parents' home in Missouri, summer of 1961.

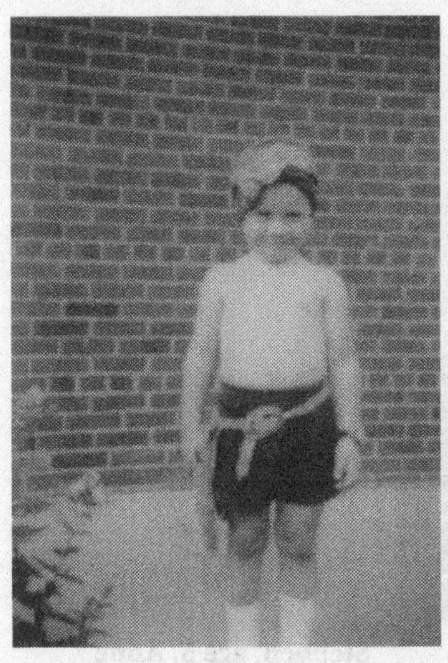

Stephen, 3½, in one of his many attires, 1962.

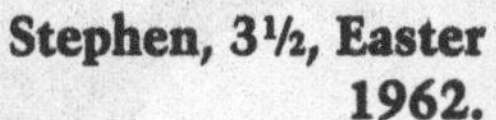

Stephen, 3½, Easter 1962.

Stephen's first fish, age 4.

Stephen, age 5, Anne and Bobby, age 8, December 1963.

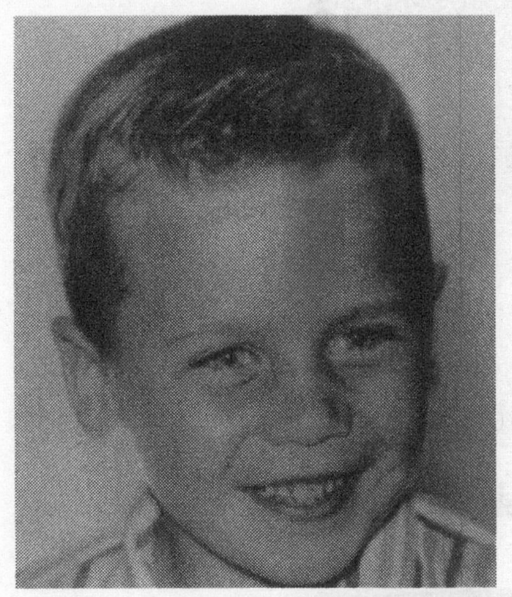

Stephen, 6 years old, 1964.

Stephen, 6, wearing his gladiator helmet and cape.

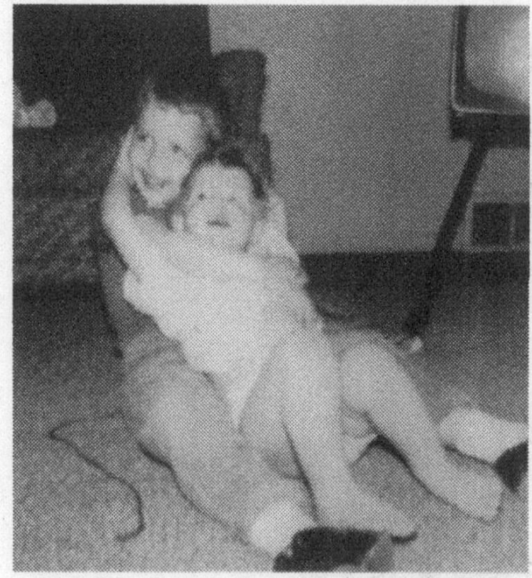

Stephen, 6, with his sister Andrea, 3, in 1964.

Stephen, 10, playing trumpet solo at church in Washington, D.C., 1968.

Stephen, 10, winning his junior high basketball trophy, 1968.

Eleven years old, 1969.

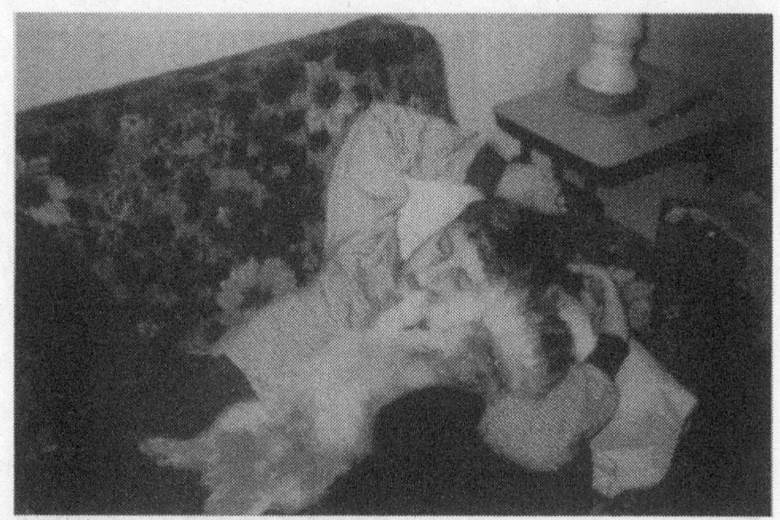

Stephen, 11, asleep with his Pekingese, "Pudgie."

Bob, 14, Debbie, 3, Stephen, 11, Andrea, 8, in 1969.

Debbie, 4, with Stephen, 12, in Rockville, Maryland.

Stephen, nearly 13, on the first day of school, 1971.

Stephen at 13.

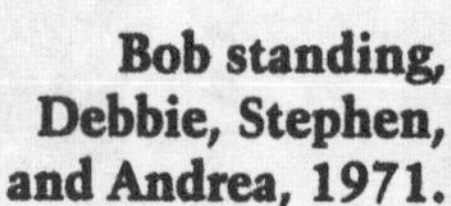

Bob standing, Debbie, Stephen, and Andrea, 1971.

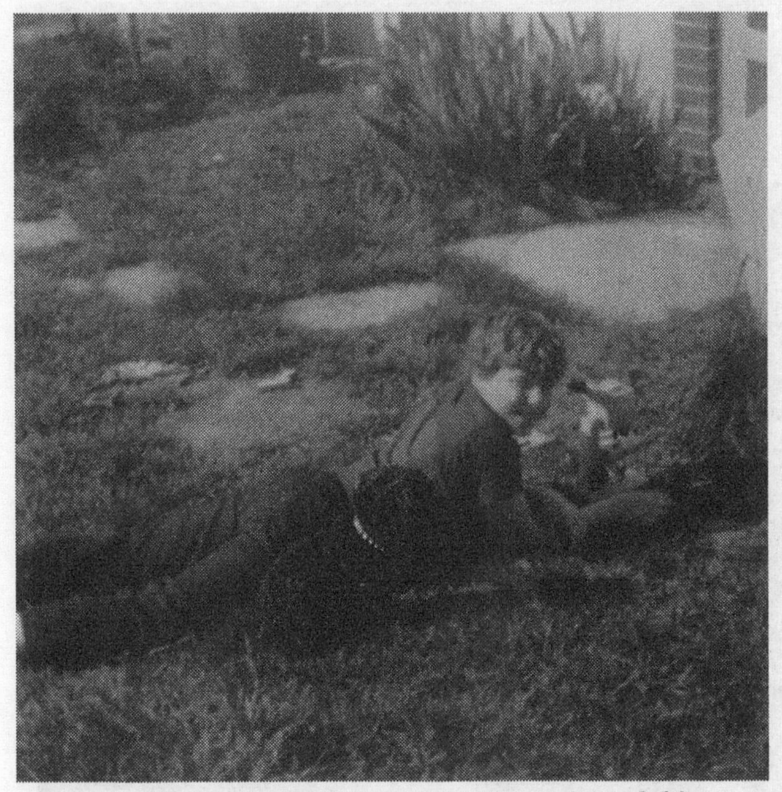

Stephen, age 12, examining insects and grass through his microscope with his "Pekapoo" dog, 1971.

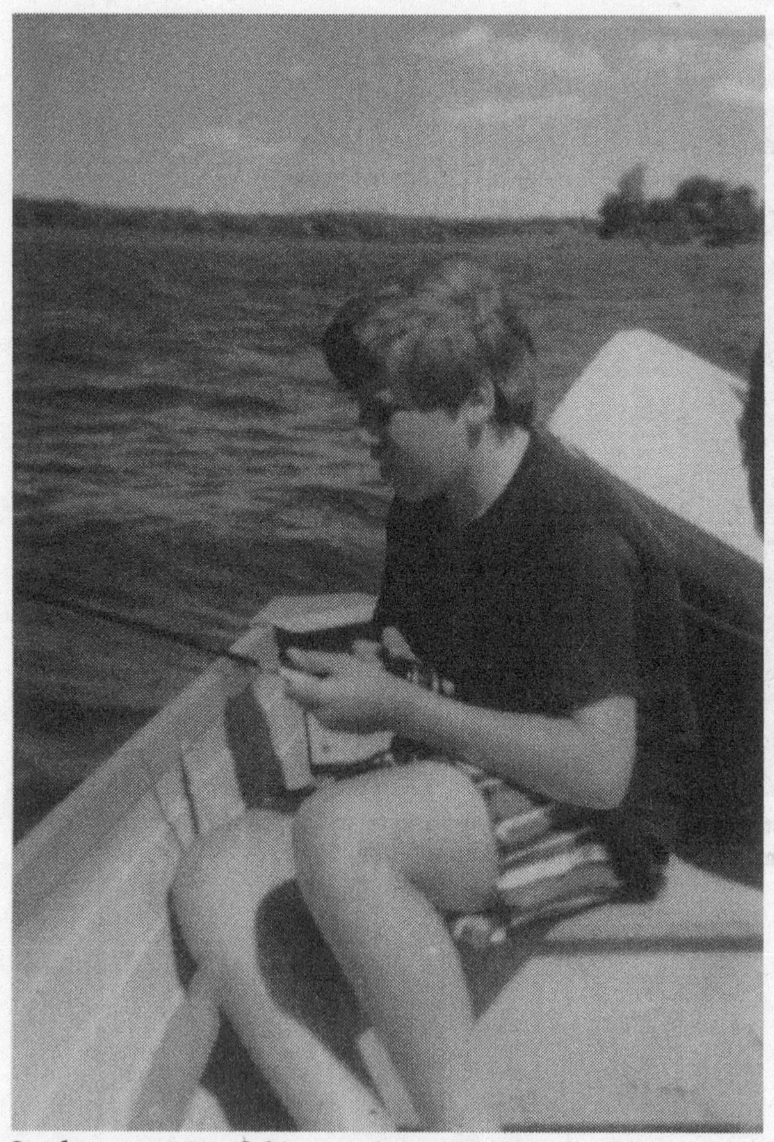

Stephen, age 12½, fishing at Algonquin Park, Canada, summer 1971.

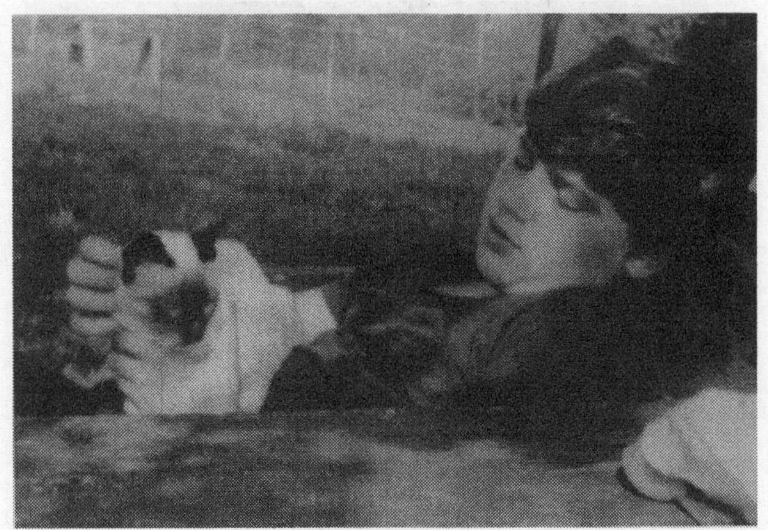

Stephen with Debbie's cat, 1971.

Stephen's last school picture, almost 14 years old, 1972.

Stephen, at 15, in his last photograph, Christmas 1973.

Our family today—back row: Bob, Andrea, Anne, Herb; second row: Bob's daughter Melissa, Debbie, Bob's daughter Vanessa and his son Robert. Seated on Debbie's lap is her daughter Krystalyn.

I Like School

I like everything about School. It is a wonderful place. Im glad I can go to School. I like my techer veary much. Sudjeks in shhol are interesting to me. Work is hard that is true but it is good you have work to do I like home work.

I like reading and math and spelling and the other Subjeks in scholl. Reses is fun that is true. We play all sorts of games at school Add that all together I dont think you can add all the things you do at shool together. but add as much as you can and you will find a good School I think

Steve D

Written about his love of school when Stephen was 8.

IM NOT
GOING IN
TODAY! I
WILL NOT BE
MISSING ANYTHING
IMPORTANT! AND I
JUST CANT GET
IT TOGETHER TODAY

The note Stephen left on my bedroom door in early 1974.

DEAR KATHRINE E▬▬▬

IN THE YEAR 1974, ON THE 26TH DAY, SECOND MONTH, THERE SAT IN A CERTAIN KINGDOM KNOWN AS SIXTH PERIOD ALGEBRA CLASS A CERTAIN REAL LIVE PERSON NAMELY SIR STEVEN, A NOBLE YET ACUTELY INSANE KNIGHT. UPON BECOMEING HIGHLY BORED THIS PARTICULAR KNIGHT TOOK PEN IN HAND, AND THINKING HIGHLY SEX ORIENTED THOUGHTS HE DID DICTATE A LETTER OF PARCHMENT TO THE MOST LOVELY AND KIND PRINCESS IN THE ENTIRE KINGDOM. THIS LETTER DID CONTAIN UTTER GIBBERISH AND THUS BEING COULD ONLY BE DECIPHERED BY A SPEAKER OF FLUENT CHIPMUNK. UPON BEING TRANSLATED THE LETTER PRECEDED AS THUS: ⟶

\$* TURN UNTO SECOND PAGE OF PARCHMENT

NOT BEING ABLE TO CALL,
I MISS YOU VERY MUCH AND
I WOULD LIKE TO SAY A
FEW THINGS THAT I PROBABLY
COULDNT TELL YOU ON THE
PHONE, TO ME YOU ARE THE
MOST BUITIFUL PERSON I KNOW
AND ALTHOUGH YOU DENY IT YOU
ARE VERY KIND AND SENSITIVE

Stephen's unfinished letter to a young girl, written on February 26, 1974 . . . just twenty days before he died.

SEVEN

✦

THE SEARCH FOR STEPHEN

I do not know why sorrows come
and burning teardrops fall;
I only know God still is God
And watches over all.

—John Gilbert

While everyone else was watching TV, I climbed the stairs to Stephen's room, closed his door, and sat at his typewriter. It had been three weeks since his death, and the room was still filled with his smell. I glanced at the treasures that he would never touch again. Usually, that made me cry, but I felt strangely comforted and at peace. This was a rare state for me.

I began to feel a sense of excitement and anticipation. The conviction was growing inside me that soon I would be able to hear and talk to Stephen. Beginning as I had always done in the months before, I prayed, "God, I ask for the highest spiritual guidance. . . . " Then, I asked to speak with Stephen. I placed my fingers on the keyboard to type what I heard, and concentrated on becoming very still. Why hadn't I done this sooner? My guides were on the other side, too, and I could hear them. It would be easy for them to help me talk to Stephen.

I waited. Nothing happened. I prayed and waited some more. Nothing. I thought I heard a few words, then absolutely nothing. I couldn't keep my thoughts still. My mind darted everywhere and gathered each memory, each thought of Stephen, and raced them through my brain. I placed my fingers on the typewriter keys again and again, pleading with my guides to speak to me, to tell me about Stephen, to bring him there to talk to me.

I heard nothing. I sensed no presence. I couldn't feel or identify anything out of the ordinary. What was wrong with me? Where had my guides gone? Where was everyone? Where was Stephen? I felt absolutely deserted. It was bad enough that Stephen was gone. Now my helpers had left, too. I waited awhile and tried again. Still nothing. Then I cried.

In the next days I told my teachers and classmates about this void when I went to school and church. I bared my soul to them, saying how worried I was that the pathway to Stephen was silent. They assured me that Stephen would talk to me when he was able. One kind friend suggested that I was still too emotionally raw to tune in. Everyone said the same thing: Stephen was fine and he continued to live in spirit. I just needed to be patient. But their words didn't help.

I was beginning to doubt the path I had taken. I had lost all of my friends in the old church by following this direction. It had previously filled me with such joy. I loved what I was learning. But maybe I had been wrong. Maybe the church was right and this was the work of the devil. Maybe God was punishing me. I could find no peace at school or church, at home or at work. Only my children kept me hanging on. I felt dead inside. I appreciated Tom's help, but he couldn't make me forget Stephen was gone. Now my guides had deserted me, too.

✦

Stephen had been dead exactly one month to the day. It was a horrible anniversary and my grief was worse than ever. It was early in the evening and dark outside. Everyone was gone somewhere—Tom with his children, the girls with Richard. I wanted to stay home. I went into the family room and sat in the blue chair where Stephen had loved to watch TV. I had rearranged the room, just as I had rearranged almost every other room in the house, except Stephen's. The memories seemed easier to bear when things weren't exactly where they had been when Stephen was alive. I turned the table lamp low, leaned my head against the back of the chair and began to pray and meditate.

I prayed for Stephen, asking God to take care of him since I hadn't done a very good job of it. I asked Him to tell Stephen how much I loved him. As an afterthought, I asked for a sign that Stephen was okay, that death wasn't really the end and that Stephen really *did* continue in spirit. "Please, God, give me a sign that Stephen is okay, and that only his body is dead." A few seconds after I finished my plea, the lightbulb in the lamp next to my chair exploded with a loud crack. The room went black.

I jumped up, ran down the hall, dove into bed, and pulled the covers over my head. I was terrified. I had asked for a sign, but I was scared out of my wits. With no one in the house but me, I didn't come out from under the covers until I heard a car pulling in the driveway. Then I got the courage to go back into the room. I found the broken glass from the bulb in an orderly pattern on the table around the lamp, not scattered on the floor. Tom and the friends I told about it suggested that I had received my sign. I wasn't sure. It was probably a coincidence.

Finally, almost a week later, I again sat alone in the family room. This time, I left two lights on. I felt more at peace than I had in a while. I prayed to God to take care of Stephen. I asked Him to tell Stephen how much I loved him.

About ten minutes passed as I sat there quietly, eyes closed, praying. I felt a hand touch my right shoulder, from behind the chair. One finger after another, then the impress of the full palm as a hand was gently laid on my shoulder. I turned to see who it was. No one was there. I felt no fear. I just closed my eyes and the hand stayed on my shoulder. I felt comforted. I didn't cry. Perhaps it was Stephen, perhaps not. I had no idea whose hand it was, and that did not frighten me either. Soon the pressure of the hand stopped. I turned again to look. No one was there. I went to bed and slept soundly for the first time since Stephen's death.

A few evenings later, lying on my bed, I heard my guides speak. Their voices came into my head from three directions and overshadowed my own thoughts. They told me Stephen was fine but that it wouldn't be that easy to talk with him yet until he learned how to communicate better from that dimension. They said he was being taught by helpers and was reviewing his life. He had been at his memorial service. My guides promised they would talk to me again soon and let me know what was happening with Stephen and help me understand things better. I was so thankful, so relieved, that I began to cry. I asked them why I hadn't been able to hear them. They said my emotions were so intense they were unable to get through to me.

As I continued to speak to my guides, I asked why they didn't warn me that Stephen was going to kill himself. They explained that because of my intense involvement with daily activities and the great stress in my life, I was simply not listening to them or even recording my dreams during that period of time. They tried to get through to me in my thoughts, and even in dreams, but they could not gain my attention. My guides also said that it would have been difficult to change the course of events since this dire pattern was firmly set in place by Stephen.

When the voices stopped, I began to doubt. What if I was imagining their voices because I wanted to hear something? What if Stephen was suffering the hell and damnation that so many churches said was the consequence of suicide? After all, even the metaphysical literature I was reading differed from book to book about the afterlife of a suicide. In some books, like Dante's *Inferno*, the dead agonized in a fiery hell. In others, suicides watched the suffering of their loved ones still living, and that became their hell. Other writers said suicides slept, awoke, and slept until they could understand their horrible deed and prepare to incarnate in another body to make up for their error. Some wrote that "self-murderers" could make no progress in the spirit realm until the years of their normal earthly span were over.

This drove me crazy. Many of the beautiful things in metaphysics gave me such hope, but I wasn't finding that same comfort and understanding about suicide. Nothing was written about *children* killing themselves. What happened to them? I read everything I could find. There was no source of hope or comfort. There was *nothing*.

As the weeks went by, the fog in my mind cleared somewhat, and I began to hear my guides more frequently. Stephen was fine, they said. He was still being worked with and was reviewing his life. He would speak to me when he could. He had not suffered, and he was not being punished or tortured in hell. They told me that Stephen was often brought to us to visit, but we were seldom aware of his presence.

I prayed that what I was hearing was true. Why hadn't one of my guides *told* me when Stephen was in the room so I could have felt him, talked to him? It didn't seem fair. I asked them why.

They said they often tried to let me know they had brought Stephen to me, and they said that sometimes when Stephen entered the room, I would start thinking about him and begin to cry. Some of my tears were an intuitive response to his presence. They also told me Stephen *had* been able to let me know he was in the room once and spoke out loud to me and called my name.

Suddenly I remembered! There was an incident two weeks before. I was sitting in the middle of my king-size bed one night, feeling awful. I was alone, crying, praying, confused, and in such emotional pain, I could hardly function. I spoke out loud to Stephen, as I often did. I called him to come to me. I begged him to be there. As usual, nothing happened.

Then from the left side of the bedroom, from what seemed to be near the top of the ceiling, I heard a distinct call, "Mom!" I turned in the direction of the voice and no one was there. I said out loud, "Stephen, is that you? Is that *you?*"

The voice didn't answer, and I kept looking at the place from where it seemed to come, and then all around the room. I kept trying to talk to Stephen, to hear him. Then I realized it hadn't sounded exactly like his voice. I sat there for a long time, believing, doubting, and unconvinced of *who* it was. I was too wrapped up in myself and my thoughts to try to attune to my guides. I never doubted what I had heard. That was simply a fact. If it had been Stephen, I reasoned, it would have *sounded* like him. I replayed the experience over and over in my mind, but it wasn't clear enough to give me real hope. Now my guides were telling me it *was* Stephen. I felt a rush of renewed hope.

As I searched for answers, I remembered hearing that some psychics could contact the dead. Maybe I could find a psychic who had this gift and make contact with Stephen. I wouldn't give the psychic any information about Stephen or why I was there. I'd see what happened. When I asked around, several psychics, or "sensitives," were recommended by classmates.

I made an appointment with one at her home. When I arrived, I was surprised to be met by a very ordinary-looking woman, dressed in casual clothing. I guess I expected her to appear more exotic. She welcomed me in and explained that she listened to the "spirits," as she called them.

She began, "You've lost someone you loved."

I excitedly answered, "Yes."

"Your father died?"

"No," I said.

"Your grandmother, or is it your grandfather?" she went on.

"No."

"Oh yes, I see now, it's a child," she said, beaming. "You've lost a child."

My heart lifted. "Yes."

She continued, "I can see now—a little one." She indicated someone three feet tall with a wave of her hand.

My hopes plummeted. "No." I sighed. Stephen was no baby and certainly taller than three feet. I left as soon as I could without being too rude, for there was nothing else she was accurate about. I was quite discouraged, but I continued searching.

I went to a half-dozen other psychics. No one brought Stephen through. I didn't doubt that there were people who really could contact the dead. I just didn't know where to find them.

Then someone gave me a book, *Always, Karen*, by Jeanne Walker. It was the story of a couple who had lost their beloved only daughter, Karen, to cancer, and in their sorrow wanted to end their own lives. Then they came in contact with Reverend George Daisley, a minister and sensitive who lived in Santa Barbara, California. Daisley had revealed hundreds of evidential pieces of information about Karen—without previously having been given any information. Reading the story, I believed that Reverend Daisley had actually made such a contact with someone in the spirit plane.

I was filled with hope again. Now to locate George Daisley. I wrote to Jeanne Walker and told her about my son. She sent me Reverend Daisley's address and phone number.

I called him. His voice over the phone was strong and kind. He explained that he did not give readings at a distance, but assured me that if I ever came to California he would be happy to see me. I didn't tell him why I wanted a session but assured him I would be out one day. It gave me something to hold on to. Despite living 3,000 miles away, I vowed one day to find a way to have a session with Daisley.

In the meantime, my guides assured me that Stephen was fine and he would talk to me very soon. Things were looking up.

Then why couldn't I stop grieving and crying? Why did I miss him so much? It was like he had gone to camp, had stayed too long, and I was ready for him to come home. And he wasn't coming home. Ever. I couldn't stand not seeing him, not holding him, not talking to him. Sometimes it seemed it would be easier if I could just believe as most churches taught: He was dead, in the ground, sleeping, and would rise again on judgment day.

I knew that wasn't true, or anyway, not *my* truth. I had read too much, had too many experiences to believe that anymore. I knew that only Stephen's body had died. I knew his soul was somewhere else. What I didn't know yet was *where* and how to find him. It was almost like he had been kidnapped, and I didn't know where he was being kept. I was sure he was "alive," but my mind, like the minds of parents whose children are abducted, would play hundreds of scenarios about Stephen's fate. Where was he? Who was he with? Was he happy, sad, hurting, safe? It was tormenting, but in the torment was the hope that one day I would find him and know how he was.

I admit that I tended to make Stephen somewhat of a hero during those months. As I have researched suicide and death and had training in counseling the years since, I have learned that temporarily sainting a dead child is a fairly normal occurrence. I was probably trying to make something special of his suicide so it wouldn't be like that of the hundreds of other kids who took their lives. It was my way of coping, of stopping some of the pain, but it also kept me from understanding and from healing for a long time.

In the meantime, our ministerial classes continued. When I wasn't studying, I read every book I could find about life after death. I still couldn't find much about suicide, and nothing about teenage suicide. I did not even know there were teenage suicide statistics. No one I knew had a child who had committed suicide—or an adult family member or friend, for that matter. I knew of no organizations to seek out. No one I asked knew either. I felt as though I was the only one who was experiencing this. The isolation added to my guilt. I began to think that nobody but me had been such a failure as a mother that it had caused her child to kill himself.

✦

There were few places to turn. There was little use in my going to psychic after psychic, since the disappointments were worse than the anticipation. Some brought through excellent information about me and about us, but their expertise was not in communicating with the dead. I was seeking information about Stephen, and none was given. Many psychics were sincere and genuine and very clairvoyant but were unable to bring any word from Stephen. All I had were the few messages from my guides and the promise of future communications. Sometimes I doubted the guidance because it came through *me*.

The other children needed my care. They seemed to be adjusting fairly well, but I would never again be so confident about the state of their lives. We talked about Stephen but it was difficult for them. They still couldn't understand why he killed himself. I tried to explain, but the words sounded empty. I didn't understand either.

One day when I was vacuuming, I found a heartbreaking note in Andrea's room. On a small crumpled sheet of lined paper, stained with tears, she had written, "March 20, 1974. Stephen, I will always love you. Please try to tell me why. I don't understand. It may be dumb, but I don't. Loving Always, Andrea."

✦

Most evenings, I sat in Stephen's room, stretched out on his bed, touched his things, and tried to imagine when he used to be there. I listened again and again to the two tapes he had made—straining to hear his solemn voice as he gave himself positive affirmations about exercising, weight loss, and building his strength.

As I listened to one of the tapes, I could feel Stephen's pain, his dreams, his fears. This was at our home in Alexandria, Virginia, and Stephen was fourteen at the time. His voice slow and measured, spoke as I remembered it:

April 4, 1973. I decided to start, every day, if possible, talking into the tape recorder and writing down my thoughts. I know I'm not perfect right now, but I am going to start right now trying to be better. No one is ever perfect, people always make mistakes. I hope this talking will help, maybe. Sure can't hurt.

Most of my problems right now center around my losing weight. But I haven't been doing too hot on it; that's the cruddy part. Like today. I didn't eat anything all day except sunflower seeds, except when I got home. Then I had three eggs, four pieces of toast—which is very bad right there—plus I had some cereal and a peanut butter and jelly sandwich and a Pop-Tart and I had two pieces of bread with peanut butter on them today, and milk and . . . it's not doing much good, but it's got to come from me, from inside.

Some of the things I've been doing are, I take karate, I try to learn other things—judo, aikido. I'm sort of upset because of my weight. It sort of throws everything out of proportion. I mean it doesn't work good. And I don't do my karate as good, I don't feel I'm in as good a shape. I feel very self-conscious, around girls especially. I like girls, I think they're cool and all, but I sorta get all tightened up when I even think about 'em. Or swimming, 'cause I should lose about thirty pounds. Now, I'm going to try to plan a program where I can exercise and learn to just generally improve myself. I'm going to practice karate, because I want to be very good at karate when I grow up. I've been reading the book, *Billy Jack*, and that's who I'd like to be: Billy Jack. And live on the reservation or something, or start a school of my own, and help kids who have problems. There are so many stupid people in this world, I've been drawn in with them. And some of the guys think I'm stupid, too, so that's part of it. . . .

His voice did not come on again but was followed by a recording of songs: "I believe, I believe, I believe, I believe, I'm falling in love. It's too late to turn back now. . . ." Then, "I can't get you out of my mind. . . ." "There's something wrong with me, something in your face that keeps me hanging around, something wrong . . . I want to live, I want to give. . . ."

On one side of the other cassette, he had made himself a self-help, suggestion tape:

Concentrate, clear your mind of everything else and concentrate. Clear your mind and breathe deep, very deep. Breathe deeper, breathe from the lowest point you can and force the air up and out. Breathe deeply, have a clear mind and concentrate on what I'm about to say.

You have the chance to become the greatest person of all your dreams and hopes. It's going to take work and you're going to have to do this work. Now concentrate and listen to what you should do. You should stop eating. You don't want to eat. Eating is bad for you. You don't want to eat. You don't need to eat for a couple of days at a time. You don't want to eat, you don't want food at all. Food tastes bad. It slows you down. You want to exercise. You want to be moving. Moving, building your body up until [you have] the proportions of Conan the Barbarian. You want to move and not eat. You don't want food. Food is bad for you. It makes you fat and ugly. It makes you ugly and fat. Feed your body so that you are built like Spiderman and Conan the Barbarian, because when you don't eat you lose weight and when you exercise you build your body to become fast and powerful. So powerful. So powerful that you will fear no one. People will fear you terribly. You'll be all power. You'll be good-looking, girls will be attracted to you.

Just think of Lynn and Kathy, and how the girls will feel if you're good-looking. They'll be attracted to you, you'll be happier. You don't want food, food is *bad* for you. It tastes terrible now. When you wake up in the morning you will not want food. Through the morning and the afternoon, you will not be hungry. You will be itching to exercise. You'll want to exercise and move and build your body. Every morning for the next three weeks when you get up, you will not want food. The only food that you will want to eat is grapefruit and apples and fruits and juices. No fattening food. You'll be ugly if you eat fattening food, you'll be ugly and fat. You'll be just hanging all over and people will turn away from you. You don't want to eat, you want to be good-looking and handsome. You will not even think of food when you wake up in the morning. You will want to exercise. Exercise will be good for you.

Concentrate and think of all the benefits. A strong, powerful body, fast speed, girls attracted to you, being good-looking, being happy. Concentrate. You have concentrated in thought of your new body and of the girls being attracted to you and of the exercise and then you will come out of it slowly, you will feel refreshed, and you will want to exercise and move. You'll be free to move and you will not be hungry.

How he suffered inside without any of us being aware! Mealtimes had been such hell for him. He had been reminded so many times that he was fat, or would get fat, and chastised for eating. His self-confidence slowly eroded away. So much emphasis was put on the outside looks by Richard as he grew up, that he had lost touch with the greater importance of the inner Stephen. Richard and I had destroyed this sensitive child. He through humiliation and emotional abuse; I through my neglect and lack of awareness of Stephen's sensitivity and needs.

Memories came flooding back as I heard his familiar voice. I wanted to see him just one more time. I was tormented by thoughts I couldn't control. Was Stephen mentally ill, as Richard said and as others hinted? "All suicides are mentally ill," I heard more than once. He didn't act mentally ill—depressed somewhat, but not mentally ill in my estimation. I couldn't be one hundred percent sure, so that tormented me. He was so loved. Didn't he know that? Hadn't I told him every day of his life how much I loved him? Was he really going to dictate some books from the other side as he said? I didn't know and my brain was mush trying to analyze and reanalyze it all.

It has been said that a suicide dies only once, but the survivors have him die a thousand times in their minds. I didn't know that then. When I thought of Stephen, I saw him hanging, dangling, eyes out, tongue out, neck broken, suffocating, twisting in agony, or dying quickly. Pictures came into my mind of him suffering for hours, over and over and over again.

It is also written that suicides leave open the door to the closet of their lives with the skeletons of the family showing for everyone to see. How true. Every negative, bad, or uncaring deed was taken from the closet into the bright light of day for scrutiny. Every childhood action, interaction, every word was remembered. Every activity in which I participated was taken apart, put back, and taken apart again. Each time I saw Stephen killing himself, I experienced the same agony again in full measure. I couldn't stop thinking about it and torturing myself. I tried to put it out of my mind, to pray, to heal. The memories wouldn't stop. Sometimes it felt like they were searing my brain. On the rare times I could get them to stop, it was as if there was *nothing* left of Stephen. Memories—any memories—were better than nothing. Memories were all I had left.

All of us who loved him searched our hearts to see what we had done to push him over the brink. Then we searched some more. It was easy to find guilt. It was harder to remember anything positive we had ever done. Especially for me. I had given him birth. He had chosen to end his life at fifteen. I had failed as a mother, as a parent, as a human being. I should be dead, he should be alive. I offered an exchange with God for the miracle of his return. He had everything to live for, my life was over. No matter how I rationalized it, the fact was: Stephen killed himself rather than be with us, with me. I must have made life totally unbearable for him.

How I longed to answer the phone at work and hear, "Hi, Mom, it's me." I looked for Stephen in every crowd. I never saw anyone who looked like him. A former employee stopped by to see us a couple of months after Stephen's death. This was the first time I had seen anyone who even vaguely reminded me of him. There were some haunting similarities. I realized, with a start, that his name was Steve, too. They didn't look that much alike, but whenever I saw him for months afterward I couldn't stop looking at him.

One day in May, I answered the phone at work and Debbie was almost screaming on the other end. "Come home quick! Come home quick, Mom!" I told her I would leave right then and asked what had happened. She said, "Mom, Stephen was here. I saw him. He had on his karate gi, standing behind the stove, cooking. He looked at me and I looked at him. He didn't say anything. Then he disappeared. Come home quick!"

I got in the car and raced home. Debbie met me at the door and I held her. She was talking so fast I could barely understand her. She told me she was sitting in the family room and looked up and saw Stephen standing behind the stove in the kitchen, dressed in his white karate gi. He smiled at her and then he disappeared.

I questioned Debbie as she told the story repeatedly in the same detail. She was frightened, but she was also sure now that Stephen was okay, that he was alive. She was sad, but never so worried about his death after that. She would tell the story often. There was a definite healing and change in her. She stopped being frightened about being in the house alone.

Why hadn't Stephen appeared to me, too? I was thankful he appeared to Debbie. But in my grief, I still longed for an experience with Stephen, a chance to see him once more.

✦

Things had been so gloomy for so long that Tom decided to plan a month-long trip across country in July. We would take the children, see all the western states, visit Tom's mother in California, and, if we could get an appointment, see George Daisley. I did not feel like taking a long trip with a car full of children. I wasn't in a sightseeing mood. But I very much wanted to see Reverend Daisley, so I was willing to endure almost anything to get to him. I called and scheduled an appointment with him for when we planned to be there. Again, I only told him my name, nothing else. If he could really contact the dead, he would have to prove it, with no help from me.

July came and we packed the station wagon for the long trip. All the children came with us except Bob. He was working and had a place of his own. There were six children and two adults in a station wagon for three weeks. I fixed lunches on the tailgate, and we drove at least eight hours or longer each day. We shared one motel room every evening on beds and sleeping bags. It was not my idea of fun. I was exhausted.

Stephen had been dead only four months. I was still in the throes of grieving. Tom's children were as demanding of him as ever. Their mother had made them fearful of me, so they never warmed up to me fully, no matter how much I played with them or cared for them. My only real comfort and joy on the trip were Andrea and Debbie. Everyone seemed to be having a good time except me. I tried to act happy so they wouldn't know, but all I could do at each beautiful vista was think how much Stephen would have loved the trip. It wasn't fair, God. It wasn't fair that he wasn't with us. Why were Tom's children alive and Stephen wasn't? Stephen was more kind, more caring than any of them. Why Stephen? I knew my reasoning was warped, and I didn't think that way often, but I was hurting so badly. Every little thing would remind me of Stephen. I knew I should snap out of it, but I couldn't. The four months Stephen had been gone seemed like forever.

My spirit was broken. I had failed as a mother, as a person. I had lost my enthusiasm for life and living. I didn't want to die and leave my other children, but living hurt too much. I felt such guilt that I couldn't stop grieving. I tried but I couldn't get the pain to stop.

EIGHT

✦

STEPHEN, IT'S YOU!

Our birth is but a sleep and a forgetting.
The soul that rises with us, our life's star,
hath had elsewhere its setting and cometh from afar.
Not in entire forgetfulness and not in utter
nakedness, but trailing clouds of glory do we
come from God who is our home.

—WORDSWORTH

I had always wanted to see the western United States. It was beautiful beyond description, but the trip was no fun without Stephen. By the time we got to California, I was so demoralized I had lost all of my enthusiasm for seeing George Daisley. No psychic had brought Stephen through yet and probably none ever would. Even when my guides told me how Stephen was doing and encouraged me that he was trying to communicate with me, I didn't believe it. I couldn't always hear them, and what I did hear, because of my skepticism, didn't always comfort me. I couldn't be sure I really heard Stephen either. The things I thought were from him were probably my imagination or what I *wanted* to hear.

Maybe people just died and that was the end. Maybe this whole metaphysical field was garbage. I was almost finished with my ministerial program. I would graduate soon, and I wasn't even sure I believed what I had been studying. Why did I think Stephen, who had killed himself intentionally, would be allowed to help from the other side? Maybe he was suffering hell and damnation and I just didn't want to believe it. Maybe I was trying to keep him alive because I couldn't face the reality that he was dead. I was haunted by doubt.

We drove from Los Angeles, to Daisley's home in Santa Barbara. It was a lovely day and a beautiful drive, and we talked about the trees. We had the children with us and we stopped to take pictures. I took hundreds of photos of the children during the trip and after Stephen died to make up for all I had neglected taking of him.

Daisley's address was on a quiet, tree-lined street, with large homes built back from the road on grassy lawns, surrounded by large trees and lovely flowers. Reverend Daisley's home was well-kept and felt very peaceful even before we stepped out of the car. A well-groomed, white-haired man with a youthful walk and manner and a golden tan came to greet us. He introduced himself as George Daisley. He appeared to be in his sixties and spoke with a delightful British accent. His friendliness made us feel very relaxed. He told the children they could play in the yard until we were through. We followed him to a small guest house down the hill from his home. He would do the reading there.

I had told Daisley nothing about why we had come. If he was authentic, he would know. We sat on a couch opposite him. He sat on a metal folding chair in the center of the room. He explained how he was able to be an alert, conscious channel and to report on what he saw and heard from the spirit realm. He asked us to confirm things immediately that were correct and to tell him if any of his messages weren't correct. He asked us no questions and suggested we take notes as he did not allow tape recording. Tom offered to be the scribe.

Reverend Daisley began with a prayer and invited those in spirit to be with us. I was cautiously optimistic, but I had been disappointed so many times that I wasn't expecting very much. My faith was shaken.

In addition, I had done something that I knew was unfair, but I still did it. I had taken a picture of Stephen out of my billfold and placed it in my flowered makeup case. "Okay, Stephen," I said as I sat and prayed alone before we drove to Santa Barbara, "if you are there and you can come through and it's really you, then tell Reverend Daisley about this test I'm doing and get him to mention where I've put your picture."

Reverend Daisley began to turn his head and look around, eyes fully open. "Steve. Who is Steve? Steve is here." Hearing his name surprised me. I answered that it was my son, Stephen. He said, "He wants you to know he's fine. You're such a worrier. He thinks you're the world's worst worrier. He wants to thank you for talking out loud to him when you sit on the bed in your room. He likes it when you talk to him out loud. But he wants you to open the drawer in the bottom of the bedside stand and get rid of all the things of his you have stored there. He doesn't need those things anymore and neither do you. Give them away."

I began to sob out loud. Besides the evidential information, I began to feel Stephen's presence in the room. He would, of course, call himself Steve, not Stephen, as I always did. I *did* talk out loud to him almost every night. I *had* put all his precious treasures in the bottom drawer of the nightstand, just as he said.

Daisley continued, "Stephen says you have eight bicycles in the garage and he watched Tom fixing the lock on the garage door the other day." Controlling my tears, I turned to Tom and said, "Is that right? Was the lock broken?" He said, "Yes." Still a little skeptical, I acknowledged that we did have eight bicycles, and I thought to myself that it could be a lucky guess. Though, I reasoned, how many people have eight bicycles?

"Stephen said he's glad Tom can wear some of his clothes." So many psychics had described Stephen as a little child, I assumed they didn't think I looked old enough to have a child his size. Reverend Daisley was correct; Tom could wear many of Stephen's clothes. "Steve says he was with you in the car on your drive here and loved the trees, too. He says to tell Mike hello." Mike was Tom's oldest son and Stephen had been fond of him.

I cannot explain it. A part of me questioned each piece of information Daisley brought through, yet I could feel the presence of Stephen—his soul or his spirit or something. I realized I had sometimes felt this same thing in the room at home since he died, but didn't trust that it was him. Now I couldn't deny it. I couldn't stop crying. I was so thankful, so touched by the spiritual feeling in the room and Stephen's presence.

Stephen continued to speak through the reverend. "You know, I always wanted a motorcycle, and I have one here now when I want to use it."

I said, "I don't think he ever mentioned wanting a motorcycle."

Tom interrupted, "Oh, yes, he did—we talked about it several times."

Then Stephen said, "Thank you for the roses at my service."

Oh, no, this simply wasn't accurate. "We didn't have flowers at his service, we just had a memorial service and no flowers," I told Reverend Daisley.

"Stephen," Daisley questioned, turning and directing his voice to his right. "Your mother says there were no flowers."

Reverend Daisley paused and began again, "He is telling me to tell you, 'Remember the pink roses on the mantel, Mom?' "

The pink roses! The ones I had bought in the grocery and put on the mantel. I had forgotten. He couldn't be reading my mind—I had forgotten. I sobbed uncontrollably.

"Please try not to be too emotional. It makes it harder for me to keep the contact," Reverend Daisley requested.

I tried. I really tried. But I was full of the feeling of Stephen's presence and his love, so it was hard not to be overcome with emotion. Then Daisley said, "Stephen says open your purse and pull out the flowered container and show me the picture you put there." The flowered what? What picture? For a moment I had forgotten the "test." I then opened my purse to confirm the information. I laughed for the first time. Bless you, Stephen. You *are* here—you heard me!

Stephen continued with information about people we knew, about the family, about himself, and the work ahead. "I told you, Mom, that I was going to help you write some books. Keep the channel open. Stop doubting so much."

Reverend Daisley spoke to me, "You know, my dear, *you* can do what I'm doing and many *other* things. Stephen will help you. You have a strong work ahead and a lot of helpers to work with you. Edgar Cayce is even here. He tells me he is going to work with you."

Oh, no! Not Edgar Cayce! Why did he have to say that? Lots of psychics thought they had to bring through some well-known person like Cayce, I thought to myself.

"Cayce has a message for you, but first he wants to prove to you it's him," he continued. A message from Stephen was one thing, but from Cayce, that was something different. I became doubtful again.

Cayce, through Daisley, told about five books we had in our library, giving us their titles and then saying that I had read a certain one, Tom another, neither of us a third, and both of us the last two. He was correct on every count. Two of the books were not well known, one being *How to Develop Your ESP*, by Suzy Smith, who had personally autographed our copy recently.

Cayce added, "You have three cameras on the trip with you. Neither of you is a particularly good photographer, like I was." He laughed. "Now that you think it *might* be me, I have a message for you." Edgar Cayce paused, then through Daisley spoke loudly and firmly, "I will work with you, and

I have a work for you to do in my work." He ended by saying he would keep in touch with me and help me.

I was amazed. What in the world did that mean, a work to do in his work?

The session ended. My heart overflowed with thanks for this wonderful man who had such a helpful gift, which he used so lovingly and spiritually. There *was* a bridge between earth and spirit that could be traveled upon. There was! There was true hope in my heart for the first time since black Monday, March 18.

The trip back home was much better. It was time to get about my work, our work—Stephen's and mine. Stephen no longer had an earthly body, there was no longer a physical Stephen Christopher, my beloved son. I would have to learn to accept that and live without the touch of his body. I could never again embrace him and feel his warmth and tenderness. Stephen now wore a spiritual form that I couldn't see. Nevertheless, I could sense his presence and hear and feel him in a different way. Now we could begin our two-way conversations. It would not be the same, but it would have to be enough. I began to sense that something really helpful and hopeful to others could come from Stephen's and my painful experiences.

✦

I was at last beginning to really use and appreciate the spiritual opening and psychic gifts I had received. After my meeting with George Daisley, Stephen and I began to talk, slowly building a bridge between our two dimensions.

Sometimes the experiences with Stephen were so clear that my faith was strengthened, and I believed totally and completely. Other times, I floundered in doubt, thinking I might be losing my mind. I sat at my typewriter whenever I could. I prayed and asked that Stephen be allowed to communicate with me. Then I got quiet, meditated, and listened. Most of the time I felt his presence within a few moments. I spoke to him out loud, "Oh, Stephen. I can feel you. I love you. I love you. I'm so sorry for all I did to hurt you. I love you so."

He would often say, "I love you, too, Mom," just as he always had. I would hear his voice inside of my head, "overshadowing my thoughts," as he put it. The communications were much like telepathy. I could hear the words inside my head—words I wasn't forming or thinking, that moved my own thoughts aside. Stephen told me that those like himself vibrated at a different, faster rate than when in an earthly body. Therefore, it was very difficult to see them with out physical eyes. Not impossible, but very difficult. He explained that at times when we raised our own energy vibrations with prayer, meditation, or other means, we could see and hear that dimension as well as other dimensions.

When I was able to hear clearly and fully, the information Stephen shared was always interesting and helpful. Many times it was very evidential. On the occasions when I wanted him to give me something to "prove" our communications were valid and true, it seemed as if nothing came through. Only when I let go of the need to "prove" anything, would a series of things be given that were verified beyond doubt.

I have tried and tested the guidance he has shared with me in every conceivable way. Doubt and skepticism have battled within me against hope and trust, each claiming a victory at times.

NINE

LISTENING TO STEPHEN

"Though I am dead, grieve not for me with tears,
Think not of death with sorrowing and fears,
I am so near that every tear you shed
Touches and tortures me, though you think me dead . . .
But when you laugh and sing in glad delight,
My soul is lifted upward to the light;
Laugh and be glad for all that
Life is giving,
And I though dead will share your joy in LIVING!"

—Author unknown

What I will share with you now comes not from me, but through me, from Stephen. It strikes a chord of truth within my own heart and soul. This information has helped me understand life more fully by understanding the transition we call death.

I have extensively researched suicide. I have studied why adults and young people kill themselves and I have asked Stephen to share his insights from that dimension. Through this, I have been able to see and understand much more. I know he lives, yet I will not pretend for a moment that I wouldn't prefer to have Stephen sitting across from me with his "old" body, talking and sharing as we once did.

At first, telepathic communication is much harder and takes far more time and effort than talking out loud. But I believe it's well worth the effort to learn how. And once learned, it becomes easier and easier.

Stephen and my guides say this way of communicating is

the bridge between our dimensions, to which we all have access. It is that same bridge that connects us as we sleep at night, then often disappears from our consciousness as we awaken, the same bridge that connects us with all other souls, living and dead. They say we can become fully awake in our sleep and in our conscious states. We can experience not only communication with loved ones who no longer have physical bodies, but we can also remember and use that awareness to access the untapped powers of our minds.

As Stephen continued to speak to me, I grew daily to trust more and more. Let me share his words to me:

"Mom, I can't say enough times—I'm here! I am not dead. I'm alive! More free and alive than when I had a body. Only my physical body is gone. I want you to bring to people a greater knowing of the state and dimension they call death. Death is not the end, it is simply walking out of the physical form and into the spirit realm, which is our true home. It's going back home. For a while, all of us share a temporary home in the earth dimension with each other, learning and growing together. When it's time, we go back to our real home. We unzip the body, so to speak, let it fall to the ground and walk through the next door clothed in our spiritual form, which was always there inside the physical body.

"I want to tell you what led up to my death and explain to you what happened when I died. I know you want to know, even though you are fearful about hearing. You see, the missing link for most parents is that they find their child dead and they don't get to say good-bye. There is no farewell hug. They do not know why the child killed himself. Many kids don't leave notes, or if they do leave them, they're angry and want to strike out or blame someone, so the notes reflect that. The parents are in anguish. None of their questions can be answered. Their plea, sometimes for years, is: 'Why? Why? Why did he do it? Why didn't I stop him? Why did I drive him to his death?' Since all the notes are written in the young person's moments of anguish and lack of hope, the very information in the notes can be misleading and cause the parents untold guilt all their lives. After all, many of the notes left either imply or clearly state, that they, the parents or family or friends, were to blame.

"What I want to explain to you is why I did it—why I took my own life. I can give you a perspective about my suicide and the suicide of other young people, too. Along with the hundreds of books you have now read, it will enable us—that's right, Mom, you and me, together—to help other parents as well as children who feel killing themselves is the only solution to their problems.

"I feel you bracing yourself, Mom, tightening up your stomach because you don't know if you can handle what I'm going to say. Some of what I have to tell you is not going to be easy to hear. Some of it has to do with mistakes that you've made. Some of it has to do with a lot of other things. You're not to blame for the choice I exercised in taking my life. It was my decision, right or wrong. I know it was a totally wrong decision. I have to accept the responsibility for what I did."

✦

Stephen was right. I *was* afraid. To hear about Stephen's suffering would be like a stab to the heart. But his presence gave me courage to continue listening.

"You often said that there were no clues or indications that I was unhappy or suicidal, and you know that's not true now, as you have looked back," Stephen went on. "You see things a lot differently than you did. At the time I died, you didn't see any clues. You could find nothing to read. There were almost no books out about adolescent suicide and the signs to look for. I think that if you could have located and read the little that was written, you would have gone through the grieving process sooner and understood better.

On the other hand, you might not have tried to communicate with me. You could easily have wanted to put it all behind you. In some ways you were kept from reading things that would do that to you. Your guides tried to keep the books that would discourage you too much away from you. Others, we tried to help you find. We sometimes succeeded and sometimes not.

"My decision to take my life was wrong, but out of that wrong choice, I have been blessed here with a chance to work with you and others. And we have a chance to help others together. You from your side, me from mine. We're not that far apart, actually."

✦

Stephen then began to share some truths about our lives—and about *his* life.

✦

"Let me tell you some of the things I have come to a greater understanding of here. When you left Dad, I hated all that happened. Dad always made me feel bad about myself. He was so critical that sometimes I hurt so much I would go in my room and crawl under the covers and cry. Sometimes I wished he was dead, then felt horrible guilt about my thoughts. But at least I knew what to expect. When you left him, I understood how miserable you were, but my world crumbled. I didn't mind Dad moving out, but we had to move away from my friends and out of our home. None of us wanted to leave the house. You knew you should have fought harder to keep us there, but you didn't and that began the difficulties.

"Remember how the church people condemned you for all the things you were reading and studying? Then when you and Tom got together, it got worse. I didn't like him and I hoped you two would break up and we could move back in the house without Dad. I didn't trust Tom from the beginning. After I was dead and you stayed with him because of how good he treated you, I wanted to barf, because he didn't treat me very well when I lived. And I knew you couldn't trust him."

✦

His words about Tom struck an uneasy chord with me. Perhaps I had known all along that something was not right with this man. But this was the hardest thing of all to see. It would be some time before I recognized the truth behind Stephen's words.

"As long as I can remember, Bobby used to hurt and torment me," Stephen continued. "I wanted him to love me because I really loved him. I remember when I killed his gerbils. I felt awful, but he had pushed me and pushed me for so many days that I was in a rage. I couldn't stand up to him, so I killed something of his that would hurt him. I felt sick afterward because I loved those little animals. It wasn't that there was anything wrong with me mentally as much as I was under such incredible pressure from Bob.

"You see, Mom, Dad was so faultfinding, overbearing, and cruel to all of us and especially Bob, that Bob struck out at me to stop some of his own pain. You even knew that and went out of your way to help Bob and me, but you were in pain, too. You hurt and you would sometimes take your pain and anger out on us. I can see it all more clearly from here and can explain it to you better. Dad was the victim of victims. His parents, bruised emotionally by their parents, took their anger and frustration out on him. He took it out on you and all of us. Sins of the parents visited upon the children . . . right? Some of this you understood back then, but you were helpless to change it."

His words rang so true. I hated to admit that I had raised my precious children in a home where the violence and despair were so great.

◆

Stephen went on to say, "I want to tell you how I felt about my childhood and then what I have seen as I have reviewed my records in this dimension. I'll share with you what I went through on the day I killed myself. I want to be able to do this honestly, even if it hurts you. My hope is that this information will help kids like me, so they will not kill themselves. Maybe it can help parents to understand their children better, and keep them from killing themselves. If only one person reads this book and pauses to think things through and doesn't kill himself, or if only one person starts listening to and understands their child better and the child doesn't kill himself, or herself, then my foolish act and our work on the book will not have been in vain.

"You did not cause my death. What happened the morning of the day I decided to take my life contributed somewhat to my decision, but by no means was it the only factor. Nor was it Dad's fault or Tom's or my teachers' who ignored me. Each of you played a role in my life and in my death, but it was my choice and mine alone. That is always true no matter what notes are left blaming others. It is always the soul's responsibility, no matter what age, for even a young child is an old soul. Blaming oneself adds to the pain and guilt that the individual or family feels they deserve for what they did or did not do that caused the death."

◆

As Stephen spoke, I realized that he was saying something very profound and true. He had not *belonged* to me; he had belonged to himself—an independent soul. How difficult it is for parents to understand that about their children! In fact, Stephen's revelations about his own birth cleared up many questions for me.

◆

"Mom, as I looked back over the records, there was a terrible time getting me in to be born to you," Stephen said knowingly, and I flashed suddenly to the agony I experienced during my pregnancy. "You didn't want another child, and you were extremely careful not to get pregnant. Yet, we had set up the possibility of this work before you incarnated. By we, I mean a group of us souls that had a work to do together. First Bob would probably come, then me. We all had lessons to learn with each other—karma it's sometimes called. Karma can be positive or negative. So we had some good karma and some not so good karma to deal with. As a soul without a body yet, waiting to enter through you, I could only use thought to impress information to you. When you did get pregnant it was because we worked hard to see that you slipped up.

"Remember, we all meet when we sleep and dream, whether we are incarnate in bodies or not and we see certain patterns unfold, choices we may make. We always have the free will to choose differently, and that's why we have certain feelings to do or not do things. We don't quite know why we feel this way or that, but it's the intuition, carried over from our higher mind or residue from our dream states. Because of your sensitivity, you knew that I might not stay with you long. You were shown that I had some lessons that I might not meet well and might choose not to reach adulthood. You also knew that you and Bill would not stay together and you were shown possibilities of other things that would not be easy.

"You created all kinds of ailments during your pregnancy with me, even armoring yourself with weight to try and stop the pain you were feeling both physically and emotionally from this unconscious awareness. Your guides and I worked diligently with you to get you to listen to us, but you were far less aware then and would not, so I watched you suffer and struggle and was unable to help. While you were pregnant with me, you were taught and instructed, both during sleep and while conscious, on other levels, about my life and our potential future.

"We thought it was funny that you were convinced you

would die giving birth to me. It was just your fear because you loved Bobby so much and were so uninformed about pregnancy. You would not have fared well in natural childbirth at that time, with your fear of pain and death. We were all there during the labor and delivery, and you were out of your body a lot, talking with us.

"I had some mixed feelings about coming back in a little body again as a baby and having to grow up. Before I entered, I reviewed my past lives and lessons I hadn't learned and would have to meet in this experience. I also reviewed my gifts and strengths and saw that I was to have a good brain and a strong body, that my nature would be kind and loving. I saw that people would like me but I would not like myself. Issues of self-esteem and loving myself needed to be dealt with. I saw that I might turn to food as a crutch, under stress, and have a battle with my weight if I wasn't careful. Worries and fears about what others thought about me were strong lessons to learn, not to mention lessons with Bob and Dad. It may help you to know, Mom, that most of the karma you and I had was good.

"When I was born, there was a beautiful bond between Bobby and me. I talked with him with my mind and he heard and talked back to me the same way. Babies are almost always totally aware. That may surprise you, but it's true. They hear and experience everything going on around them, whether it's said aloud or just thought. If parents were aware that every argument, every word said *and* thought is heard and deeply impressed upon an infant's mind, they would guard their words and thoughts carefully.

"I have to tell you, Mom, that I almost let myself die that time I fell down the stairs when I was two. I could see some of my life pathway ahead, and I didn't want to go on. When I was asleep, my spiritual helpers would assure me I could make it. I wasn't so sure. I didn't try to kill myself, but a part of my life force was ebbing away. When I slipped on the stairs, I was unlinking from my body. My helpers and your prayers and the prayers of the church people tilted the scales. I reviewed my options and with help, I chose to stay."

Stephen went on to describe secrets that few parents understood. "Actually, all of us hear each other's thoughts all the time, and it's why you have certain feelings, for instance, that someone says one thing and means another. You hear and you know, but you deny it. You are far more than just physical bodies. Newborn babies, being totally aware from birth, are just more susceptible and sensitive to the positive and negative thoughts and energies from everyone.

"Those parents who begin to work with the soul of the child before conception, during pregnancy, and in the very early years can truly help direct the new age soul. It enables that soul to be of greater spiritual service and mental awareness to help change the world. Or at least their corner of the world. Ideally, a parent should not leave the child with someone else and be away often until the child is at least five years old. This will not be appreciated by modern parents, but for the sake of the child, it's true. This is not to say that the mother or father should give up all their interests, but that the responsibility of bringing in a new soul is of such importance that it should be a high priority. If parents truly knew and believed how critical the first five years were for the right foundation, they would sacrifice and devote those years to full parenting, whenever possible. Or, if they were unable to spend this time, they would opt not to bring in a soul until they could. You were unable to do this with Bob or me and it weakened our foundation."

Stephen's further insight about the link between diet and conduct in the young confirmed a fact that many people have long suspected. I wasn't surprised that he had investigated this subject in the afterlife. It had been a consuming matter for him on earth.

✦

"The correct diet will help with juvenile delinquency, lethargy, hyperactivity, and disease," Stephen said. "By training the parents to greater awareness in helping their children eat correctly, be fed correctly, the entire planet can be helped! Those who say correct diet is *the* way, *the* answer to everything are incorrect. It is a big piece of the puzzle, but not the whole puzzle.

"If enough parents banded together, as has been done in some places, the horrendous diets in the school cafeterias and day care centers could be changed," Stephen pointed out. "Children are being fed the equivalent of poison with sugared cereals, soft drinks, white flour, and processed foods. What is taken into the body is very, very important, for the soul can have a great purpose and be mired down by the lack of energy and vitality to do the work. I was one of these.

"In my case, I was hypoglycemic," he explained. "My blood sugar was low and erratic, from my faulty diet. The first couple of years of my life, you gave me exactly what the doctor ordered. Unfortunately, it was food without any life in it. Jars of baby food, white bread, sugar, and bottled milk were not healthy choices. Breast milk is so important for infants. If I had been a car needing leaded gas, what you gave me was equivalent to filling the car with kerosene and expecting it to run.

"Even later when you cooked everything from scratch, there was too much sugar and wheat and not enough fresh vegetables and fruits. You didn't know that then and didn't understand. It is foolish to say if the diet is right there would be no suicides. Of course, that isn't true. However, a better national diet would drop the percentages considerably. There are many other factors, even if the diet is ideal, but a proper diet helps you think more clearly, have more energy, and stay well and feel better about yourself. It helps your brain chemistry to function better. These things could be the difference many times between choosing death and choosing to live.

"Mealtime was my personal hell for as long as I can remember. Dad was always on us about eating and meals were awful. That's where my problems with digestion and assimilation began. My stomach churned during his lengthy lectures almost every meal. None of us knew then how bad it was to eat under those circumstances. I would be forced to clean my plate. Lots of times I was stuffed and didn't want any more food. Other times I wasn't hungry to begin with. There were times when certain foods were so repulsive to me, I would gag. I knew, and children know, sometimes intuitively, which foods they shouldn't be eating. I was given no choice, except by you when Dad wasn't around. I was often hungry after I left the table because of the stress or inadequate diet. I wanted to eat all the time because I was actually not getting enough vitamins and minerals. Those I did get weren't assimilated correctly. You had a sweet tooth and made too many baked goodies and homemade bread. We drank diet cola, which made it worse.

"You always said I didn't need to lose weight, and I always thought I did. Dad had this thing about us all keeping slim, and you and I just ate more when he nagged. There was stress and tension all the time. I didn't even know why I was always hungry and couldn't stop eating. I thought I had no willpower. It made me feel awful about myself."

"Oh, Stephen," I cried. "Is this what caused you to commit suicide? Tell me, Stephen. How did it happen?"

TEN

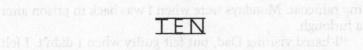

STEPHEN TELLS ME ABOUT HIS DEATH

He that knows how to live does not fear death.
—Ancient Shaolin saying

"I thought about killing myself when I ran away the first time, when we lived in Virginia," Stephen said. "Things had been real bad for me for months. You could tell from the note I left for you, which said, among other things, 'I don't feel like going on, life's not worth living.' I just didn't have the courage to do it then. I had been reading a lot of literature on different Oriental philosophies, and suicide was considered an honorable death in many cultures. Perhaps in certain cases it is, but I need to tell you this and hope you believe it. Suicide is never, ever, the correct decision for a young person. It wasn't for me, it isn't for any child. It's understandable in many cases, but it's never right.

"The day I died, here's what was happening. Remember, I see it now from a clearer perspective than when it happened. It was Monday and I hated Mondays. The weekends were all that kept me alive for weeks. Mondays were when I had to go back to school and try to hide my fat body under my raincoat. Mondays were when I was back in prison after a furlough.

"I hated visiting Dad, but felt guilty when I didn't. I felt sorry for him, but he made me feel like shit. Leave that in—'like shit.' He found fault with everything I did. I know he loved me in his way, but being around him was crazy-making. Every time I let down my guard and felt sorry for him or was caring, he shoved the knife in when I was least expecting it. His girlfriends were nice and he was nicer around them, just like you were sometimes nicer around Tom. I just wanted him to like me and tell me he was proud of me. I felt like a fat pig around him and food was an obsession with him. 'Don't eat that, don't eat this . . . you've had enough to eat. . . .' I was fifteen and he treated me like I was five. After a visit with him I felt like I had been beaten with a broom. I really did. Tom made me sick, too. He was Mr. Macho all the time. He wasn't much fun to play sports with. You always thought how great he was, playing sports with us kids, but he was mean. He would do anything to win. He didn't exactly cheat, but he stretched everything to the limit of cheating. He was so determined to win whatever we played, that it was never any fun. I didn't like him. I didn't trust him. I watched how he looked at girls and women, and I thought he was a lech. He treated his kids like little kings and us like peasants. I liked his kids, I really did. They were sneaky little rascals, always doing things that were just on the edge of trouble, but we had lots of fun. I liked them better when they weren't around their dad. Around him they were whiny, demanding, and acted like babies.

"Andrea was my good friend. I liked her a lot, and I loved her. Things were rough on her, too. She never did complain much, and she and I did lots of things together. Debbie was a brat sometimes, but I couldn't help loving her. We all spoiled her when she was little, she was so cute. She could really be mouthy when she wanted something. You let her get by with a lot, but mostly none of us minded too much. Most of the things she did were so funny. I think we all understood she was the baby and her ways made Dad laugh, which was cool. So weekends were my salvation. I loved Friday nights and Saturdays. I started feeling stressed by Sunday afternoons because Monday was coming.

"The last weekend was not all that different from most except Bob was home. He wanted everything done his way. It really worried me, all that he was going through. We went to the movies that Sunday, and he wanted to go to one and I wanted to go to the other, and we went to the one he wanted, but that was okay. I wanted us to be friends. I still loved him, but I irritated him so much. I wanted him to like me, like he used to.

"Sunday night I felt fat—really fat. I had eaten all weekend and my stomach was sticking out and my pants were tight. I felt awful. I still kept snacking. I couldn't stop. I was getting hot in school wearing my raincoat every day. Soon I would have to take it off or die. Pardon the pun, Mom. It was my security blanket, without it everyone would see how fat, fat, fat I really was.

"Now, reviewing all that happened from here, I see things differently. It is not easy having a physical body. It weighs you down. You get obsessed about it. Particularly if you have low blood sugar and vitamin deficiencies, allergies, and excessive insulin release, which I didn't know I had and you didn't know I had. You know how it was, Mom. The mealtimes with Dad were torture and everything you ate was commented on or you were always told *not* to eat things when you were hungry or thirsty, and to eat them when you were full. It also creates a lot of stress and strain and some real bad thinking.

"I look at my records here whenever I want. You can see them just like watching movies, except you can become part of the experience when you want to get into the feelings more. I see now, I wasn't that fat. In my head I was fat. I did need to lose about twenty pounds, but I didn't look like I thought I looked. I didn't see all the good things about myself. All I saw was fat.

"Somewhere in my warped thinking, I thought that if I got slim everything would get better. Everyone would speak to me, girls would like me more, and all that. So my way of getting slim was to stop eating. That was great for one meal, but by the time I got home from school, I was so hungry I ate three times as much. Then I hated myself and ate more.

"About this time, Kathy told me she might be pregnant. I had such a crush on her. I was crazy about her, but I handled it real well on the phone with her when she told me. Afterward, I felt like someone had kicked me. I would never have touched her if I'd been her boyfriend and here some jerk had taken advantage of her. I was hurt and jealous and protective. I didn't have a car and couldn't get to her, and our phone conversations left me very frustrated. I was the only one she could talk to, so she told me every detail, which hurt me even more.

"Lynn was so cute, and I liked her a lot, but I only saw her when she and her mom were with Dad. She was nice enough, but I called her and she would be busy or have to get off the phone. So it felt like I didn't have anybody. No car, no friends, nobody. Just a fat, ugly body."

"You had me, Stephen. I loved you."

"Mom, you just weren't enough then. You were busy. You were my mother. Part of being my age and growing up was to pull away a little anyway, to become a little independent. Kids do that in preparation for leaving home in the years ahead. I know that now, I didn't then. I just knew that how much you loved me and how good-looking you thought I was didn't mean much. I actually thought that you loved me no matter how fat I was and wouldn't tell me how awful I really looked.

"I went to bed that night wishing I were dead. I was not going to school ever again and be embarrassed and lonesome and ignored. I had decided to stay home Monday. When I told you, you insisted I go in, but I went back to bed. Tom came to my room to tell me you said I had to go to school. He said you all knew I had shoplifted some things. He told me not to take my gym bag to school or anywhere and you would both talk to me that night when you got home.

"I didn't know why I took things occasionally. Many of the kids did, and I guess it seemed like I was more part of things with them. We'd all sneak things out of the store. We'd all laugh and grin at each other. We only took little things, not expensive things, but for that little while, I felt like one of them, like everybody else. They'd leave the store and go off with their friends, and I'd come home and here would be this stuff in my gym bag and I felt awful. I'd try to enjoy whatever it was, but it made me feel worse. I didn't even need the stuff. That's no excuse. I'm not trying to excuse what I did.

"Well, anyway, that did it! I thought, that son of a bitch, Tom, had no right to make me feel bad. Who was he? Nothing but a creep. I was humiliated. Nothing I ever did was okay with him and now he rubbed it in by telling me I had shoplifted. I *had* to have my bag. It went everywhere with me. I was sick about getting caught. I had only lifted a few things from the drugstore, some tanning stuff to make me look darker and a few things. I knew I shouldn't have, but I did and now I was caught. I would probably be made to take them back and feel like a fool. I felt like a fool now. A fool. A fat fool. I wanted to die from embarrassment.

"I couldn't tell you I wasn't going to school now. You would both make me go or make me feel worse. I would *have* to go. I would show you both, I would pretend to go and stay home. But you messed that up, Mom. You wouldn't let me walk and you wouldn't leave before I left, so I was stuck with getting in the car with you. I had decided I wouldn't stay, no matter what. You said, 'Stephen, you just can't take things from the store. We can pay for them.

It's not right. We'll talk tonight. I love you, honey. We have to get these things straightened out.' Right in front of Tom. I was hurt and angry. I would show you both. I turned right around and didn't go to school when you let me off. I sneaked back home. I ate and watched TV and felt worse and worse. I decided not to be humiliated anymore. I would be gone when you got home. I decided to go to the woods and spend the night where you couldn't talk to me. I might even kill myself.

"I gathered together some of my things. I packed enough food to last a few meals. So, you could see how ambivalent I was. I found my little hideaway in the woods, sat down, and began to think about killing myself. My thinking was muddled. I could hang myself and then you'd all be sorry. I would never again have to go to school and be humiliated there. Nobody cared anyway. You had Tom. He didn't care about any of us. The girls didn't care. Dad didn't care, for sure. I was just an embarrassment to him. Maybe I could help more from the other side. For sure I couldn't do anything here.

"My thinking changed from wanting to show you and hurt you, to how free I would be dead, and how much I could do and help from the other side. I had been reading things about life after death, and we had talked about it. It would be better than what I was going through. I honestly didn't even consider the finality of it all. In my mind it was like—I'd show all of you. I wouldn't be a bother anymore, and maybe I could help. You had said that people don't die, they continued on the other side. I could do something there. I couldn't do anything alive. As I thought further I imagined you'd all regret what you did, and I'd come back and you'd appreciate me more. After all, in the movies and on TV people got killed one night and were on another program the next. I didn't specifically think that, but my consciousness was like that. Death and its real meaning were somewhat cloudy then. I didn't think how absolutely irreversible and final it would be.

"My plan caused me to feel better, almost excited, with something to aim for. Something I could do, something I had some control over. The more I thought about it, the better it seemed. I began to write notes to everyone. As I wrote them I had some funny feelings. I felt important but I felt sad. I felt people would sit up and listen, but I felt a pain in the pit of my stomach. I felt like crying, and I felt sorry for myself; then I changed and felt strong and brave. My feelings were like a merry-go-round: up and down and around and around.

"I had brought a rope along, not to hang myself especially, but I always brought a rope camping. Remember, Dad taught us that. So I began to plan and practice certain knots with it. Then I wrote a few things, then I would think. I climbed up the tree. It was getting late in the afternoon, dusk, almost dark. I sat on the limb and let the rope down to touch the ground, then shortened it so that my body wouldn't touch the ground when I jumped. I might jump and hit the ground if it weren't just right. So I climbed up on a higher limb. That ought to work for sure. I knotted the rope around the tree limb, so it wouldn't come undone. Then I put the other end around my neck with a perfect slipknot.

"I stood up on the tree. I had on my navy blue shirt, and I was writing the notes in my little spiral book. I put it in my pocket before I jumped so that someone would find it. I had been indecisive about whether I'd do it or not. I'd been thinking about it for a long time now, it seemed. So I wrote more notes and went into a state of elation almost, of real high-pitched, false, and intense joy.

"Now that's the real danger stage, I've learned. If someone had been there to help me through that stage, I would not have killed myself. But there was nobody there, and I had made some pretty final choices. There I was, writing the last notes and I was feeling so high about it, like maybe I could really help from the other side. I felt impotent about helping as a fifteen-year-old with my ugly, overweight body.

So I began to feel sure I could help from the other side. There was a sense of excitement, of going on a journey. There was also that fear in the pit of my stomach that moved like an electric basketball.

"I didn't sense any presences around me. As you read the one note you thought that a guide or being was there telling me the things I wrote. (Stephen had written in a booklet separate from his notes: "Getting scared will syke you out and may make you lose. Avoid confrontation during this time, breathe deeply and clear mind of thought of losing, then practice to overcome fear.") Actually, I was just giving myself a suggestion so I wouldn't back out. I had written that much earlier.

"Later, I discovered that even before I left my body, there were all kinds of beings around me—angels and guides—and they all helped me. At that time I couldn't see any. I had some moments of real doubt and fear. And then I had some moments of real courage. And my courage fought with my fear. There was a war on that tree. What I thought was that my courage won. What I see now is that my fear won.

"I was writing the notes before I got up on the tree, and then up on the tree I took the pad and pen with me. It was exactly like you thought—I flipped to the back of the book, and I started writing. I was scared then and started to cry; you can see the change in my handwriting. I'm sitting there with the rope around my neck, wanting to be stopped, and yet not wanting to be a coward by backing out, like when I was little and Dad told me not to be a coward and to jump into the swimming pool. I don't think at that time I had any thought that someone might come and find me. There were other times I did, but I didn't at that time. I was pretty far back in the woods and nothing could have stopped me then.

"So I finished the notes, and I asked *God* to stop me. It was the final thing. I asked God to stop me if I shouldn't kill myself. That was probably the hardest note for you, Mom. You had some anger toward God at times for not doing what I asked. You were mad at yourself for not teaching me that God would not step in and stop me if I did something foolish. I finished the last note and was shaking and crying. I kind of expected God to step out of the woods and stop me, and I waited but He didn't. I waited a few minutes more. I even said out loud, 'Now, God, its up to you. Stop me if I shouldn't do this.' Then I put the notebook in my shirt pocket. I was shaking so bad that I dropped the pen and it fell on the ground. I started to go down and get it but I didn't.

"First I was going to jump. I stood up. It looked so far down, it scared me. I started crying. So I sat down. I kept trying to make myself do it and couldn't. Then I forced myself and jumped. Not a real jump, just a kind of slide and easing-myself-over-the-limb jump. I died instantly. I did feel a moment of pain. I'm not going to tell you I didn't. There was a moment of blinding pain. The pain only lasted for a little bit and it stopped.

"I felt like I was floating up. I was like an air bubble under the water. It felt like I had dived into deep water and was coming up, but I could breathe in the water. I floated up out of my body and it felt like there was somebody at each elbow, but I couldn't see anybody. And I looked around and there were kind of mistylike forms, but I couldn't see them very clearly. I floated above my body. I looked down. I could see the top of a head, and then I kind of floated away and I could see this body hanging there by the neck. For a moment I couldn't figure out who it was. It didn't look familiar.

"When I realized it was me, panic took over. I mean *panic*. Instead of being excited that I was out of my body and was still alive and could see and think, I suddenly realized how mad you and Tom were going to be. I had this moment of feeling like a kid that had done some bad thing and was going to be caught and punished for it. I didn't realize that there was no way you could punish me for this. I had created my own punishment. I started to really cry; tears filled my eyes and I sobbed. I hurt so bad, and my heart was pounding—I felt like I still had a body. I felt just like I always did, except that I wasn't touching the ground. I was suspended in the air somehow, without falling.

"And as I looked around, the forms around me began to become clearer. I saw Grandfather H. I didn't even remember him except from his pictures, and there he was. I saw your grandfathers. I saw a lot of people that I'd only seen pictures of in the albums. I saw a couple of friends of mine—not real friends, but acquaintances that I had known, and I remembered that they were dead. I saw a whole lot of people I didn't know, but I felt like I knew them from somewhere. I was confused and didn't know what to think. I was sad, but I was also surprised, and I was kind of excited. I guess I stopped crying. Some of them came up to me and hugged me. Others said, 'Hi, Steve.' All I could see were the people. I felt so much better. Then when I looked, I could see the body hanging there. It gave me a terrible feeling each time I saw it. It grossed me out. I didn't want to look at it. It was strange. I knew it was my body, but it didn't look like my body. I had my body, it seemed. It was confusing.

"Panic set in again. Then this cold feeling all over. Maybe I was going to throw up. Then I began to feel I was going to sleep. I just felt myself kind of moving upward and away. Kind of a swishing sound. I just moved upward and away and fell asleep. There was a lady there helping me, a sweet and kind lady dressed in white, who held my hand.

"The next thing I knew, I woke up and it was daylight, and I felt so good. I just felt wonderful. I looked around and there was kind of a misty look everywhere, then it got clearer. I looked closer. I was lying down on my bed, and there was a window. I could see the sun outside. And I tried to remember where I was. You know how you wake up in a strange room and you don't know where you are? I couldn't remember where I was. I had some vague thought come to me that I had seen somebody hanging on a tree, and I fell back asleep.

"They tell me that you woke up in the middle of the night after I had hanged myself, crying and very sad. It was raining outside and you were concerned that I was getting wet. I wasn't consciously there, and I didn't know that. I think you've always thought that I came to your bed after I did it and tried to tell you, but I really didn't. That's not what happened. What you felt was the bond between us severed. Your intuition being so strong, you sensed something had happened. But you didn't consciously know what, only that it made you cry. Later, I was taken to you by some helpers and we were together a little while, but neither of us remembered. It was just to prepare you until you were informed the next day about me.

"I kept waking up and getting afraid and then very gently going back to sleep. Someone came and sat by me. I could hear them talking to me, then I'd go back to sleep. I didn't really want to hear what they were saying to me. You know how sometimes you wake up for school and you don't really want to go, so you go back to sleep, but you're aware of what's going on even though you're still not ready to get up. It was that kind of a feeling.

"Mom, I know this isn't easy. I know how it hurts and how sad it makes you. Just kind of breathe deeply and relax. I remember waking up again and this really nice lady was sitting beside me. I thought at first she was a nurse. She had on a white dress. Just a sweet, nice lady. She didn't say her name, but she talked to me quite a while. It felt like I knew her. She said, 'Would you like to go for a few minutes and see your mother? She has just been told what happened to you. She's hurting a lot.' And I said, 'Yeah, how do we get there?' She said 'Just come with me,' and she took my hand and it seemed like the next minute I was in the living room standing beside her as you sat on the couch, and two men sat across from you.

"I was so shocked, I didn't say anything for a second, and then I said, 'Mom, Mom! It's me, Steve. Mom! You won't believe what happened!' You didn't answer me. You didn't even look over. I thought you were too busy talking to them to see me. I didn't want to interrupt you, so I saw Tom and said, 'What's wrong, Tom? Tom, what's wrong?' He didn't look at me or answer either. I looked around. There were Andrea and Debbie, and Tom's kids. I turned to Andrea and said, 'What's wrong, Andrea?' She was crying and she didn't answer me either. The woman very gently put her arm around me and said, 'They can't see you. They can't hear you. But we brought you here to see your mother and to be with her.'

"I said, 'Am I dead? I *am* dead, aren't I?' And she said, 'That's what they would say.' I said, 'Oh, no!' Suddenly I felt so embarrassed to be there, because I felt like you and Tom could see me, and how irritated and angry you must be. Then somehow, even though you weren't crying, I could feel your hurting inside, your heart inside my heart. I had never hurt so bad, *ever.* Not even when I jumped from the tree.

"Then I remembered again the pain and jumping off the tree. It had been like standing by a cold pool and dreading jumping in the cold water. Thinking I *had* to, then doing it and feeling the shock of the cold water when I hit. Then the pain stops and you get used to the water. Only this pain wasn't stopping. I wished I could go back and not jump. I must have been crazy.

"I felt sick. I wished I could kill myself to stop hurting. Funny statement, huh? Here I am 'dead' and wishing I could kill myself. Not so funny in this dimension, by the way. No matter how much you hurt or how bad you feel, you can't kill yourself here. I hated what I had done to you. I never realized how much I loved you and you loved me. I never realized how much I loved my home and the girls and Bob. I wanted to be back. I screamed at you, 'Mom! Mom! I'm here! I'm here, Mom! Look! I'm not dead! I'm *here!*' You turned as if you heard me and looked away. I went over and grabbed your shoulder, then hugged you and hugged you, but you didn't even know I was there. It was strange, you didn't feel the same. In fact I could hardly feel your body.

"I began to cry. I couldn't stop. I hated to cry in front of anyone. Here I was blubbering in front of the men and Tom and you and all the kids, and the woman with me. I still couldn't stop. I cried and cried. It hurt so bad. I forgot that no one could even hear me. The lady could, though, and said, 'Steve, let's go now.' I said, 'No! I want to stay.'

"I remembered when I was born, for some reason. I was scared and wanted to cry then, too. It felt like I was in a tight box being held against my will when I entered into my body as it was being born. I couldn't stop crying, and I wanted out of there, but no one heard me. Then some angels came and sang to me and held me and rocked me back and forth, and I was better. They stayed with me until I was taken to you, then stood around, and I watched them while you held me. Then when the nurse took me back to the nursery, I was scared again and started to cry. They sang to me and made nice sounds and held me.

"The lady with me was like an angel. She was the only one who seemed to hear me, to know I needed something, that I was alive. But I was obsessed with letting you know I was okay. I tried again, 'Mom! Mom! Listen! I'm here. I'm sorry! I'm sorry! I didn't mean to do this! I'm really sorry.' I went to Andrea and begged her to tell you. She was still crying and didn't hear me either. I tried all Tom's kids, then Debbie as a last resort. Debbie heard me! She didn't know what to say. You've forgotten this, but she came over to you and sat in your lap and hugged you and said, 'Mom, don't be sad, Stephen's okay. He's not dead. He's here with us.' You hugged her and said, 'I know, honey, don't you be sad either.' You thought she was just being sweet and trying to make you feel better. She could hear me. I tried to get through to her again, but it was no use.

"I was standing there crying like a baby, but so many things became clearer. I discovered that I could read all your minds. At first I didn't know that. I thought you were all saying the things I heard. I began to realize that I could hear what you were saying and what you were thinking.

"Tom's kids were wondering about getting some of my things—my weight bench and stuff. I told them they could have the stuff, but they didn't hear. Andrea was blaming herself for me being dead. She was thinking how she could have stopped me from going to the woods and that she hadn't been a good sister to me. Your mind was racing like a roller coaster. You covered everything from calling people to thinking about my body, to doubting I was dead, to wondering why the pain in your stomach wouldn't stop, and even to what the neighbors would think. Debbie was actually wondering why everyone was so sad. She knew I was alive. Later she doubted that, but not then.

"The lady asked me again if I was ready to leave. I didn't want to go. I said, 'Where is my body? I want to see my body.' She nodded and I followed her. There was something on a stretcher. Tom came out and they pulled the cover down and there I was. Yuk. It grossed me out. I looked awful. My hair was all messed up and my skin was strange looking. It didn't look like me at all. I didn't want anyone to see me looking like that. Suddenly I had a thought! What if I jumped back into my body and then I couldn't be dead? I would just sit up and walk in the house and say, 'Fooled you, I'm alive.'

"I tried it, I went over and tried to squeeze into my body, but I kept slipping out. I finally made it but nothing happened. I could see and hear just like I was in it, and I could sit up, but the body didn't move. I tried and tried. I tried pulling my hand up, getting under my shoulders, and pushing myself up. I couldn't budge my body. I couldn't even lift the sheet covering it. I thought I was so weak that I couldn't even lift my own hand.

"I turned around and said, 'Help me,' The men in the ambulance didn't hear me but the lady did. 'Please help me get back in my body,' I begged her. 'I can't do that,' she said.

'You can't stay in your body anymore. You will have to stay here with me. Let's go and we'll talk about it some more. They can't hear you right now. There'll be a time when they *can* hear you, but they just can't right now. Let's go, dear, and . . .'

"I tried not to be impolite but said firmly, 'I don't want to go. I want to stay here where I belong. I am not *dead.* I did a dumb, stupid thing jumping off the tree with the rope around my neck. I'm really sorry. I want another chance. Just help me get in my body and make it move, and I *promise* you, I won't do anything dumb like that again. Please! I promise if you'll help me, I'll do anything you want.'

"She was compassionate but firm. 'Steve,' she said, 'you can't undo what you've done. You can't use this body anymore. There is nothing I can do. There is nothing *you* can do here. Come with me and we'll get you settled and talk about all this.'

" 'I am not leaving here!' I screamed. Mom, you know how polite I always tried to be, but I just knew if we left I wouldn't be able to find my body and have another chance. So I refused to leave. She said okay and stayed with me. I went back inside to try and talk to all of you again. It was getting more and more frustrating. I felt like crying, then I felt like yelling. I thought if I could just sit by you and have you hug me and tell me everything was going to be okay, it would be. So I sat down by you and snuggled against you, but I realized again that I couldn't exactly feel you, even though I was sitting right there touching you. I guessed you couldn't feel me either. You ignored me.

" 'Oh God, NO! What have I done? I *am* dead. I'm sorry! I made a mistake. Help me stay here.' I started to cry like I never cried in all my life. Then, everything went blank."

✦

I could barely listen, I was sobbing so hard. My poor child. It was wrenching to hear the details of his suffering. If only I had known—if only I could have reached out and drawn him back. I would never let him go.

"Don't cry, Mom." Stephen's voice was clear and gentle. "Let me tell you the rest."

ELEVEN

STEPHEN'S HOMECOMING

"For life and death are one, even as the river and the sea are one."
—Kahlil Gibran

"I woke up later in the same room I had been in before and looked around," Stephen went on. "It wasn't a strange room after all; it was like my room at home. Only as I looked, it was different. I looked out the window and it wasn't my backyard.

"The lady was sitting in the chair near my bed. 'What's going on? Tell me what's going on.' I was disoriented and confused.

" 'Steve, you aren't using your physical body anymore," she told me. "You were feeling very, very badly and you ended your earthly life. Now you are going to be living here with us. I'll tell you again what it's like here. You've forgotten our conversations. I'll help you meet some of your old friends and relatives and get acquainted.'

" 'But I don't want to be here,' I said. 'Is this heaven or hell? Are you an angel? Where is my family? Why isn't my backyard outside, and why is my room different?' I tried to be nice but I was feeling scared. Maybe this was a dream and I was going to wake up. 'Is this a dream?'

" 'No, my dear, this isn't a dream,' she said. 'This isn't heaven or hell. This is a wonderful place where we can have one foot a little on earth and another a little in heaven, I guess you could say. It's certainly not hell—there really isn't a hell unless someone wants to create that. You don't need to create that. We thought you might enjoy a room like the one you had. Let' go outside and I'll show you around.'

" 'I don't want to see anything,' I cried. 'Can you show me where my family is and let me visit them?"

" 'It would be better if you waited, Steve. Then you can see everyone if you like. There are a lot of people here who want to see you and welcome you.'

" 'Why are you here?' I persisted. 'Are you an angel? If you aren't an angel, then why are you here? Are you dead?'

" 'I guess people would say I'm dead,' she said, laughing. 'But don't I look alive? You will discover that dead doesn't mean what you have always thought. And I'm here because my job is to help young people like yourself, who come here to visit a little too early, get adjusted and acquainted. I am not an angel, but there are angels here.'

"She was trying to be so nice, and I hated to make her feel bad, so I agreed to go with her. First I asked her all kinds of questions and we talked for a long time. She took me to see Grandfather H. again. He and I talked about my real dad and lots of things. He was very nice and he looked just like his pictures. I met your mother's mother and father and talked with them and we talked about the family. I met lots of your relatives that I didn't know and barely remembered from the photos you and Grandmother had of them. It felt like I knew them and they treated me like I was one of the family. I thought about some people I knew who were dead, but I didn't see them.

"I looked around and it wasn't all that different from where we lived except that it wasn't familiar. There were trees and birds and streets and houses and people everywhere. Some were friendly and happy, some spoke to us, some walked by without speaking, others waved. There were kids my age and every age, playing and running and walking with their friends. There were some old people, but not many. Later, the lady told me people evolved from their ages at death to an ideal age they create for a while.

"I was miserable. I tried to act happy, but there were things I needed to take care of back home. This was not where I was supposed to be and I knew it, even if the lady didn't, and I was going to find some way to get back. This was not heaven. In heaven, angels floated around on clouds playing harps. Here nobody had wings; nobody was on a cloud. They were just ordinary people like at home. Only this wasn't home and I didn't like it here. It was okay for someone else but not for me. I wanted to go home—*now*.

"I decided to go back to my room and lie down to think. Then I was there. I didn't know how I got there. I hadn't walked, I was sure. The lady was there, too. She explained, 'You can use your mind here because you don't have a body anymore. You actually do have a body for now, but it's a finer, etheric body, and you won't be limited like you were with a physical body.'

"I looked down and was shocked. I wasn't fat. I was lean like I'd been working out on weights and not eating. I stood up. I wondered how come my clothes fit. I must have lost thirty pounds. I looked in the mirror on my wall. Neat-o! I said, 'Wait till the kids see me. Wait till Lynn and Kathy see me!'

" 'Stephen,' the lady told me gently, 'you look wonderful and you'll feel better soon. But your friends back home will not be able to see you. This is what's sometimes called your spiritual body and your thoughts create exactly what you want. We can see your body here, but your family and friends will usually not be able to.'

"I laid back down on the bed, sick at my stomach, and fell asleep. I woke up and remembered the woods and what I had done. I got sicker. I was going to throw up. Suddenly I was there in the woods. What had happened? I could see the tree where I hanged myself, but the rope was gone. I wondered if it had left a mark. When I thought that, I kind of floated up to the branch and could see that there was bark missing from the tree. Nothing else was around. Everything else was gone. For sure I'd throw up, I thought. I was back on the bed, but I didn't throw up.

"The lady said, 'They are going to have a memorial service for you. Would you like to attend? You can see everyone, and it may help you feel better.'

" 'Yeah, but they can't see me, right? I don't want to go, I'll stay here.' I thought about it for a while and decided I did want to go, so I told her I'd changed my mind. She explained that the service would be in a few days and she would help me get prepared. I asked her if I could go see my brother. She agreed, and we started walking out of the room and almost immediately we were with Bob.

"Bob was lying in his bed, smoking. I said, 'Hi, Bob.' He glanced over at me and I said, 'Hi, Bob,' again. 'It's me, Steve.' I said to the woman, 'He can see me, he heard me.' She said, 'Not really. He doesn't even know you're here with us yet. He will be told very soon, but right now he doesn't know you're dead.' I felt lousy. I thought, Bob has enough problems to deal with and when he finds out what I did, he is going to feel terrible. He will hate my guts and think I'm stupid.

"I started to leave, but I went over and hugged him because I realized how much I loved him and wanted us to be friends. He didn't even know I was there. I started remembering all the good times we had had together, then some of the pain. It was hard to let go, but we had to leave.

"I thought that since we were close by, I would visit you at the house again, Mom. As I thought that, there we were. Right at the door. I tried the doorknob to open it and found myself inside. The door didn't open, but I was inside. I realized I had gone through it.

"I walked through the house looking for you, but no one

was there. I felt so lonesome and homesick—worse than when I had been at camp and was ready to come home. I walked up to my room and everything was like I left it—a mess. But someone had gone through my things and they were piled up on my bed. Some of my clothes were in big plastic bags on the bed. All of my private papers were stacked and moved around. Nobody was supposed to touch my private things. I bent to pick them up and put them back and couldn't move them. I couldn't lift a little piece of paper. This wasn't fair. These were my private things. Who had a right to mess with my things?

"I stormed down the steps to complain, but had forgotten that no one was there. Even the lady was nowhere to be seen. I went into every room, just looking, until you got back from wherever you were. I decided to lie down and watch TV or open the refrigerator. I could lie down on my chair, but that was all.

"I heard the car pull up and looked out the window. You were home! You and Tom and Andrea and Debbie. I ran out to meet you. 'Mom, it's me, I'm back.' You stared right through me. You looked awful. Your eyes were swollen and your shoulders were slumped over and you started crying on the way in the door and ran up to my room and fell on my bed. I followed you. You grabbed a shirt of mine on the bed and tucked it under your face and cried and cried. I held you, but I still couldn't really feel you and you couldn't feel me, and that made me crazy. I really was dead. Dead. Dead was supposed to be *dead*. I could hear and see and do everything I had ever done. I was not really dead. I knew I wasn't, but everyone else thought I was. What could I do? This was awful. You were crying because you thought I was dead. I was hugging you and trying to tell you I'm not, and you didn't even know it.

"I am explaining all this to you, Mom, because it's important to understand the unbelievable pain and frustration I felt. Most of us, no matter how we die, go through this agony. Usually, when you have a body, if you do something you shouldn't, it's rough for a while, but it gets better and you can make up for it. When you kill yourself, it's over. It's final. Anything you loved and enjoyed on earth is finished. No matter how hard you try to change it, there is nothing you can do.

"It was a very difficult time for me. Back in my new room, I asked to go see Dad and the lady said, 'Let's wait a bit. Let me take you somewhere.' We walked down the hall of this house where my room was until we came to a big building. We entered a large room, like a library. There were tables and people sitting around reading and looking at things. I asked her if this was a library, and she suggested maybe I'd like to find something to read. I went over to a group of books on a shelf. I wasn't really interested in reading, but I didn't want to make her feel bad, so I looked at different books. I spotted a book on life after death. When I picked it up, it had a funny feeling to it, like a little electrical jolt on my hand. I opened it, and as I looked at the words, I could read them and feel them go inside my head. It was the strangest sensation—like the words becoming pictures in my head. I could read and see and hear at the same time. The book was about the changes that accompany death and how you need to prepare yourself for what it's like not to have a body. At the time, I thought it was a strange coincidence to find that specific book. Now I know it was part of what I had to learn if I were to grow. It was no coincidence at all.

"I became very aware of my body again. My stomach was lean and flat. I touched my body and it was firm and solid. I thought dead people had bodies like ghosts but mine was a real body or so it felt. The book said the world in this dimension was very much the same as when we had a physical body until we got acclimated to not having such a body. I read the whole book, but even in reading it, I was being prepared for other ways of learning. I realized I had read the entire book in just a few minutes, and I didn't even skim through it.

"I saw a library full of people, yet I later learned it was more a thought form created by a lot of other people. It wasn't my imagination. It was actually created out of the needs many of us had at the time. The same as my bedroom and chest and clothes—everything. After a while I didn't need to create these things anymore.

"You know how I hated to hurt anything or anyone. Yet I had done something so awful by killing myself, that it had hurt everyone I knew a hundred times more than if I had beaten them. Every time I got to visit someone, they were crying or talking about what I had done or carrying on terribly. Some of the things they said and thought were not very nice. I heard myself and my act analyzed, picked apart, judged, criticized in the worst terms, and talked about with fear and disgust. Almost no one understood except you and a few others. I got so I dreaded visiting anyone else.

"You tried to make me a saint for a while out of your lack of understanding. I kept sending you messages about how I really was and not to do that. My friends' families tried to convince them I was mentally disturbed and very sick. Everyone became an expert on why I had done what I did. Some said they had always known I was disturbed. A few were compassionate, saying, 'It's a wonder one of our children hasn't done the same thing after all they went through. It's a rough time at that age,' or 'I wish I had known how to help him.' Some said it was the satanic things you believed, others said God was punishing the family for you leaving Dad. It was awful to hear some of the lies and not be able to say anything back.

"At school, rumors went around about what I had and hadn't done. I thought that was the most disgusting because *nobody* ever gave a damn. Teachers, to add to the gossip, said they had watched me and known there was a problem there. Some kids made up lies about things I had drawn or done or said, just to get attention. You know the truth—not one, not *one* even remembered me clearly.

"My notes were another thing, Mom. I meant them

when I wrote them, and they made sense. Then I realized I should have written other things, different things, things I really meant and felt more strongly about. You should know that's pretty typical of suicide notes. There is truth in the notes, but they were written in the emotion of the moment, and I was not in a clear state of mind. I'm working a lot now with kids who take their lives, and a lot of them leave horrible blaming notes to hurt someone, when they didn't feel that way most of the time. The people reading them are devastated, sometimes for the rest of their lives, and carry terrible guilt. Most of these notes are written in a very unclear, emotional, and fragile state of mind.

"As I got to know the lady who helped me over and took such loving care of me, I found out a lot about her. She was a mother. All her own children had been killed in a fire, and then her husband left her before she died. On this side, she was able to reconnect with her children and then, out of agony she had experienced, volunteered to be trained to help young people like myself. Her role wasn't just to meet me when I died. As I began to make choices, which could end in suicide, she was assigned to me to try to help me choose differently. She did all she could, but I was beyond listening. She was there to help me once I made the final decision. I knew you will think this strange, but I never called her by name nor asked her name. I didn't need to.

"It won't be easy for some parents to hear that their children will be in the watch-care of angels and guides. Or that these helpers will assist in preparing them either to return or, when the time is correct, to go to other realms. If families knew they can always contact their children, and *do* when asleep, or meditating, and even when awake—in other bodies—that knowledge could be very healing for them. Some parents will be watching for their children to come back as grandchildren or other children, and could become too possessive with them. I hope when we get through with all this information we're going to include, that that won't be a problem. Many of the kids will not come back during the lifetime of their families, so there's no reason to watch for them. It usually takes longer to prepare suicides to return than that. A lot of parents and relatives will meet their children immediately after they themselves die. Together they will prepare to come back in family units to try to change and strengthen some of these patterns together.

"Lots of parents whose children die, want to die, too. Some let themselves grieve so much they do get sick and die. Others create accidents to die because they don't care anymore, and others take their own lives. None of these are good or correct choices. True, they will see their child when they come here, but not as much and as fully, usually, as when they are still in their earth bodies and the child is in its spirit body. Here, they will miss the ones who remain alive, just like they missed the child who died. Their child is learning and growing, and a parent dying in these ways must also learn and grow, and may be working on totally different issues. This means they may be about their business in different ways and in different realms much of the time. If the parents will keep themselves safe and well and remain in their bodies, they will visit these children in dreams, meditations, and in other realms of consciousness far more frequently than if they come here. Also, sometimes parents let themselves die prematurely or commit suicide, to be with the child that died, and that child has reincarnated, or is in other realms and they aren't able to be with them much at all. Better to live fully and help others as a gift to the dead child, and know with a certainty that you are meeting them, and can begin to remember those meetings."

✦

"Stephen," I said, "people are going to think this is crazy. What do I say, 'Hey, do you know I talk to my son who died? He killed himself, but he's okay. He's not in hell. He says it's a lot different than we can imagine. He says, if your kid died, you can talk to him. . . .' "

✦

Stephen laughed and answered, "Yeah, Mom, something like that. I know how hard it has been for you to learn to hear me well, then how hard it was to learn to trust what you received, and now I'm asking you to tell the world. I know how you feel. I have given you so much information, and the others you talk to here have brought you such proof that you can't deny it, can you? Trust that those who read what we share will sense the truth and let it transform their thinking and their lives.

"We need to build the bridge between the living and the world of spirit, between the fundamentalist thinking and new thought. The bridge has actually always been there, as written about in many religions and teachings, but has been obstructed from the view of most by dogma and fear. We can open that bridge again—you and I."

TWELVE

✦

THE STRENGTH TO HEAL

To live in hearts we leave behind is not to die

—Campbell

I was healing more each month, aided by frequent communications from Stephen. I understood many things now that I had been unable to grasp before. But my heart and mind were still full of questions.

I still struggled with doubt and skepticism, but it was lessening. I still grieved and sometimes it was overwhelming. The eighteenth of every month was an anniversary I dreaded. Birthdays and holidays were difficult, too. The first Christmas without Stephen was awful. We spent even more money than usual on the children, perhaps trying to fill the void left by his death.

In the beginning, I told everyone that Stephen had a right to take his own life, whether we agreed with his choice or not. Only much later did I realize I had missed the point. The suicidal state is a transient state. Had Stephen received counseling or help, his suicide might have easily been prevented. Since most potential suicides are ambivalent, help before and during the crisis can often prevent the final act. Further counseling after the episode can stabilize the child, and he may never consider suicide again. I had no awareness of that at the time. Stephen taught me much about the nature of suicide, the landscape of what we call the afterlife, and reincarnation. Through Stephen's words, I learned about the beautiful logic of life and death—the benevolent cycle.

"Reincarnation is true," he said. "Think about it, Mom. It's the only thing that makes sense and shows how just and fair God is. People do not come back in the bodies of animals—that's called transmigration and simply is not true, nor do they become rocks or trees. All these have a vibration or lower form of consciousness. Anyone who thinks they remember being an animal or plant has simply attuned themselves to that kingdom and become in such rapport as to identify with it this way. Some can take their consciousness into plants and animals for brief periods of time. People come back as people. The bodies change but the soul returns again and again to learn and grow. I've loved looking at past lives here, both mine and others. Sometime I'll talk to you about that in greater depth and we'll write about it.

"There would be no fairness or justice in the world if a baby entered and was killed or died at three years old, and a Mafia leader who kills and has people killed, lived to be ninety, and seemingly gets away with it. The child will have other opportunities to reincarnate in other bodies, and the criminal will some day, some life, be made accountable for what he has done. It is not God measuring out punishment—it is the law of cause and effect. Humankind is given free will. Choices made create growth and strength, or lessons to be met and relationships to be resolved.

"Your guides and I live in this dimension close to the earth, actually existing in your exact space but at a different vibratory speed. Some call it the astral plane, but it's known by many names. Within this dimension are many levels; plus there are higher planes with many levels, and other even higher planes.

"In this plane we create the reality we desire. That is why so many books, written by those who have been here, or brought through from those who are here, describe things so differently. If we want a beach and sunshine, warmth and lots of food around, then we will see and experience that as long as it's needed. If we want clothes, a home, furniture, just like we had on the earth plane, we can learn to manifest that with thought, or our helpers can do it for us when we arrive. If we have negative thoughts, they will be manifested as well. As we grow in awareness, what we desire and what we create changes.

"Some of those entering here have places prepared for them by others already here for their own good while they learn. They do not understand their ability to create all that they desire at any time. Some would create things to hinder their progress. Some do not know they are dead. Others will not accept that they are dead for a long time. Many, who were so dogmatically positive that their religion was correct, flounder when "heaven" isn't what they expected.

"What happens to the suicide is not much different from what happens to someone who dies of old age or in an accident. Your guides and angels are with you at the moment of death, usually helping your soul release from the body, just before you die. Usually you can see your body when you leave it but don't always know it's you for a few moments, then reactions differ. Some cry, some get frightened, some turn away; everyone reacts in their own way. Your helpers move you to another place and you are met by friends and loved ones who have preceded you—a kind of welcoming party. You see hazy forms around you that become clearer. You find it hard to believe you're dead because you feel so alive, so free, so light, and aware. There is no feeling of weight because you have shed your physical form, and that feels wonderful once you become aware of it fully. You have a body but it is weightless and finer, lighter. It may look the same for a while until you discard that form for another even lighter and finer one.

"You may want to have explained to you what has happened, or you may yourself try to explain to whoever is near you. It can be overwhelming or it can by joyful, depending upon the circumstances of your death and your consciousness and awareness while you were in the physical body. Often you want to sit down and rest or sleep. When you are ready, your helpers discuss this new dimension with you, your death, and how you planned this trip. There are rarely ever any real 'accidents.' Whether suicide or a natural death, you have helped in the planning of it for some time, and you become conscious of that after you arrive in this dimension.

"Your consciousness, your state of mind, determines the course the next days and weeks take. Most souls want to see loved ones left behind to see how they are, to see how they are taking the death, and to tell their families and friends they are okay. You feel the same emotions you always did; things don't change much for quite a while. You may cry or laugh, be fearful or sad, be playful or shy. Your personality continues pretty much the same.

"Many souls are encouraged to attend their funerals or memorial services, if there is one. Most want to. It can be a very difficult time emotionally, or a very healing time. Sometimes the number of people who come to the service to pay their respects, and what you can hear them thinking and saying aloud about you, makes you feel great. You know how much you were cared for. It works the other way also. You may not have treated others very well during your life, and few people may care that you're gone. Or those who do attend may not be thinking wonderful things about you. There are these experiences at both ends and many in between."

✦

Stephen went on to describe the process of learning that then occurred.

✦

"Sometime after we arrive and are ready, we begin to review the lifetime we have just experienced. We do this in stages for no one could handle it all at once. We begin to look at specific things honestly and clearly, not fogged over as we often did when we were in our physical bodies. We see what we did correctly and incorrectly. No one sits in judgment on us. Though we judge ourselves very harshly at first, we soon begin to ease up and see what we can learn from reviewing our mistakes and our strengths. There are those who piously felt they had done such good that they expected to receive their rewards at God's throne the moment they arrived. Boy, are they disappointed when they review their life. All the judgment and deceit they've hidden is fully revealed.

"At first, it is very emotional because you see all the people you have interacted with, helped, hurt, and forgotten. You see clearly all the things you so carefully hid from others. Unfortunately, everyone around you sees them, too. Soon, what others see about you is unimportant. What you see about yourself, how far you fell short, and what golden opportunities you failed to use, is heartbreaking. You feel such shame, other times anger. Later, there is a little more detachment, almost like studying a subject in school—but that subject is you. All of it is something you know must be worked with and understood before you can advance further. Or before you can again claim a physical body to return and get about what you have left undone.

"Depending upon the consciousness of the person arriving here, the degree of enlightenment, choices made, and the work accomplished, some souls can quickly claim a body and return for the next experience. Others may have to wait years and years to reincarnate for a variety of reasons, such as needing longer to learn and grow in preparation for returning, or to be taught and helped to correct serious character flaws that have slowed the soul's progress. There are lots of reasons.

"The more aware soul selects the parents and circumstances for the next incarnation carefully, for he knows that if too many obstacles are put in the way, it may be difficult to accomplish all he came in to do. On the other hand, some souls choose extremely difficult situations for just that reason. If those opportunities can be handled right, great and rapid soul growth can be made in that one incarnation.

"Some souls select parents where there will be damage to the chromosomes of the fetus, knowing in advance that there will be grave physical or mental difficulties. In such adverse circumstances there is possible rapid and great growth for the soul, and perhaps a wonderful opportunity to help teach the parents and family. However, there are souls sent into those circumstances because of a need to learn lessons they have ignored.

"Others seeing in advance a pattern where their parents may divorce, need to experience that particular set of circumstances. Many choose vehicles knowing they will be given up for adoption, so they can get with the correct parents for their soul growth. Others choose parents to enter, knowing they will be left for years in difficult foster homes or orphanages or neglected, so they may learn particular lessons.

"The soul choosing, either knows beforehand the patterns that will happen, or that the possibility of those happening is very high. They need these particular experiences for growth, not having learned them correctly before. Or being the perpetrator of these very things, need to experience them and make amends. There are other souls who do not have difficult karma to work with but choose a family or situation to be teachers, to give those around them a chance to choose better."

✦

"And you, Stephen?" I wanted to know. "Why did you choose me?" When I asked the question, a wave of sadness came over me. In the aftermath of his life and suicide, I wondered if he had made the right choice. As much as I loved him, perhaps he would have been better off elsewhere.

"I was a soul preparing to enter, choosing you as a parent, seeing the roadway ahead with all its boulders, feeling I was strong enough to climb over them. After I was born and grew older, I chose unwisely many times because of my sensitivity. My last choice, to take my own life, ended my opportunity for growth. There was also part of the teacher in me for Dad, that was to show him love. I did that to the best of my ability. I gave him my devoted love and adoration. It may look like it didn't help at all, but as I reviewed our records, I saw that it did.

"The love I gave and the little he let himself receive, caused him to be gentler than in his last lifetime. In his last incarnation, he physically and emotionally abused his six children, even causing brain damage in two of them. His records show he disfigured his wife with his fist. He callously starved and tortured his horses. No one called him friend and no one grieved when he died. It may seem hard to believe, but I have seen these records. I was one of the children. I learned much tolerance and unconditional love for him this lifetime. My karma with him is finished, especially as I have understood and forgiven him since I have been here. His karma continues."

I asked, "Stephen, is that why he had such violent streaks and was so cruel?"

"Yes, Mom, but not nearly as bad as in his last life. So some good was done.

"Let's talk about you a minute, Mom. The reason you chose your parents was to get a strong physical body from your dad, because your mother had weak lungs and tuberculosis, which would be inherited. This was eliminated by the strength of your father's genes. You chose your mother because you would be loved so totally and taught sensitivity and empathy to prepare you for your work. You also would meet some other lessons, which you can see more clearly now. You saw the pattern where you might choose to get pregnant too early.

"Always you had free will and choice, though. Bob and I would have been born to you with another father, later, had you chosen differently. So few things are 'destined.' There is so much free will and it is not always exercised in the wisest or best way. When you made choices that set up the patterns you experienced, we reviewed things, learned all we could to prepare, and did all we could to enter, even though circumstances were less than ideal. We could have chosen other parents, but all things considered, wanted to be with you. You would be our strength and stability, we felt, as we grew.

"Want to know why *I* chose you? Well, we go way back. I have been your brother, father, mother, aunt, uncle, husband, and on and on. We had some great experiences, and we had some less than great ones. Overall, you had encouraged me, supported me, and inspired me. Most of all, you had loved me even during lifetimes when I wasn't so lovable. I knew I could count on you."

"Oh, Stephen, you couldn't count on me. I let you down."

"You did and you didn't. You got so caught up in all the emotions and stress that you weren't sensitive to my needs. You always made me feel loved, but you weren't always strong enough to help me when I most needed it. You would try to please everyone around you and forget about us sometimes."

✦

"I'm so sorry, honey. Forgive me."

✦

"Mom, I'm not telling you this to make you feel bad or to blame you. I want you to see the bigger picture, the pieces to the puzzle that make a whole. Not only about us, but about our connected dimensions.

"And, no, I did not have to die. I did not have to take my own life. While the scales were tilted somewhat in the direction of such a choice when I incarnated, it did not have to occur. But so many things had weakened my spirit that eventually the scales tipped, and I made an unnecessary and incorrect choice. I considered creating what would have seemed to be an accident instead of hanging myself. With all the stigma associated with suicide, I started to think that perhaps you and I could bring it out of the closet and into the light of day, and help more people this way. My hope and prayer is that we can."

✦

"Yes, Stephen," I agreed. "But I admit that I still struggle with the question of suicide. How can I help others when I feel so lost myself?"

✦

"I will help you," Stephen promised. "This book will cause people to treasure their lives more, take better care of themselves, do all they can to make the best of this life. It will bring hope to people who have had a loved one die at their own hand. It will bring reassurance knowing that these souls who leave in such a way are not suffering the hell and damnation that many churches preach, but that they continue. They are learning, being taught, and being helped. They are helping others."

✦

"Stephen," I asked, "if you can talk to me, why can't others talk to the people they left behind and give them comfort?"

✦

"The souls here try very hard to reach the people they knew," Stephen replied. "But hundreds of souls simply never get through to anyone because those they are trying to reach don't know that it's really possible to talk to us in this dimension. It can be very frustrating."

"There are astral places or houses here specifically to act as communication stations between dimensions. We can go to these places for help when we are unable to make the link by ourselves. Despite this, and all the efforts made in these places, consistent and clear communications are difficult. It's akin to trying to locate a station on a radio and then losing it, or having static disrupt the reception.

"You can perhaps understand two things now. One, how fortunate I am to have you listen, and, two, how important it is despite your worries and doubts that you get the message out to others. What I have given you is very simple, truly just an overview of what one may experience no matter what type of death."

In spite of the joy of being able to communicate with Stephen, the first anniversary of his death was very hard. All the pain and agony were replayed during the two days I associated with his death—the eighteenth, when he killed himself, and the nineteenth, when his body was found. Although I found great comfort and strength in my conversations with Stephen and my guides, the sadness triggered by this anniversary continued for weeks afterward.

It was also at that time that I began to hear troubling messages from Stephen and my guides about Tom. They lovingly suggested that Tom wasn't as I thought, that he was doing things that were harmful and that could cause great trouble. I saw graphic pictures in my mind that shocked me. These were the kind of visions I had that so frequently proved to be true. Deeply troubled, I went to Tom and told him about my visions. He denied that there was any validity to my impressions. He told me I was getting crazy guidance, that none of it was true. He convinced me that I was jealous, insecure, and imagining things. He was so convincing, and I wanted so much to believe him.

A deep rift grew between my trust in Tom, my husband, and the trust I had developed in my guides and Stephen. I began to think that maybe Tom was right—I was getting false guidance. The thought horrified me.

I kept all of my communications from Stephen and my guides in boxes—hundreds of typed sheets, notebooks, and papers. In a moment of despair, I emptied the boxes in a metal trash can, lit a match, and slowly burned them all to ashes. I cried and cried as my guidance turned to dust.

For months, I didn't listen or get guidance for myself. I didn't talk with Stephen. I gave readings for others, wondering if I was misleading them. Finally, I was moved to sit at my typewriter and began again to listen. My guides told me I had made an error in destroying the guidance, that several books I was to write were destroyed. They did not again mention Tom. When I asked them why they misled me about him, they only said, "We're sorry for your pain. Let's begin."

Little by little, I began to trust them again because so much evidential information was coming through. Stephen shared many helpful things with me in the following months, but nothing was mentioned about Tom. It was as if they knew I was not ready to hear the truth, so they kept a distance.

Then, Tom confessed that he had been having affairs—even bringing a woman with whom we worked into our home several times. I was stunned. There weren't enough words to describe what I felt. I was numb with pain and in complete shock. I kept asking him over and over, "Why? Why?" He said he didn't know, that he was so sorry. He said he loved me and pleaded for me to forgive him and give him another chance.

My brain and heart went dead. A hundred times I cried out, "Why?" All night I lay awake. "God, what is this? First Stephen, then this. What have I done to deserve such hell? I must be the worst person on earth to have all this happen. I must be so awful that God hates me and wants to hurt me until I just give up and die."

Crazy thoughts such as these raced through my mind until, by morning, I had convinced myself that I had driven Tom into the arms of others. I had been grieving for Stephen for a year, and I must have neglected Tom. It was my fault.

In that state of mind, I devoted myself to Tom. I took care of him like a mother. And he let me. I promised myself I would be such a good wife. I would stop grieving for Stephen. I would do everything I could to keep him close. After all, I reasoned, I was responsible for Stephen's death. I must be responsible for Tom's unfaithfulness, too. As I write it now, I realize how utterly mixed up I was. In my grief and guilt about Stephen, I was willing to be the scapegoat for everything.

My guides had been right about Tom, and so had Stephen, but I could not see it that way. I was still unable and unwilling to face the truth.

We had been talking about moving West since our trip across country. After this trauma, the West began to look more and more appealing. I loved what I had seen of Phoenix, and I thought it was a good choice. It was so difficult to live in a house where the child you loved had filled each room with his laughter and was now no more. Every room still held precious and painful memories of Stephen. Each time I stepped out the front door, the woods across the street stood as a sentinel to bear witness to the place where Stephen had walked to hang himself and die.

It was also difficult to walk through a living room where my husband had brought another woman to have sex. That realization often pushed away the tender thoughts of the times Stephen had filled the room with his presence. I was hurt and raw from the pain. I wanted to get away. I just couldn't tolerate any more of the memories the house held.

Just before we left for Phoenix, I went up to Stephen's now vacant room and said good-bye. Soon no one would even remember that a loving teenage boy lived and dreamed and suffered there. I took one last look from the front door of the house across the field to the woods where Stephen had breathed his last breath. I closed the door and walked to the car. I hoped that Stephen could find me in Arizona.

One Sunday afternoon, shortly after our arrival in Phoenix, I opened the newspaper and was idly looking at the want ads. As I was turning the pages, I saw an ad that was glowing with light. It literally looked as if a spotlight framed the inch-square ad. I turned around to see if there was a light shining from behind me on the paper, but there wasn't. My heart began to beat rapidly. Something strange was going on.

The ad was for a secretary to the director of a holistic medical clinic. I had worked as a secretary before, but I was a minister now. I had been doing counseling and lecturing, and I had also developed a reputation on the East Coast as a psychic. I could do life readings—"tune in" to someone and tell them things that I "saw" and knew intuitively. This was the work I was to do. Being a secretary again was not an option.

Nevertheless, there was something intriguing about the way the light illuminated that particular ad. I stopped reading and began to meditate. Immediately my guides started speaking. I didn't even know what holistic meant, and they explained that it had to do with healing the body, mind, and spirit. My guides instructed me to call for an appointment. They said that I would be called back before 2:00 P.M. and would go in for an interview and be hired by Dr. M——. They instructed me not to tell my employer-to-be about my psychic abilities. They would tell me when it was the right time to mention it. Until then I was to do whatever secretarial work he needed and to help in whatever way I could. They said this was a part of the next step toward what I had incarnated to do.

If I called the number and it was true, I would never doubt their guidance again. This was my usual vow, which I always broke. However, this guidance was so far-fetched, that I fully expected the voice at the other end of the phone to say, "Are you kidding? Doctor Who?" Instead, the voice confirmed my guides' information and said someone would call me back to schedule an interview. The phone rang just before 2:00 P.M. The manager was on the line. He set up the initial interview, and I went to meet with the doctor.

As instructed, I did not tell him what I did, just my genuine interest in his work. We talked for an hour. He hired me on the spot, and I began to work for him the next week.

How about that! My guides had been right! I began my secretarial job. Transcribing dictation and doing secretarial work was boring after the work I had been doing the last years, although I liked the organization and the people. I kept asking my guides if I couldn't tell the doctor what I *really* did. They encouraged me to be patient.

Within a few months at the clinic, we began to plan a seventeen-day holistic medical program. About fifteen patients were to participate in each of the intensive residential healing programs. It was suggested that one component of the program should be for each patient to receive a psychic reading. The doctors believed it could be very helpful to people. One woman on staff could see auras and they thought perhaps they could work that in, too.

Here was my chance at last, to tell them I could see auras, too, and knew what the colors meant. I could tell them I saw other things as well. My guides cautioned me to wait until the time was right. I finally got the okay, met with the doctor, and told him about myself. By then, he trusted me; we were friends and he never questioned that I was telling the truth. Little by little, he worked me into the program, and I began to give life readings for every patient.

My work at the clinic was to extend over four years. Those years were good for me. We traveled overseas, and we met hundreds of fine people, many of whom still remain friends. People who had readings referred their friends. I did counseling and readings five days a week. I also worked in the special programs on weekends when those were scheduled. I taught meditation, visualization, and psychic development to the groups and classes.

I found comfort and a lessening of my grief in my work. From my pain and healing, I saw how I could help others. Tom was also hired by the clinic as director of patient care. Our marriage seemed to be healing. There were no more warning messages from Stephen or my guides—at least, none that I could hear.

At the end of a particularly busy seventeen-day in-patient program, Tom and I had taken the patients to their farewell dinner at a restaurant. We would bid them good-bye the next morning.

Tom and I came home and sat down in the living room to read the paper. Debbie was doing homework on the floor near us. It was ten days until Christmas 1979, and the house was already decorated with some of our holiday treasures.

Across the room, on a table, there was a ceramic Christmas tree with a music box that played "Silent Night." Suddenly it began to play on its own. It had never done that before. It played and played, as if someone had wound it to its limit. We all looked up and listened, very surprised. The energy in the room became very electrically charged. I could feel a presence—Stephen's presence.

Before I could speak, Debbie said, "Mom, Stephen's here." Immediately the music box stopped. Stephen? Stephen! I, too, knew he was there. I could feel him, too. Tom went back to reading. I said, "I can hear him speak. Can you hear him?" They couldn't, but Debbie asked me to see what Stephen had to say. I got a steno pad and pen and began to listen. His message, as usual, overshadowed my own thoughts.

Stephen said he and I needed to start writing a book together very soon. There was much we had to tell the world. He had told me this before, but I had always put it in the back of my mind.

As if reading my thoughts, Stephen said, "Mom, I know how hard it is for you to believe that we can talk to you like we do and to know you're not fooling yourself. I know how you don't want to mislead anyone, and I know what a doubter you are." He laughed affectionately. "So here's something you can *prove.* At the medical program today, you were listening to the girl play the piano and wishing you had a piano to learn to play. We're going to work on some people to impress them to give you a piano; you'll get it just before Christmas. That should prove to you we're real and you're not crazy."

I read Stephen's words to Tom and Debbie. Debbie squealed, "Yea! We're going to get a piano. If Stephen says we are, we are."

I said, "If we get a piano, I will *never* doubt again." Famous last words!

The experience with Stephen had been so overpowering, yet I didn't want to get my hopes up watching for a sign. A piano? We had wanted a piano for a long time, but it was way down on our list of priorities. I thanked Stephen for talking to me, no matter what happened, and I went to bed.

The next morning, Tom and I dressed and went to say good-bye to the patients. After being together for seventeen days, it was always sad to see the program end. One of the couples, a businessman who had sold his company back East, and his wife, who were retiring to Arizona, handed me an envelope. Inside was a note telling me they wanted me to get a piano and were impressed to give me enough money to buy one. Enough $100 bills were folded in the envelope to purchase a piano.

It was difficult to talk, to even thank them. I protested, saying that I couldn't accept the money. They insisted. So I told them what had happened the night before. They made me promise never to reveal who they were, that it would remain our secret—theirs, mine, and Stephen's. We went out the next day and bought a marvelous piano. It was delivered just before Christmas.

Those might have been happy days. But during that period, Tom returned from a business trip to Virginia Beach and confessed that he had met a woman and he was in love with her. He wanted a divorce so he and the other woman could be married. To deepen my hurt, Tom also bragged that he had slept with other women since we moved to Arizona.

I collapsed once again. I had not even suspected anything since there was never a letup in Tom's constant affirmations of his undying love or his desire for me. How could he betray me in this way? It didn't seem possible

After much soul-searching and prayer, I decided I would give Tom his freedom. I was tired of wondering who he was having sex with every time he went out the door.

I could see no hope that the marriage could continue. What Tom had done hurt too badly. I realized I loved myself too much to put up with it any longer. I finally saw that the problem might be Tom and the way *he* was, instead of me and my grief over Stephen. Maybe I would never be enough for him. I needed to begin being enough for myself. Then and there, I determined that I would end my marriage with Tom very soon.

I could also see that my days at the clinic were coming to an end. Stephen and my guides began to prepare me for changes that were to occur in all areas of my life. Frankly, I told them, there had already been enough changes in my life for one incarnation. But they assured me there were more to come.

THIRTEEN

MATCHMAKING FROM THE SPIRIT PLANE

When the one man loves the one woman and the one woman loves the one man, the very angels leave HEAVEN and come and sit in the house and sing for joy.

—AUTHOR UNKNOWN

My personal strength began to grow. Not only was I getting stronger, but I was also less tolerant of people who tried to take advantage of me. I was taking my power back, and it felt wonderful. At last, I was really listening to my guides and to Stephen and trusting their guidance.

In the midst of everything, I was preparing to leave Tom. We were still living in the same house, but now we moved in separate orbits. Our marriage was over in every way but appearance.

Stephen and my guides advised me almost daily during this time. I said to Stephen several times that I would never marry again. I meant it. I didn't ever want to be hurt again the way Tom hurt me.

Quite unexpectedly, in January of 1982, a good friend asked me for a personal favor. He knew that I gave life readings like Edgar Cayce. Would I do a reading for a friend of his and the friend's wife? His friend was a man named Dr.

Herbert Bruce Puryear, a psychologist and one of the directors of the Edgar Cayce organization in Virginia Beach. He had written a number of popular books about Cayce, including *Meditation and the Mind of Man,* which I used as a textbook in the meditation classes I taught.

I had seen Dr. Puryear only at a distance when I was working at the clinic. He always gave the keynote address at the annual medical symposium the clinic sponsored. A year or two earlier, the doctor I worked for turned to me after Dr. Puryear had spoken and said, "He may be the best speaker in the country." I replied, "He *is* good, but he seems rather cold." "Cold?" he responded in surprise. "He's not cold at all. He's very warm and caring. Let me introduce you." Somehow he never did, so we didn't meet.

Now I had to give Dr. Puryear a reading. I didn't want to do it, and I was nervous. I didn't want to be a specimen he was examining. Maybe he would change his mind. But he came to Phoenix in late January, and he still wanted the reading. My friend told me that Dr. Puryear's wife Meredith wasn't very interested in the psychic field and was very skeptical about psychics, but she had agreed to have a reading also. Oh great, I thought! She didn't believe in this work. I couldn't figure a way to get out of doing the readings and I didn't want to disappoint my friend. He loved the work I did and was always bringing people around for readings, probably whether they wanted to come or not.

My friend arrived at the center with Dr. Puryear and his wife. As I moved to shake hands with Dr. Puryear, he gave me a hug and insisted that I call him Herb. I was surprised. He was very nice and friendly.

I worked with Meredith first. I could see from her aura that she had some healing ability and also that she carried a great deal of anger. After the reading, I asked Meredith how she reconciled her healing work and her anger. She denied the anger—a common response. She said that she was a skeptic but added that the reading was interesting. That didn't bother me. What people did with the guidance was their choice.

I always prayed and asked God to speak through me to bring help and hope to people seeking spiritual guidance; the rest was up to the person. Of the hundreds of readings I had given, the feedback had almost always been positive. I knew it was not me but God working through me. So, in that altered state, I just let go and let God. My responsibility was to stay spiritually grounded and clear.

I then gave Herb a reading. I turned on the two tape recorders and began. Herb had a most unusual aura with a double rainbow of light around him. The pink in his aura was all filmed over, and across his heart was a block of energy. I told him this. He said that over a half dozen other psychics had told him the same thing. He knew there was a blockage in his heart center and he was working on clearing it. I went into a deeper altered state.

When I gave readings, I could not hear my voice when I was in the altered state, so afterward clients would comment on what came through. On rare occasions, I would play the second tape after they were gone and listen to what they had been given. The information that came through always amazed me. It was obviously from a source beyond myself.

Herb and I talked about a few of the things in the reading. He gave me some feedback and was warm and friendly. He said he had been researching psychics since the 1950s, and we talked about his interest in the metaphysical field. He was very interesting to talk with about his research and experiences. He seemed to be a nice person after all, not as I had judged him. He wasn't cold, just somewhat reserved.

I wondered how he and his wife got along, since they were so totally different; he had none of the anger she manifested. I wondered what had caused him to close down emotionally with such a blocked heart center. Oh well, it was none of my business, and we didn't talk about it.

Two months later, Herb sent me a series of questions in

a letter, and asked me to do another reading for him at a distance. It was the first time I had heard from him. He wrote that his mother had died during that time. He called a few days later to see when the reading could be done. My schedule was full for months in advance, but I promised him I would work it in just as soon as I could. A few weeks later, he called about a client of his who was having some serious emotional problems and asked if I could tune in briefly and share with him whatever I received. I did. He thanked me.

Herb called several other times. Each time, it was about someone he was counseling. He gave me the name, asking me to share whatever I received. When I called him with the information, he thanked me, with little comment.

Many months afterward, Herb confessed that at the same time he called me, he also called several other sensitives, asking the same questions about his clients. He used all of the information he received as perspectives with his own counseling; but, he said, the information he received from my Source was always the most consistent, helpful, and verifiably correct.

I was finally able to do Herb's second reading in April. I listened to it afterward to see what the answers had been to his questions, in case he called and wanted to discuss it. It was not particularly meaningful to me since I didn't know the people or situations about whom he asked. Later he told me he had listened to it many times, and it gave him hope for the work he had come in to do.

I didn't hear from Herb for quite a while. Then he called one day in June. A minister friend had invited him to Arizona to attend a Tibetan Hopi meeting over the Fourth of July holiday. He asked me to get some guidance about whether he should come and how important it was. He would add my guidance to that of others and make a decision.

I told him I was so busy that I didn't know when I could get to it, but I would try to tune in as soon as I possibly could. A week passed and I almost forgot to do what he asked. I was at home working when Stephen and my guides reminded me that Herb needed some guidance. The typewriter wasn't working, so I sat down with a pen and paper to listen and ask for any information that could be helpful for him. My guides said Herb should make the trip—it was going to turn his life around. Afterward, he would begin to do the rest of what he was meant to do with his life. They shared some other guidance for him, which I wrote down. Then I called Herb and read it to him over the phone and mailed him a copy.

I was planning a party for the holiday Herb would be in town. When Herb's chiropractor friend called to tell me Herb had decided to come to Phoenix, I asked him to join us and bring him along. He wasn't sure they'd have time, but he said he'd try.

On July 4, I played hostess to dozens of people eating outside on the patio and swimming in the pool. I was winding down a ten-day juice fast and feeling clear and strong. I was taking control of my life and I felt good. I would soon be free of the emotional stress of living with Tom. I felt at peace. I didn't know what the future held, but as the saying went, I knew *Who* held the future.

Halfway through the party, there was a knock on the door. In came our chiropractor friend with Herb. They had managed to make it, after all. During the remainder of the afternoon, Herb and I kept gravitating toward each other. We were drawn together by an unexplainable force.

Toward the end of the day, as Herb and I were talking by the pool, I became light-headed from the fast. He brought me fruit and gave me his sunglasses. He was really nice. This was strange. What was happening? We were definitely attracted to each other. He didn't even know I was leaving Tom, and he was married. What in the world was going on?

The party broke up, and Herb told me the Tibetan Hopi meeting had been canceled but that he had decided to come anyway and meet with some people. He asked if we could get together and talk since he would have some extra time. I agreed and said I'd call him and let him know when.

I was shaken. I had never felt like this. Herb and I could talk—really talk—about anything and everything. As much as I liked him and enjoyed being with him, I was afraid of where our relationship would lead us. I decided not to meet him, and that would end that. I went upstairs and laid down on the bed. Stephen and my guides began to speak to me. I got paper and pen, said a prayer, then listened.

They revealed that everything had been planned to bring Herb to Arizona. Herb's own guides helped to get him a free airline ticket to Phoenix, knowing the meeting would be canceled. They said neither of us was accomplishing what we had incarnated to do. They also said that Herb and I would be involved in work with many others, and that work could be of help to a lot of people. Oh, I thought, with a sense of relief. It wasn't a personal thing, after all. I had been reading the feelings all wrong. It was work that had to do with our life's mission. I could handle that.

Herb and I met the next day at our center. He began by saying that for years psychics and sensitives had told him a marriage separation was in the future; he acknowledged to each of them that he knew that to be true. He said that he had been very unhappy in his marriage for years, and had known from the beginning they should not have been married. For the last fifteen years, he had known he wouldn't remain in the marriage. He had suggested a separation numerous times, and Meredith had threatened to leave many times. She hated living in Virginia Beach, resented the organization he worked for, and hated his work. She told him she would not live in his shadow anymore.

Two months earlier, a sense of finality and clarity had come to Herb. He decided that it was time for them to permanently separate. The heart of his life work was to live by his own spiritual guidance and to teach others how to do the same. He always cautioned people to seek guidance for themselves and not to use it to control others. The way in which Meredith always ridiculed him for his work and made light of his guidance was becoming intolerable. He told her that he was no longer going to live like that.

I told Herb about Tom and me. We talked and shared as if we had known each other for years. We discovered, to our absolute amazement, that we had gone through the identical things in our marriages. He had experienced, except for the suicide of a child, everything that I had. Everything! When I told him what I had been through, he understood—really understood. He had been through it, too. Something very special was happening. We meditated and prayed together several times, and we knew there was work for us to do together. We didn't yet know what that work would be, but there was a peaceful feeling of "coming home," of being with your dearest friend.

Something totally unexpected was happening between Herb and me. I began to be filled with a knowing that we would be together, and the idea filled me with awe and apprehension. I had never felt this way before, and yet I had promised myself I would never marry again.

I prayed for guidance and the signs became vividly clear. Herb asked me to marry him and I said yes without hesitation. Before Herb had left to come to Arizona he had asked the board to place him in one of the top three leadership positions of the organization, since the leader Hugh Lynn Cayce was dying. Cayce's son, C.T., who was in one of the leadership roles, told Herb that he would fight to keep him out of any leadership position. Herb then knew it was time to continue the "Work" in another place and in another way. Herb made the decision to join me in Arizona.

Our relationship was wonderfully romantic, lit by the energy of our spirits. We belonged together. There was no doubt. Not only were we deeply in love, that love was heightened by a shared sense of mission. It was the most beautiful relationship one could imagine. We knew we would marry—and this time it would be forever.

✦

Stephen was delighted about my plans to marry Herb, and he gave me frequent guidance and insights. He liked him so much that sometimes I suspected Stephen of orchestrating the whole thing. I had to laugh. Now my son was matchmaking from the spirit plane. He said he had been shown that Herb and I had been making plans for years at the soul level during our dream states, to find each other and be together when the time was correct. He said that we had a work to do that was beyond what we could fully understand at that time, but that later he and my guides would elaborate. I was so in love that the work now paled in comparison to just seeing Herb again.

We hadn't set a date for the wedding, but we were certain that we would spend the rest of our lives together. There was a knowing of the depth and strength of this relationship that was like no other we had ever experienced. All lovers feel this way, I'm sure, but we also felt a deep soul commitment to our work.

We were married with great joy on Christmas Eve, right after midnight, at an Eastern Orthodox monastery where the chapel was a converted stable that could seat only seventy people. The sanctuary was filled with our friends. Before the service, a Pavoratti tape poured out Christmas music. Afterward, we had a reception at our home that began at 2:00 A.M. with French champagne, enough food to feed an army, and a wedding cake made from a recipe used at the Greek Olympics over 3,000 years ago.

With both excitement and trepidation, we began our new lives and our new work together. Herb was given the name Logos in a meditation, and we decided that would be the name of our organization. Logos Center became incorporated as a church and foundation in Arizona, on May 26, 1983. We planned three divisions for Logos: an interfaith church, a holistic center, and a university of educational outreach. We began a private practice using offices in our home. We saw clients, gave readings, and started weekly study group and meditation meetings.

In 1985, we moved into an acre facility with two buildings, several blocks from the home we had bought the year before. The facility had been a Baptist church and school. We began offering Sunday services, classes for children, and educational programs.

In 1986, just before Christmas, Herb and I were sitting in the living room, talking. The doorbell rang. Herb got up to answer it. No one was there when he opened the door. He sat down to talk and it rang again. I answered it and again no one was there. The next time it rang, I jumped up quickly and opened the door to catch whoever was playing a joke. No one was there. As we both stood at the door looking, it rang again and again. I said, "Stephen's here." We could feel him so clearly. We were delighted. When I asked Stephen about it, he said he just wanted to wish us a Merry Christmas. The doorbell never rang like that before, nor has it since.

FOURTEEN

✦

CHOOSE LIFE!

And ever near us, though unseen,
The fair immortal spirits tread;
For all the boundless universe
Is life; there are no dead!

—"RESERGAM" ATTRIBUTED TO BULWER-LYTTON

"Mom," Stephen told me one day, "this is our first book together, and I can only skim the surface and share such a small bit of information about so many things with you. You can't possibly put in all I have already shared, and there is so much more. This is a start.

"I want you to leave in this book the things I've told you to write about yourself—don't edit them out. As hard as it is for you to be that honest and revealing, my life and death can't be understood as well without knowing about your life. Your sense of guilt is something parents and families can relate to. Some of your choices and actions did contribute to my overall pattern and the action I took to end my life. How you have understood this and resolved it and how you have grown can give hope to others."

✦

I understood what Stephen meant. In the beginning, it had been so hard for me to look honestly at my life and the choices I had made. After Stephen committed suicide, I wanted to die myself. I couldn't stand the intense feelings of guilt and despair. But remarkably, the more I began to view my life with honesty, the stronger I became. Over time, the rawness of guilt was replaced by the growing realization that, with Stephen's help, I could use my pain to help others.

✦

"You *know* death isn't the end," Stephen reminded me many times. "We who die really can and do communicate with those who remain, if they let us. Mom, when you lost the fear of death, you began to truly live. This knowledge will usher in a new age of hope and understanding.

"Mom, don't be concerned about how some will react when they read this. To those who will not open their minds to truth, nothing can be written or said to pry that closed mind ajar. But many who read what we are sharing with you will resonate to the truth in their hearts and it will bring them peace and understanding about their children who have died such as nothing else has. This guidance then is the healing balm for those ready to hear.

"Right now, the earth is shadowed by fear and despair. The suicide statistics are evidence of that. Suicide is on the rise—and the most heartbreaking of all is the increase in suicide among the young.

"If someone says a person killed himself because of this book, don't believe it for a second, because some people would use anything as an excuse for doing the act rather than getting help. This book will not be a catalyst for people killing themselves. So you must have no guilt nor pride because this book comes not from you but from my soul to yours. It is not of us but through us and our pain.

"Since I've been on this side, I've been taught and instructed about suicide and my own choices. My helpers have shown me why suicide is never correct for young people. The reason I say 'young' is because they have shown me, also, that suicide is sometimes the spiritually correct decision for the elderly and the terminally ill, where the choice to take one's life may free the soul from a body where it's not making any growth, allowing the person to die with dignity. This enables the person to move to the spirit plane where they can learn and grow, and prepare for their future incarnation.

"The truth is, most deaths are some form of suicide, either conscious or subconscious. For instance, cancer is considered an 'acceptable form of death,' but often the condition has been created or activated by the individual as a way to escape intolerable conditions or because they have lost hope. This is not true for every case of cancer, of course, but for a great many, and for other terminal diseases, too. The diseases are not visited upon people by some unloving god. They enter bodies where choices are being made many times as to whether to live or die. The person would never overtly take his own life, and an incurable disease is an acceptable way to release. How can anyone blame someone for dying of a disease they aren't responsible for? But they *are* responsible. Emotions and stress left unattended, unhealed, open the door to disease entering and viruses being activated, when the door could be shut. But 'miraculous' healings occur when people change their thinking—choosing life instead of death. This very knowledge is the bridge in understanding suicides. The person who kills himself has taken a deliberate action to release from his body. Those who die from disease, or even from many accidents, have done exactly the same, but do it in a more subtle or covert way. Some are aware they want to die and leave signs, hints, and messages.

"Some of the death wishes are more subconscious, but even then there is an awareness somewhere on the conscious level. Thoughts may have come to the persons to change or do something differently, and they didn't heed them. Other thoughts, perhaps, had come from time to time about the foolishness of what was being eaten, smoked, or done incorrectly. Many fool themselves into thinking their diseases have appeared against their will. Others who die 'accidentally,' whether through car wrecks, drug overdose, or some 'freak' accident that is unexplainable, nevertheless have been instrumental in creating their own death. When they reach this side, they are able to view the whole experience and cannot then deny their own active role.

"Perhaps the hardest thing for parents to accept is the death of a very young child. Let me share a new perspective. Many young children who drown or have accidents, voluntarily release from the body, subconsciously, or even consciously at times, for a higher purpose. They see and are instructed on the spiritual level, usually during sleep, that they cannot accomplish what they came to do because of the situations around them. They become aware that they will be unable to change these situations. They see that, even when they're older, they will be unable to accomplish what they came for. Other souls enter knowing that they will only be in physical bodies for a period of time, because their early death can teach valuable lessons to the parents or those who remain. Others, experiencing diseases that will be fatal, know that their death may serve to save scores of other lives. Some children who are killed, come into the world knowing that their deaths may affect public consciousness for the better. What is amazing, I have discovered, is that the parents, in their higher consciousness while asleep and in other states of awareness, are also aware that the child will release from his body long before they actually die and are preparing for it. This isn't conscious, although the rare parent is sometimes aware consciously.

"I know this is hard to accept, but there can be a gift in the death of each child if the survivors will look for it. It will not ease the pain totally, but can bring understanding and comfort. Parents whose children drown, for instance, could spare themselves much guilt by knowing they did not cause the accident by looking away for a few moments when a child is in danger. This is where there will always be confusion and controversy, for parents should always be watchful of their children so that they are protected in every possible way. But if the child is part of a work or a plan to teach, some accidents cannot be prevented no matter how careful the parents are. While it is not always true for adults, almost all deaths of children under twelve, and some even years older, are a part of the soul plan of the incarnating soul. They enter, most often, as teachers to teach the adults around them, then release in various ways when they are finished. Crib deaths are not 'accidents' as such but should be looked at for the lessons to be learned by the adults and families remaining alive. Often times these very souls that leave at such a young age, reincarnate into the same family with the same parents at the next pregnancy.

"Young children are old souls. They are growing in small bodies, but they are, in consciousness, every bit as mature as, or more mature than, the adults around them. This is not to say treat the children like adults, for they need to be nurtured as children, but realize there is the soul part of them that is mature, that is not a child.

"When children die very young, their helpers and others on our side, work with them until they manifest that old soul quality, that maturity in spirit. To be more easily recognized, they may appear to those left behind as the young child they were, but they actually reach their soul maturity rather quickly. Parents grieving for the young babies they held, who seemed to be snatched from them by death, should know three things—first, that they were only babies in that particular incarnation and are old souls; secondly, that they are being cared for in spirit with every bit as much love and caring as the parent gave them; and third, that at night or when the parent sleeps, they connect with that child all during the sleep state. There is no feeling by the child of being deserted, nor a feeling of the loss by the child in that state of the parent. It's the very reason that a person very close to a child who has died, mothers in particular, may desire to sleep a great deal after the child's death. In sleep, she is nurturing, holding, and being with that one she loves and misses. What is even more interesting, is that even when the parent isn't sleeping, the 'higher self' or another level of the mind is in constant connection with the higher self of the child at *all* times. There is absolutely no feeling of separation in that state. The more aware individuals become of themselves as multidimensional, the more conscious memory they can have of that state. With this awareness, the pain of death and separation would be greatly eased.

"A parent may feel the presence of the child or imagine they heard them, after they die. It is not imagination. There are often dreams of the loved one that indicate the connection in the dream state. Not that the events in the dream necessarily happen as they are remembered, but rather are filtered from the experience and are a sure sign of a connection. The dreams of the meetings may not be remembered, but there is still the coming together. Children are often brought to see the remaining family, especially until the parents are more aware of how to commune with them with the higher mind. They may speak to someone in the family, and the person may feel their presence and actually hear their voices. Usually the family member thinks it's their imagination, but sometimes they *know* they are not hallucinating.

"In other words, there is no separation, no feeling of loss in the higher realms. The awareness of that coming together and what is shared at those times is only lost when you awaken, because you have forgotten how to remember fully. So never say I *lost* a child, or *lost* a loved one. No one is ever lost to anyone they love.

"Now, these deaths are not suicides. They are planned, on the bridge between earth and spirit, as part of a greater work, either before entering, or as conditions change, by the souls of the child, family members, and others associated with the child. This is different from young people who have a mission to fulfill in a physical body, and a full life to lead, who overtly take their lives and 'check out' prematurely. I can't emphasize this enough: Suicide by children is not part of a spiritual plan. This is taking the gift of life and destroying a great soul opportunity. There is a big difference. Whether the young person is 'terminally' ill, depressed, or overloaded with burdens, there is always a better way than 'self-murder.' There is such a life force in a young person, that with visualization, holistic healing, changed diet, or whatever is best for their own particular healing, they can often get well mentally and physically.

"I can't say it strongly enough—it is never right for a young person to commit suicide. There is always a way they can be helped. There is always someone who cares. It isn't easy, and it will take a lot of work, but there is always a way. Mom, I want you to help bring this understanding and guidance to parents and children who are suffering. Just a little awareness of the many influences in a young person's life can help prevent the needless deaths of thousands of precious lives.

"I think it will help you understand what happened to me—and help other parents understand, too—if I paint a picture. Let's say I was born with a large backpack on my back that contained a few stones—stones from past-life experiences and stones from genetic things, from both you and Bill. Let's call these stones emotional weights. The first few years living with you added another stone or two to the pack. When you left Bill, a couple more stones were added because I was dealing with feeling deserted and pulled away from the ones I loved. The years I spent with uncaring babysitters added a few more stones. When you married Dad, those years added a bunch of stones. Dad was not good about helping build our self-esteem.

"There was a weakness in you of not knowing how to stand up to Dad; your weakness added more stones. And Bob took out his aggression and frustration on me; that added stones, too.

"As the situation got worse with Dad, and he forced us to do things that were naturally against the pattern of our growth and development, more stones. Then I hit adolescence and all the hormonal changes happened, and that added another stone. It may surprise you that no stones were added from your divorce from Dad. But when Tom came into the picture with all his kids and the chaos, a couple of stones got added to the pack.

"You sometimes wondered if I would still be alive if you hadn't left Dad. I wouldn't. The things that were created in that relationship added so many stones that by then the weight was getting so heavy I wasn't able to reach around in back to remove stones and ease the load. I seldom knew how to get the backpack off to release the weight. It was strapped too tightly, held by my own feelings of inferiority.

"The people at church who came down so hard on us added stones. When I agreed with them and said things I didn't mean, I added my own stones. The mess with Tom added a lot in a short time. He didn't like me and he didn't like Deb. He liked Bob some and Andrea okay. The backpack became so full, so heavy, that I could hardly carry it during the week, but I felt I could rest it a little on the weekends.

"The situation at school with the kids teasing me, hurting me, and ignoring me added more stones. And some of my own bad choices and reactions threw in more stones, too. When you sent Tom to tell me about not taking my gym bag to school and that you knew I had shoplifted, I lost face. There was a smugness about the way Tom said it. With Kathy pregnant, no girls who liked me for a boyfriend, no friends around, being ugly and overweight, the pack got so overloaded that as I sat on the tree, it just weighed me down—pushed me over and down I went. I'm not blaming anyone for my choice, but maybe if people understood this, it could prevent other kids from getting so weighted down that they make this wrong choice.

"Tell the world, Mom: If you can reach kids soon enough,

get them counseling, relieve some of the peer pressure, help them change to healthier diets, and help them develop self-esteem, you can prevent ninety percent of the suicides in kids. Some of their backpacks are getting overloaded. Parents think that one problem or one act makes a kid kill himself. It doesn't. It just adds that extra stone that tilts the scales to overload. This is the message I want you to send in your book—in *our* book."

✦

"We finally did it—you and I, Mom. We wrote the book. Sometimes I thought we'd never get it done, and I got as discouraged as you did. But we did it! You learned to listen, and I found a way to speak to you in a different way.

"Tell other parents: If a child has died, or killed himself or herself, don't forget them. Pray for them, listen for them. Get on with your own life, but keep the connection open with their dimension. It won't slow their progress or yours if you let yourself 'visit' with them from time to time, just like when they were still alive. Some of them may even help you communicate your experiences, so from your pain, you might offer comfort to others. Don't grieve and mourn and stop living. Do all you can to help everyone around you. Your loved one in spirit will know your good works, and it will be like a gift to them and make them very happy. One day you'll be together again even more so than when they were alive.

"Most of all, to any of you, especially young people, who read this and are thinking about taking your own life, please listen to me for a moment. Don't do it. Please, don't do it. There are other options. Talk to your parents if you possibly can. Let them know how you're feeling. Let them get you help. Don't downplay how unhappy and discouraged you are. Tell them just how badly you feel. Don't tell them that everything is okay just to make them feel better when it isn't. This is your *life*. Ask them to help you. Maybe you think they will yell at you and not understand. Well, try to make them understand. Maybe you think it will hurt them too much. If you kill yourself, it will hurt them a thousand times more.

"If you can't talk to your parents, call your minister or a hot line or a counselor or an older friend. Sometimes kids your own age are too frightened of their own feelings. They have no idea what to do so they aren't much help to you, either. Find someone, *anyone,* who will first listen, then get help, and keep in touch with you until you are thinking more clearly.

"I'm having my mother put some resources in this book. Use them. Or call her and the organization she and Herb are directors of—The Logos Center. They care and will either help you or direct you to someone who will. But don't try to handle it by yourself. Sometimes you can't. I couldn't. It's nothing to be ashamed of. We all need help. If you get yourself help, then you will stay alive to help someone else later in your life.

"Suicide is so final. Once you do it, that's it. You can't change your mind. Remember how hard I tried to undo what I did? Trying to climb back in my body? The depression and agony I suffered when I realized I was dead? There was no going back and it was a hundred times worse than the feelings that made me kill myself.

"Besides, once you are out of your body and in this dimension, everything doesn't change. You don't suddenly feel perfect and excited about this new adventure. Not at all. You really want to kill yourself then, but that's impossible here. It takes months to get to feeling okay and you never get over longing for your family or those you leave behind. Especially because *you* can see and hear *them,* but rarely are they aware that they can see and hear *you.*

"Don't do it. Please, don't do it. Pray and ask your guides and angels to help you through the crisis. You will be throwing away God's gift to you—your life. This life is your chance to *do* something, to grow and become the best you can, to help someone who is hurting worse than you are.

When it's not your time to be here yet, it is *not* better than where you are right now. It's much, much harder.

"There are groups of us who hear you cry. We are assigned to help you if you ask us, and we will try to support you through the bad times. Sometimes we will comfort you, sometimes we will send a thought of someone you should contact, sometimes we will tell you of foods that are literally 'driving you crazy.' If you don't think you can hear us, it's not because we're not there. You have to keep trying, and learn to listen in a different way. Other times we will try to impress upon you that there are disruptive energies coming from people around you who try to discourage you with negative thoughts and actions. So, there are times when bad thoughts you have are 'sent' to you and they're not your own at all. If you think there is the slightest possibility that is true, then ask God and your angels to stand between you and those thoughts, and they will lessen.

"Don't do it! Maybe the worst is true, that no one in your family loves you and you don't have any friends. Maybe. But God loves you. And you must learn to love yourself. You're okay. God doesn't make *junk*. And he loves you enough to give you the greatest gift he can give—life. Treasure it. He loves you as if you were His only child. When you go to sleep, ask God to send his angels to heal you and to help you see things differently. He *does* and *will* answer your prayers. He won't stop you from a wrong act once you set it in motion, but He will try in a hundred ways to direct you away from taking your own life. Ultimately, only *you* can make the final decision. To take your life is never right. To live life fully, to love yourself like God loves you, to become the best you can be, to be filled with joy, and to help others is His plan for you. He created you to succeed, to be triumphant—not to fail. He created you to know that He loves you. There is nothing you and He can't do together.

"So, Please . . . DO NOT KILL YOURSELF!

Steve"

◆

Finally, Stephen asked me to explain to you in my own words how I get in touch with him and how we communicate. Stephen and the others taught me to do several things. I begin with a prayer. I ask God that only the very highest spiritual guidance comes through. I ask to be a clear, pure channel of truth and hope. Usually, I take my hand and make a cross from my chest to my forehead, and I make a smaller one on my head, then make the sign of two triangles to form a star of David on my forehead also. That's my personal ritual.

I work with different breathing exercises. I usually breathe in through my right nostril very slowly and out through my mouth three times for strength, then in through my left and out through my right nostril three times to open the higher spiritual centers. Other times, I use various breathing exercises until I feel relaxed.

When I begin attuning by lying on the floor or resting my head on the back of a chair, I often do a breathing exercise I love. In my mind's eye, I watch my breath going in and out for a minute. Then I inhale deeply and extend my diaphragm or stomach, hold the breath a few seconds, then exhale through my nostrils or mouth forcefully. I do this three to six times. Then I do the same breathing technique, but as I exhale, I visualize the breath as white light, going throughout my whole body, from toes to head. I see it ending at the center of my forehead and staying there until the next breath. After three to six repetitions, I am usually relaxed and beginning to slightly alter my consciousness. I either continue to rest where I am and listen, or get up and sit at the computer or typewriter. Often I stay quiet afterward and meditate or still my mind for a few more minutes, using prayer or affirmations I have memorized. Evidently, Stephen and my guides know when I am ready to listen because I begin to hear the voices, and I type what I hear.

Most of my communication with Stephen and the guides used to be done at my typewriter. Now I sit at my computer and prepare to listen. Occasionally, I use pen and paper, but that is so slow that I can't record for as long a period. After my preparations, as I am meditating or praying, thoughts will begin to come, overshadowing my own thoughts. Sometimes I receive very deliberate words, one at a time, then I usually start to hear sentences or phrases. I can interrupt the communication to ask questions, and it will continue where it left off. At times, Stephen or my guides tell me to wait and then another one of them continues. Sometimes, whole concepts are given, which I put in my own words, although if this occurs, they correct anything that isn't exactly as they want it said.

There are times when even though I'm not thinking about Stephen, I will hear him call me. We have our car conversations and our unplanned visits in this way. I've found that if I forget to record them, I don't remember part of what is said. It's like my dreams; if I don't record them, I forget most of them. I ask questions and sometimes Stephen answers, sometimes not. At times he doesn't know the answers, but says he will try to find them by speaking with other guides to get information he doesn't know.

"When you pray or meditate and call me to come and chat, I hear, or am brought the message by a helper, and try to come as soon as possible. Usually I can be with you in seconds or minutes. Occasionally, I am involved in a class or learning something and am delayed a few hours.

"I visit you in your dreams quite a bit. Unfortunately, you remember only about ten percent of your dreams. You can prepare with affirmations before sleep or specific suggestions to remember more, as can most people. You and I have great dream contact. As I've told you, most people have frequent dream contact with loved ones who are in this dimension. That bit of knowledge should comfort many parents. When a child dies, there is always contact between their souls in the dream state. It's a good place to communicate with them. Often their prayers and attunement to the child can be comforting and helpful for the child as well as themselves.

"There is a way you can communicate with missing children, with people at a distance from you, or with people with whom you want to resolve difficulties. It's called soul linking, or mind linking—which is not mind control. You can even do it in your dimension between two physical bodies. You first pray and ask to link mind to mind, or soul to soul with the person, according to their free will. When you do, it's like you pick up the receiver of a phone, dial their number, it rings, they answer, and you begin to talk to them. Then, with your mind, you can comfort them, send them healing, talk to them, even teach them, and they *will* hear. They will not be conscious of hearing, but they will hear more fully than if you spoke to them out loud. This attunement is *not* to be used to bend their will to yours or to influence them to think and believe as you do. It is *not* to be used in this way, though, of course, many working with mind-control techniques do. Much negative karma is created if this technique is used incorrectly. The person you ask to link with may not consciously remember, but they *will* hear. Most often, you begin to see changes in your relationship for the good when you are together in person. If you are apart, a feeling of peace and serenity is felt about the relationship. It can be extremely comforting to have such a link until a missing child is returned, for example.

"You can do this also with the mind and soul of a person, even if you don't know who they are, such as one who has abducted a child. Sometimes you will hear an inner 'no' when you request to link with them, and they won't allow it. If this happens, ask to meet them instead, in your dreams with your angels and theirs, and request that the angels minister to them. Usually, however, they will let you make a contact with that higher state. You can, out loud or telepathically, commune with them. You can appeal to the goodness within them, to the higher part of themselves, to release your child and cause no harm.

"Just a brief word about angels in this regard. Instead of worrying, parents would do better to ask for angels to be with their children daily at school, at home, and as they play. Angels, except for the children's specific guardians, must be called upon to help. They will not interfere unless asked. Call on angels of love and protection to stand around your loved ones at all times. If a child has disappeared, use powerful prayer and call upon protective angels and angels of all kinds and your guides or those of us here in spirit to help. Unless separation and death are part of the karmic pattern of the young entity, miracles can and do happen, and many children are returned unharmed.

"In the same manner, someone in a physical body can also soul link, meet in the dreams and send angels to someone *without* a physical body, those you call 'dead.' When you know you have established the soul link, talk to the person, tell them how you feel, and what you are wishing to communicate. Ask questions of them and listen for the answers. Ask them to tell you how they feel, what they are doing. Listen. It really works.

"It can be done by us here also. We don't need words. We think or telepathically say whatever we want to say to each other, but we can ask for fuller communication by doing the soul linking. It's a wonderful healing tool and great comfort to all who do it whether we have bodies anymore or not. It is not the imagination, but always remember that what you think to be imagination is the foundation of intuition and other soul abilities. Imagination is your golden key to unlocking your greater awareness."

The overlong pregnancy has ended, and Stephen's book has been birthed. Stephen tells me that he and I have other books to write in the next years. We still continue to meet often on the bridge between our dimensions.

Stephen has now been in the spirit plane longer than he was here in a physical body. I am thankful that we can talk often together, but I would prefer to hear the voice I remember and to hold him close to me.

I am grateful that Stephen lives, even if it's not in this realm, here with me. I am grateful that God lent him to me for a while.

Still, I may always be among the "walking wounded"—as family survivors of suicide are sometimes called. But I am blessed with children, grandchildren, family, and friends who walk beside me and share the pain. They have taught me how to find joy in life again. I am blessed with a wonderful husband who loves me deeply and who is truly my soul mate in my spiritual ideals and work.

I understand children much better now, and I am more aware of what they need spiritually, mentally, and physically, what hurts them, and hopefully, how to help them more fully. This knowledge is wonderful and I pray that I may use it in the best possible way. I learned it all too late to save Stephen's life.

There is no excuse for any of us to be so psychologically and spiritually illiterate anymore. We have all the tools we need in this day and age to become emotionally healthy adults. We can learn to apply what we know and to teach it to our families and others as we have the opportunity. We must learn to raise emotionally healthy children, filled with zest and joy for life. To raise children who have strength of character and coping skills taught to them from birth, through the love and understanding of their parents or caretakers. It is the only hope we have for saving the lives of the children we love.

Thousands of children took their lives last year. They shot themselves, hanged themselves, overdosed with drugs, drove their cars into lampposts, and slit their wrists. Even more will kill themselves each coming year. Only we, as more caring, less self-centered, better informed parents and teachers, can prevent the loss of these precious young lives.

My prayer now is that this book will offer inspiration and comfort to families in distress. I hope that those of you whose children have already committed this irreversible and heartbreaking act called suicide will find some peace in knowing that your loved ones continue. They are fully aware in spirit. Do not stop talking about them or hide the truth because of your shame and hurt. Reach out to them. They need your prayers and love, as always.

If you want to try and communicate with them, don't be discouraged if it is difficult. Trust and persevere. You are relearning telepathy, which feels awkward at first but is really the truest form of communication between souls. It won't end the pain or loneliness you feel for your child. It will, however, be another step in your healing so that you, too, can begin to live again.

I am thankful that God loves us and has prepared a way for us to grow and heal and communicate with our loved ones.

And, especially, I am forever thankful that my beloved son, Stephen, LIVES!

EPILOGUE

✦

MEMORIES OF STEPHEN

I asked Stephen's two sisters and his brother to write a few words about their brother before they read the manuscript. After I read the letters, I asked them if I could include them in the book, and they agreed.

DEBBIE'S LETTER

Being the youngest in the family, I really didn't comprehend death. I did know it was a sad thing, and I would never see my brother again. I was the last member in the family that saw him. I do clearly recall the day before his death. Stephen had packed a duffel bag and also a sleeping bag. As he left the house, I opened the door and asked him where he was going. He said, "I'm going to build a fort." My reaction was why do you need a sleeping bag. I watched him walk away. I was a bit confused about the bag. And that was the last time I saw him . . . for now.

One Christmas Stephen got me a mouse. He carried it in his pocket, trying to hide it from me so it would be a surprise. When it died, he and I put it in a small box with a poem on it and buried it.

When it snowed, Stephen and all of us kids had great fun. Steve would pull us up a hill like we were mountain climbing. He used to make me go home because my mittens got too wet.

I remember he liked karate. He had a robe he always wore. He liked cooking eggs and eating breakfast. I remember that most—him in the kitchen.

Not long after his death, he appeared to me in the kitchen, cooking. It was only a few seconds but as clear and lifelike as a "live person" standing there. I was very stunned and scared. I was convinced many years later that there really was life after death. This was only one sign at the time, but there were many later to follow. A Christmas tree music box started by itself and knowing in our hearts that somehow he had started it—a doorbell ringing by itself, musical instrument playing alone, etc. Stephen just has a way of letting his family know he is just fine.

I'll always wonder why he took his life, but someday we'll all know the answer. If it wasn't for him appearing to me, I might be very sad about his death.

ANDREA'S LETTER

The first thing that comes to mind, I suppose, is "blame"—who or what circumstances would cause someone to take their own life. The next thing that comes to mind is why should anyone be "to blame."

I can remember the day the police knocked on the door like it was yesterday. Other things have faded with the passage of time, and that makes me sad. Someone who is as important as a brother or sister should stand out but when they aren't around to remind you, it becomes more difficult to remember.

Steve was the most gentle of all of us, more introspective, I suppose. It took a lot to make him angry. Not to say that Stephen didn't have his moments, they just seemed less frequent than mine, Bob, or Deb's.

I can remember having him teach me how to mow the lawn, ride a skateboard, "throw like a boy, girls can't throw right," how to ride a two-wheeler, build a fort in the woods.

Once he even tried to teach me how to play the trumpet. At that time his favorite musician was Herb Alpert. He wanted to be able to play like that some day. For some time the martial arts were a pastime. "Kung Fu" was a favorite TV show, and karate was the focus. When he got his gi and first belt, I think it was a highlight. For days he wore the gi and practiced throwing punches "the right way." Breaking boards with his hands and feet became a goal.

Camping was special. It was special for all of us. Both Stephen and Bob liked to help build the fire and keep it going. Going for hikes to look for wood and anything else we could find. I think it gave him a chance to feel close to Dad. Something that wasn't easy for him all the time. I think he really wanted Dad to be proud of him and like him. Sometimes he didn't think Dad did or was.

I also remember times at the beach, teaching me how to body surf, looking for shark's teeth, fishing for crab with chicken legs, walking along the shore in the morning, finding the horseshoe crabs that had washed up on the shore during the night. Some things are harder to define, just vague or slight: Deer Park retreats, visiting Nanny and Poppy and going to Miller Lake. BB gun fights in back of Uncle Dean's house with Sheri, Sandi, and Tiger. Hide-and-seek with Ralph, Mary, and Joanne P. at night in the summer. Making homemade ice cream—I'd sit on the top and he'd turn the crank. Painting the house on Heathfield—we painted the house, the back porch, the scooter, and each other. Boy, Dad was pissed!

His favorite color was a deep blue, favorite song for a time was "Er Es Tu" (It Is You), favorite musicians were Herb Alpert and another trumpet player who died of cancer at the highlight of his career. The day the police knocked I remember very well.

Actually, I should go backward here to the day he left. I walked into the master bedroom to ask a question, and he was in the bathroom. His green-and-black-checkered bag was sitting on the bed. I asked him what he was doing. After a few moments, he said I had to promise not to tell Mom. He said he was going away for a couple of days to think. He'd be fine, not to worry, and not to tell Mom. Being a typical little sister, I asked if he wanted me to go along. I just didn't think about how worried you'd be about him.

The next day, Chris and I were out for a walk, and I looked over to the other side of the street where an ambulance and police cars were parked. From the trees, a guy in a suit carried a bag that looked like Stephen's. I made a comment to Chris that Stephen had a bag that looked kinda like that, and thought nothing more about it.

All the kids were in the house and Tom was making popcorn. I answered the door and two guys ID'd themselves and asked to speak with my mom. I got Mom and was asked to go into the other room. Curiosity got the best of me, and I listened at the edge of the door. It felt like my stomach dropped to the floor. After that I was kinda numb. Part of me decided that there was a mistake and he was fine. The other part knew there was no mistake.

After that, I suppose, was getting used to not seeing him anymore. And waiting for him to come to me in a dream or spirit and explain why he chose to leave that way. The next was anger for him leaving and wondering if I could have done something to prevent him from dying. There was a time I felt like he "copped out," afraid to face whatever his fears were. As for now, I wonder where he would be in his life—college grad, married, children? How would my life be different if he were still alive? Even then and still now, I have a respect for his quiet strength.

I guess that's all for now, except I miss him.

BOB'S LETTER

What can I say about a brother who we lost before he ever became a man? I could tell you how much I wish he was here now with his family. I could also tell you that if I had the ability to travel physically back through time, the first stop would be one of intervention, to keep my younger brother from doing that act which would in this life keep us ever apart. I could tell you how my heart and soul aches and how many times I've needed a brother to lean on and talk to. I could further expound on the guilt over not caring and not treating him as well as I should have while he was alive. The thing that is most distressing to me is the fact that none of us saw it coming. Looking back it's easy to say, "We all saw the patterns," but during the time preceding his death, I would have never believed any member of our family capable of taking their own life, except for myself. You see, I failed in something that Stephen did not. I remember standing in front of the bathroom mirror and taking an entire large bottle of aspirin. I remember the total hopeless feeling that life was not worth going on living. I remember lying down in bed and waiting to die. And I remember coming to the next day, vomiting blood. I also remember that my little brother took care of me that day, thinking that I had the flu. I remember that he made me bologna and cheese sandwiches and a cold glass of milk.

I also think back on the times he would just sit and watch TV alone, and I would come home and not even bother to say hello. I remember his favorite TV show was "Kung Fu" with David Carradine and how he would get up during the commercials and imitate the moves he would see on the show. I remember he would read books on the art of being a "ninja," but, most of all, I remember him not having any friends and spending most of his time by himself. I guess if I could look back and point to any one thing that was an obvious danger signal, it was him spending too much time alone.

I feel intense guilt for not having been any kind of decent brother to him. The plain fact of the matter is, I constantly picked on him. You see, shit rolls downhill, and our stepfather, Richard, was constantly on my case either physically or mentally. So I learned how to transfer some of that onto

Steve. When I would do something wrong, instead of admitting it and incurring the wrath of my stepfather, I would usually try to blame it on my little brother. I remember one instance in which Steve and I got into a fight while the folks were gone. I threw a crayon at him and he ducked and it hit the wall, leaving a purple mark. Well, it was just our luck that he noticed the mark the instant he came home. We both were so used to getting spanked with a belt, that neither one of us was about to admit it. So Richard got us up every thirty minutes throughout the night until around 3:00 A.M. when Steve couldn't take it anymore and confessed to my "crime."

Another instance that comes to mind is that one day when I was about fourteen, I decided that I couldn't take any more of Richard and decided to run away. As young as I was, I realized that I would need something to eat, so I took a huge roast out of the freezer and hid it in the bushes. Somehow, later I changed my mind and forgot about the roast outside. About a week later, Richard found the roast covered with maggots and went crazy. I knew that if he found out that I had done it, there would be hell to pay. So I denied it. But, as usual, both of us were punished until one of us broke down—Steve. Thank you, baby brother, for saving my hide all of those times.

I remember when Steve was younger that when he got spanked by Richard, he would wet himself and in return for that "crime" he would get beaten even more. I could go on and on and on and on and on, but it wouldn't bring him back, and it wouldn't change Richard from the asshole he is even still today.

Steve killed himself when I was eighteen, and my initial reaction was to cry for all of thirty minutes. Then I started to get angry and told myself over and over again that it was a chicken-shit thing to do. At the time of his death, Mom had recently and finally gotten divorced from Richard and found what we all considered at the time, an easygoing, relaxed new partner. During this period in my life, I was totally uncontrollable.

The week before Steve died, he and I went to see *Enter the Dragon* starring Bruce Lee. I remember that it was at a movie theater in the mall and that it was one of those where they have several different choices. The one next to the movie we were watching was rated "X" and I felt that it was time my little brother broadened his horizons. We snuck into the movie—more or less I dragged him into it. Well, we were only there about fifteen minutes before an usher started walking down the aisle and checking people's tickets. So we returned to the karate movie. Afterward, we hung around the mall, and I remember daring him to dump his popcorn down onto a man who was sitting on a bench on the lower level. When he did, we ran laughing. That was the last time I ever laughed with my little brother. That was also one of the few times that I remember us being really happy together and being crazy as a team.

Steve, I really need you now and wish you were here so we could do all the things that we never got the chance to do when you were alive. There's something missing in my life that only you can supply, and that something is the total love that a brother can give. I look around me and I see other people who have brothers and take them for granted, and I want to go up and shake them and say that they better pray to God that they never lose them.

I often wonder what it would be like if you were alive still. Would you be married? Would you have kids? What would you be doing for a job? But there is one thing that I know that no matter how much distance would be between us, I would still have a baby brother to call my own and he would have a big brother, who though he may be one of the world's most screwed-up people, he would always be there in a moment of need.

Steve, you know, there are three nieces and a nephew who would love you, and the sad thing is, they never knew their uncle Steve. God, I never knew how much I missed you until I wrote all this down. I always was angry and considered you a coward and now. . . well, now all I can do is cry and tell you how sorry I am that I wasn't there for you when you needed me. Steve, things change. When you get older you develop a better sense of family. I wish you could have grown old with the rest of us. There are so many things we could do together and it tears my heart in two knowing that in this life we never will. I wish I had Mom's gift and could communicate with you—maybe that would make things easier. But I haven't been able to. I want to say something to you that I could never say to you in life: I love you and miss you and hope the best for you in all you do. All I ask of you is forever to remember me as loving you . . . Your brother, Bob.

APPENDIX

Helpful Information and Resources

I. ARTICLES OF SPECIAL INTEREST REGARDING SUICIDE

"Before You Kill Yourself . . . Read These Brutal Facts About Suicide"

You've decided to do it. Life is impossible. Suicide is your way out.

Fine—but before you kill yourself, there are some things you should know. I am a psychiatric nurse, and I see the results of suicide—when it works and, more often, when it doesn't. Consider, before you act, these facts.

Suicide is usually not successful. You think you know a way to guarantee it? Ask the twenty-five-year-old who tried to electrocute himself. He lived. But both his arms are gone.

What about jumping? Ask John. He used to be intelligent, with an engaging sense of humor. That was before he leaped from a building. Now he's brain damaged and will always need care. He staggers and has seizures. He lives in a fog. But worst of all, he *knows* he used to be normal.

Even less violent methods can leave you crippled. What about pills? Ask the twelve-year-old with extensive liver damage from an overdose. Have you seen anyone die of liver damage? It takes awhile. You turn yellow. It's a hard way to go.

No method is foolproof. What about a gun? Ask the twenty-four-year-old who shot himself in the head. Now he drags one leg, has a useless arm, and no vision or hearing on one side. He lived through his "foolproof" suicide. You might, too.

Suicide is not glamorous. You may picture a movie star in a slinky negligee drifting off to eternal sleep from an overdose of pills. But your picture omits a likely sickening reality; as she dies, her sphincter muscles relax, and that beautiful gown is soiled with her excrement.

Who will clean your blood off the carpet, or scrape your brains from the ceiling? Commercial cleaning crews may refuse that job—but *someone* has to do it. Who will have to cut you down from where you hanged yourself, or identify your bloated body after you've drowned? Your mother? Your wife? Your son?

The carefully worded "loving" suicide note is no help. Those who loved you will *never* completely recover. They'll feel regret, and an unending pain. And rage, because at that moment, you cared only about yourself.

Suicide is contagious. Look around at your family: sons, daughters, brothers, sisters, husband, wife. Look closely at the four-year-old playing with his cars on the rug. Kill yourself tonight, and he may do it ten years from now. It's a fact that suicide often follows suicide in families, and kids are especially vulnerable.

You do have other choices. There are people who can help you through crisis. Call a hot line. Call a friend. Call your minister or priest. Call a doctor or hospital. Call the police.

They will tell you that there's hope. Maybe you'll find it in the mail tomorrow. Or in a phone call this weekend. Or when you meet someone shopping. You don't know—no one does. But what you're seeking could be just a minute, a day, or a month away.

You say you don't want to be stopped? Still want to do it? Well, then, I may see you in the psychiatric ward later. And we'll work with whatever you have left.

RENEE T. LUCERO

"Please, God, I'm Only Seventeen"

Suddenly I wakened. My body was mangled. I was saturated with blood. Pieces of jagged glass were sticking out all over. Strange that I couldn't feel anything.

Hey! Don't pull that sheet over my head. I can't be dead. I'm only seventeen. I've got a date tonight. I'm supposed to grow up and have a wonderful life. I haven't lived yet. I can't be dead.

Later, I was placed in a drawer. My folks had to identify me. Why did they have to see me like this? Why did I have to look at Mom's eyes when she had to face the most terrible ordeal of her life? Dad suddenly looked like an old man. He told the man in charge, "Yes, he's my son."

The funeral was a weird experience. I saw all my relatives and friends walk toward the casket. They passed by one by one and looked at me with the saddest eyes I've ever seen. Some of my buddies were crying. A few of the girls touched my hand and sobbed as they walked away.

Please, somebody wake me up. Get me out of here. I can't bear to see my mom and dad so broken up. My grandparents are so wracked with grief that they can hardly walk. My brother and sisters are like zombies, in a daze. Everybody. No one can believe this and I can't believe it either.

Please don't bury me. I'm not dead. I have a lot of living to do. I want to laugh and run again. I promise, if you give me just one more chance, God, I'll be the most careful driver in the whole world. All I want is one more chance. Please, God. I'm only seventeen.

As seen in a DEAR ABBY column by Abigail Van Buren. Dist. by UNIVERSAL PRESS SYNDICATE. Reprinted with permission.

II. INFORMATION REGARDING GRIEF

How to Help When A Child Dies

For an excellent brochure, "How Can I Help?" order from The Compassionate Friends, P.O. Box 3696, Oak Brook, IL 60522-3696, or call 708-990-0010. In addition, The Compassionate Friends offers a variety of helpful resource materials.

Among the suggestions and insights in this brochure: Grief

lasts far longer than anyone expects; don't expect your friends to be unchanged by this experience. Stay in touch with the family, and mention the child in conversations. Don't be afraid to cry with the parents. Don't say "I know how you feel." Avoid using "it was God's will" or "at least you have other children." Listen; understand that the parents have a need to talk about their child. Don't presume to offer answers about serious questions the parent may have about God's role in the child's death. Be aware of what needs to be done and offer to do specific tasks. Give special attention to surviving children who are often hurt and ignored. Don't assume the surviving children aren't hurting because they don't express their feelings. Share a fond memory of the child. Remember the family on the child's birthday and death anniversary. Take the initiative to suggest lunch or a movie as relief from the isolation of grief when appropriate. (Reprinted by permission of The Compassionate Friends.)

Suggestions for Friends and Relatives of the Grieving Survivor

1. **Get in touch.** Telephone. Speak either to the mourner or to someone close and ask when you can visit and how you might help. Even if much time has passed, it's never too late to express concern.

2. **Say little on an early visit.** In the initial period (before burial), your brief embrace, your press of the hand, your few words of affection and feeling may be all that is needed.

3. **Avoid clichés and easy answers.** "He had a good life," "He is out of pain," and "Aren't you lucky that . . ." are not likely to help. A simple "I'm sorry" is better. Likewise, spiritual sayings can even provoke anger unless the mourner shares the faith that is implied. In general, *do not attempt to minimize the loss.*

4. **Be yourself.** Show your own natural concern and sorrow in your own way and in your own words.

5. **Keep in touch.** Be available. Be there. If you are a close friend or relative, your presence might be needed from the beginning. Later, when close family may be less available, anyone's visit and phone call can be very helpful.

6. **Attend to practical matters.** Discover if you might be needed to answer the phone, usher in callers, prepare meals, clean the house, care for the children, etc. This kind of help lifts burdens

and creates a bond. It might be needed well beyond the initial period, especially for the widowed.

7. **Encourage others to visit or help.** Usually one visit will overcome a friend's discomfort and allow him or her to contribute further support. You might even be able to *schedule* some visitors, so that everyone does not come at once in the beginning or fails to come at all later on.

8. **Accept silence.** If the mourner doesn't feel like talking, don't force conversation. Silence is better than aimless chatter. The mourner should be allowed to lead.

9. **Be a good listener.** When suffering spills over in words, you can do the one thing the bereaved needs above all else at that time—*you can listen.* Is he emotional? Accept that. Does he cry? Accept that, too. Is he angry at God? God will manage without your defending him. Accept whatever feelings are expressed. Do not rebuke. Do not change the subject. Be as understanding as you can be.

10. **Do not attempt to tell the bereaved how he feels.** You can ask (without probing), but you cannot *know,* except as he tells you. Everyone, bereaved or not, resents an attempt to describe his feelings. To say, for example, "You must feel relieved now that he is out of pain," is presumptuous. Even to say, "I know just how you feel," is questionable. *Learn* from the mourner; do not *instruct* him.

11. **Do not probe for details about the death.** If the survivor offers information, listen with understanding.

12. **Comfort children in the family.** Do not assume that a seemingly calm child is not sorrowing. If you can, be a friend to whom feelings can be confided and with whom tears can be shed. In most cases, incidentally, children should be left in the home and not shielded from the grieving of others.

13. **Avoid talking to others about trivia in the presence of the recently bereaved.** Prolonged discussion of sports, weather, or stock market, for example, is resented, even if done purposely to distract the mourner.

14. **Allow the "working through of grief."** Do not whisk away clothing or hide pictures. Do not criticize seemingly morbid behavior. Young people may repeatedly visit the site of the fatal accident. A widow may sleep with her husband's pajamas as a pillow. A young child may wear his dead sibling's clothing.

15. **Write a letter.** A sympathy card is a poor substitute for your own expression. If you take time to write of your love for and memories of the one who died, your letter might be read many times and cherished, possibly into the next generation.

16. **Encourage the postponement of major decisions until after the period of intense grief.** Whatever can wait should wait.

17. **In time, gently draw the mourner into quiet, outside activity.** He may not have the initiative to go out on his own.

18. **When the mourner returns to social activity, treat him as a normal person.** Avoid pity—it destroys self-respect. Simple understanding is enough. Acknowledge the loss, the change in his life, but don't dwell on it.

19. **Be aware of needed progress through grief.** If the mourner seems unable to resolve anger or guilt, for example, you might suggest a consultation with a clergyman or other trained counselor.

A final thought: Helping must be more than following a few rules. Especially if the bereavement is devastating and you are close to the bereaved, you may have to give more time, more care, *more of yourself* than you imagined. And you will have to perceive the *special needs* of your friend and creatively attempt to meet those needs. Such commitment and effort may even save a life. At the least, you will know the satisfaction of being truly and deeply helpful.

From the folder "Is There Anything I Can Do to Help?" by Amy Hillyard Jensen, copyright © 1985, Medic Publishing Co., P.O. Box 89, Redmond, WA 98073. Reprinted by permission.

III. SUICIDE PREVENTION INFORMATION

Warning Signs and Behaviors of High-Risk Individuals Contemplating Suicide

- Major loss (of loved person, home, possessions, or status), especially if preceded by other losses. A suicide in the family.

- Neglect of appearance.
- Withdrawal from people, especially close friends or family.
- Putting oneself down. Continued lack of self-esteem.
- Unusual or extreme change in school performance or attendance.
- Change in sleep patterns—insomnia or oversleeping.
- Weight loss or gain.
- Self-injury.
- Staying away or running away from home.
- Irritability and restlessness.
- Angry outbursts at home or school.
- Use of alcohol or drugs as an escape from pain.
- Sudden beginning of self-destructive or risk-taking behavior, like fast driving.
- Intense feelings of being trapped and helpless, without any hope of changing the situation.
- Specific threats of suicide (verbal or written).
- Prior suicide attempts.
- Giving away prized possessions.
- Preoccupation with death or suicide.
- Walks slowly, talks slowly with difficulty, slumps rather than sits.
- Personality changes—nervousness, anger, apathy or cries frequently.
- Extreme sadness or hopelessness.
- Says he's hurting his loved ones by staying alive, or is a burden to them.
- Makes vague statements couched in deep misery, or prompted by guilt.

Your child or loved one may have some, and in extreme cases, all of these signs and behaviors. Some of these feelings and behaviors may be an indication of depression and suicide is not being considered. However, they are warning signs and a call for help.

Stephen manifested a number of these signs, and I didn't recognize them for what they were—that he was seriously contemplating suicide. Most suicides are ambivalent, and by becoming aware of these warning signs, you may be able to intervene and save a life.

✦

The following is excerpted from an article written by John Hudson when he was an assistant principal of Paradise Valley High School District in Arizona, regarding his establishment of a suicide prevention program in his school and other schools:

The Paradise Valley School District is meeting the problem of adolescent suicide head-on through the establishment of a suicide prevention program. . . . All too often we hear "If only I had known," "I wish there was something I could have done," in response to suicide. The truth is that, more often than not, something could have been done. Individuals in crisis do give off many signs and signals. We are capable of "reading" these, and providing support which might help to bring someone through their crisis.

The program . . . consists of a twofold training experience. The first part involves instruction dealing with classic examples of and traditional approaches to suicide. The second facet deals with an innovative approach which involves the use of intuition.

For years we have been taught to disregard the information our intuition provides us with and to opt instead for what is logical and safe. For example, when encountering a friend or acquaintance who we feel is "not himself," we often ask, "Are you OK today?" The automatic response is "Yes, I'm fine." Many times we "know" (intuitively) this person is not OK, but by accepting this response, we are "off the hook." The training participants receive in this program, sensitizes them and helps to bring these intuitive messages into focus. We are conditioned to pay attention to what these messages tell us.

In addition to the effectiveness of the intuitive training, the other major strength of this program, is its team approach. Adults and students participate in the training sessions and form a Suicide Prevention Team as *equal* partners. This provides all involved with valuable insights.

Behaviors oftentimes indicative of individuals contemplating suicide:

- A sudden change in attitude from deep depression to a calm, determined or even cheerful outlook. This can indicate a decision to solve problems through suicide.
- Ending of a relationship (boyfriend-girlfriend) particularly if this is the only supportive relationship an individual experiences.

- A sudden significant drop in grades.
- Multiple pressures: home, grades, behavior.
- Suddenly becoming accident prone.
- An inability to fit in or belong to any group, possibly leading to ridicule.
- Lethargy, lack of interest in surroundings, perhaps accompanied by excessive periods of sleep.
- A perceived inability to live up to parents/friends/personal expectations.
- Feelings of shame or guilt for having brought dishonor upon family or friends.
- Loss of supportive relationships due to family relocation.

Steps You Can Take to Help an Individual in a Suicidal Crisis

- Listen and show that you care.
- Stay with the person if you feel there is any danger.
- Ask the person to express his or her feelings. Letting out pent-up emotions is essential in resolving the stressful situation. Let the person speak about his troubles at his own speed.
- Ask open-ended questions (what, how, tell me more about).
- Paraphrase and reflect thoughts and feelings.
- Don't argue or preach.
- Determine if the person has a plan. Assume a fact-finding, problem-solving attitude. The fewer supports and the more specific the plan, the greater the suicidal risk. (Talking openly about it will not cause more trouble or give the person ideas.)
- Assess suicidal potential: ask about frequency and intensity of self-destructive thoughts and feelings; ask about stressors (recent events, circumstances, losses); ask about actual plans and means of suicide; check the person's own estimate of his/her self-control.
- Assist the person in defining alternatives and other options.
- Keep calm—at least act calm (but concerned).
- Try to detect what the person is trying to communicate, and to whom.
- Don't try to "cure" the person.
- Don't rush the person to the hospital.
- Talk to the significant other or family member of person, in the

presence of the suicidal person if possible. Do not agree to keep a secret of the suicidal intent.

- Take a break to consult with others. Facilitate getting professional help for the person (accompany if necessary).
- Call a suicide prevention hotline.

REMEMBER: NO MATTER HOW MUCH THE PERSON MAY SEEM TO WANT TO DIE, ON SOME LEVEL HE ALSO WANTS DESPERATELY TO LIVE.

When wondering how to deal with your children, perhaps these words can help to provide a perspective from a child's point of view:

- DON'T spoil me. I know quite well I shouldn't have all I ask for. I'm only testing you.
- DON'T be afraid to be firm with me. I prefer it—it makes me feel secure.
- DON'T let me form bad habits. I have to rely on you to detect them in the early stages.
- DON'T make me feel smaller than I am. It only makes me behave stupidly "big."
- DON'T correct me in front of other people if you can help it. I'll take much more notice if you talk to me quietly in private.
- DON'T protect me from consequences. I need to learn the painful way sometimes.
- DON'T make me feel my mistakes are sins. It upsets my sense of values.
- DON'T be too upset if I say "I hate you." It isn't you I hate, but your power to thwart me.
- DON'T take too much notice of my small ailments. Sometimes they get me the attention I need.
- DON'T nag. If you do, I'll have to protect myself by appearing deaf.
- DON'T make rash promises. I feel badly let down when promises are broken.
- DON'T forget that I can't explain myself as well as I'd like. This is why I'm not always accurate.

- DON'T tax my honesty too much. I'm easily frightened into telling lies.
- DON'T be inconsistent. It completely confuses me and makes me lose my faith in you.
- DON'T put me off when I ask questions. If you do, you'll find I stop asking and seek information elsewhere.
- DON'T tell me my fears are silly. They're terribly real.
- DON'T suggest that you are perfect or infallible. It gives me too great a shock when I find out you're neither.
- DON'T ever think it is beneath your dignity to apologize to me. An honest apology makes me surprisingly warm toward you.
- DON'T forget I love experimenting. I can't get on without it, so please put up with it.
- DON'T forget how quickly I'm growing up. It must be hard to keep pace with me, but please try.

—Anonymous

IV.
WHERE TO FIND HELP

Assistance and/or referrals are often available from such organizations and listings as: Suicide Prevention Centers; Crisis Intervention Centers or Crisis Centers; Mental Health Clinics; Hospitals; Family Physicians or Holistic Practitioners; Ministers, clergy, churches; New Age Churches; Metaphysical Centers; Health Food Stores (don't laugh—they often have great networking links); County Mental Health Department; and U.S. Government Printing Offices for a variety of information and pamphlets.

Specialized self-help groups are often listed in the Yellow Pages or through telephone information under: Survivors of Suicide; Alcoholics Anonymous (AA); Al-Anon; Families Anonymous; Gamblers Anonymous; Narcotics Anonymous; Overeaters Anonymous (OA); Parents Anonymous; Sex Addicts Anonymous; Sexaholics Anonymous.

If a number listed below does not work in your area, telephone 1-800-555-1212, the directory assistance number for toll-free listings. Numbers change often, and some "800" numbers are unavailable in particular areas. If you are unable to locate help, dial "911" for emergencies.

The following resources are listed in alphabetical order:

Alcoholics Anonymous (AA), General Service Headquarters, 475 Riverside Drive, New York, NY 10025, (212) 870-3400.

Al-Anon Family Group Headquarters, P.O. Box 862, Midtown Station, New York, NY 10018-0862, (212) 302-7240. For the families of alcoholics or substance abusers.

American Association of Suicidology, 4201 Connecticut Avenue, N.W., Suite 310, Washington, D.C. 20008. (202) 237-2280, FAX: (202) 237-2282 For suicide or other crisis. List of survivor groups, publications, books, films, newsletters focusing on survivors. Goal is to understand and prevent suicide. Promotes research, public awareness programs, training for professionals, volunteers, and other programs for the understanding and prevention of suicide. National clearinghouse for information on suicide. Annual conference on suicide. Publication of annual conference proceedings. Listing of Survivors of Suicide Support Groups and Suicide Prevention and Crisis Intervention Centers.

American Psychiatric Association, (202) 682-6000. Provides referral to psychiatrists in your area working with suicidal teens or others.

American Psychological Association, (202) 336-5500. Will provide a list of psychologists in your area working with suicidal teens, or others.

Anorexia Nervosa and Related Eating Disorders Information Line, P.O. Box 5102, Eugene, OR 97405, (503) 344-1144, or (503) 686-7372. Information and referral service for questions regarding eating disorders and their treatment. Leave message for information.

American Self-Help Clearinghouse, Northwest Covenant Medical Center, 25 Pocono Road, Denville, NJ 07984-2995. (201) 625-7101. They refer to self-help groups of all types, nationwide.

Anxiety Disorders Association of America, 6000 Executive Blvd., Suite 200, Rockville, MD 20852. (301) 231-9350. Offers information and resources regarding various anxiety disorders.

Childhelp USA, Child Abuse Hotline, (800) 422-4453. If you are being sexually abused and need help, or if you want to report abuse, you will be directed to the appropriate counselors. Literature available also.

Cocaine Hotline, 1-800-COCAINE, 1-800-262-2246. Referral service for drug treatment. Information.

Co-Dependents of Sexual Addicts (CoSA), P.O. Box 14537, Minneapolis, MN 55414, (612) 537-6904. Support groups for families of sexual addicts.

The Compassionate Friends National Headquarters, P.O. Box 3696, Oak Brook, IL 60522-3696, (708) 990-0010. Local chapters offering healing and hope for bereaved parents. Newsletter by subscription. Annual conference of survivors. Books and publications.

Concern for Dying, 250 W. 57th Street, New York, NY 10107. Conferences on death and dying. Distributes the Living Will. Newsletter and other material. Annual convention.

Contact USA, Pouch A, Harrisburg, PA 17105-1300, (717) 232-3501 for Helpline Telephone Numbers in your area and information. Over 73 centers. Affiliated with LifeLine International with groups in ten countries.

Covenant House, East Coast, (800) 999-9999. Help and referrals.

Empact, 24-hour crisis hot line (602) 784-1500, Tempe, Arizona.

ENcourage Newsletter, 13610 N. Scottsdale Road, Suite 10-126, Scottsdale, AZ 85254. Subscription newsletter providing information, resources and support for those experiencing panic disorder and/or agoraphobia.

Families Anonymous, P.O. Box 528, Van Nuys, CA 91408, (800) 736-9805 and (818) 989-7841. Support program for drug, alcohol, and behavior problems in children. Assists parents in developing a better understanding of the problems. 500 groups worldwide. Literature.

Grief Recovery Institute, 8306 Wilshire Blvd., Suite 21A, Beverly Hills, CA 90211. To talk with someone, no message service, Monday through Friday, 9 A.M.–5 P.M. PST: (800) 445-4808. To talk with someone during business hours or to leave a message 24 hours a day: (213) 650-1234. They believe grief is a natural reaction to loss and will try to lead people in directions of healing. Seminars, certification programs for grief counselors. They use the *Grief Recovery Handbook* by John James.

Hemlock Society, P.O. Box 66218, Los Angeles, CA 90066. Supports voluntary euthanasia for the advanced terminally ill and the seriously incurably ill. Publications.

Incest Survivors Resource Network, 15 Rutherford Place, New York, NY 10003, (212) 521-4260. Support groups for incest victims.

Link Counseling Center, 348 Mount Vernon Highway NE, Atlanta, GA 30328, (404) 256-9797. Director: Iris Bolton, author of *My Son, My Son,* book about the suicide death of her son. Counseling and referrals. Survivors of Suicide Support Groups listings.

Logos Center, P.O. Box 12880, Scottsdale, AZ 85267-2880, (602) 483-8777. Rev. Anne Puryear and Herbert B. Puryear, Ph.D., Co-Directors. Counseling and referral. Books, videos, workshops.

Mothers Against Drunk Drivers (MADD) Headquarters, 511 E. John Carpenter Freeway, #700, Irving, TX 75062. Victims Hotline: (800) 438-6233. Literature: (214) 744-6233. Referrals to groups in your state. Acts as the voice of the victim of drunk driving accidents. Information for victims and their families on bereavement groups. Newsletter and brochure.

NAR-ANON, P.O. Box 2562, San Pedro, CA 90731, (310) 547-5800. For families and friends of recovering addicts.

Narcotics Anonymous (NA), P.O. Box 9999, Van Nuys, CA 91409, (818) 773-9999. Referrals throughout the world for addicts and recovering addicts.

National AIDS Information Clearinghouse, (800) 458-5231, also in Spanish.

National Council on Sexual Addiction (NCSA), P.O. Box 20249, Wickenburg, AZ, 85354, (800) 321-2066. Send self-addressed, stamped envelope for information.

National HIV and AIDS, P.O. Box 6003, Rockville, MD 20849. Information Service Hotline: (800) 342-AIDS. General publications, AIDS packet.

National Institute of Mental Health, (301) 443-4536. Literature on mental illness, depression.

National Mental Health Association, (703) 684-7722, for community mental health clinics in your area.

National Runaway Switchboard, (800) 621-4000. Crisis hot line. Counselors trained in crisis intervention. Referrals.

National Self-Help Clearinghouse, (212) 642-2944. Send stamped, self-addressed envelope to: 25 W. 43rd Street, New York, NY 10036 for information and literature.

National Youth Crisis Hotline, (800) 448-4663.

Nationally Sexually Transmitted Disease Hotline, (800) 227-8922.

1-800-ALCOHOL. Phone (800) 252-6465 for 24-hour help and referral regarding alcohol and drug abuse.

Overeaters Anonymous (OA), (602) 831-6849. Doris, World Chairman for young people. Meetings, literature, youth newspaper, and pen pals all over the world. Help for young people with eating disorders and weight problems. Referrals to groups in your area for adults and young people.

Parents of Murdered Children, 100 E. 8th Street, B-41, Cincinnati, OH 45202, (513) 721-5683. Physical and emotional support. Information about the criminal justice system as it pertains to survivors of a homicide victim. Newsletter.

Parents United, P.O. Box 952, San Jose, CA 95108, (408) 453-7616. For those who have experienced sexual molestation. Provides assistance to families affected by incest and other types of child sexual abuse. Crisis and long-term support. Training of professionals. Literature. 24-hour coverage.

Practical Allergy Research Foundation, P.O. Box 60, Buffalo, NY 14223-0060. (800) 787-8780. Help for young people with physical and emotional problems and those who are suicidal.

Sex and Love Addicts Anonymous, P.O. Box 119, Boston, MA 02258, (617) 332-1845.

Sex Addicts Anonymous (SAA), P.O. Box 70949, Houston, TX 77270. (713) 869-4902. Support groups for sexual addicts that follow a program adapted from Twelve-Step program of AA, in dealing with sexual behavior. (Sexual addicts are people who compulsively repeat sexual behavior that is often abusive, exploitive, and damaging to their lives at home and at work.)

Sexaholics Anonymous (SA), P.O. Box 300, Simi Valley, CA 93062. Groups for individuals wanting to stop sexually self-destructive thinking and behavior such as fantasy, pornography, incest, or criminal sexual activity. The group believes that the sexaholic is addicted to lust and sex as others are to alcohol and drugs. This behavior is often followed by guilt, remorse, and depression, and may do serious damage to relationships.

Sexual Compulsives Anonymous, P.O. Box 1585, New York, NY 10113-0935, (212) 439-1123.

Society for the Right to Die, 250 W. 57th Street, New York, NY 10107, (212) 366-5540. Publications, convention. Protects the rights of dying patients.

Survivors of Suicide, Judy Lewis, Coordinator, Tempe, AZ (602) 784-1514.

Valley Hope, Chandler, AZ, (800) 252-6465. For drug and alcohol problems.

Wesom, Inc., P.O. Box 46312, Chicago, IL 60646, (312) 792-7034. Computerized service, leave a message and telephone number and your call will be returned. This is the "We Saved Our Marriage" organization founded by Richard and Elizabeth Brzeczek, authors of *Addicted to Adultery.* Groups throughout the country, based on 12-step program, for addiction to adultery and for wives or husbands whose spouses are unfaithful.

REFERENCES AND RELATED READING

As I researched suicide, explored Stephen's death, delved into our family dynamics, and tried to understand myself, I personally read every book listed here, as well as dozens of others I have not included because of lack of space. I have selected some of the books and publications that gave me special insights, broadened my understanding, and helped me to heal. Since I read these books over a period of years, I am putting an asterisk (*) beside those books that I would consider "read first." Then, as time permits, read the others that sound helpful to you.

Following these books, you will find additional resources including recommended movies, and audio and videotapes of special interest.

—Anne Puryear

Abravanel, Elliot D., M.D. and Elizabeth King. *Dr. Abravanel's Body Type Diet and Lifetime Nutrition Plan.* New York: Bantam, 1983.

*———. *Dr. Abravanel's Body Type Program for Health, Fitness and Nutrition.* New York: Bantam, 1985.

———. *Dr. Abravanel's Anti-Craving Weight Loss Diet.* New York: Bantam, 1990.

Al-Anon's Twelve Steps and Twelve Traditions. New York: Al-Anon Family Group Headquarters, Inc., 1981.

Alexander, Helen Mae. *The Angels Speak.* Denver: State of the Art, Ltd., 1984.

———. *Angels Can Light Up Your Life.* New York: Vantage Press, 1993.

*Alvarez, A. *The Savage God: A Study of Suicide.* New York: Random House, 1972.

American Psychologist Special Issue: Adolescence. Vol. 48, Number 2, February 1993. American Psychological Association.

Anderson, Dorothy, B., and Lenora J. McClean. *Identifying Suicide Potential.* New York: Behavioral Publications, 1969.
Angelou, Maya. *The Complete Collected Poems of Maya Angelou.* New York: Random House, 1994.
Atkinson, J. Maxwell. *Discovering Suicide: Studies in the Social Organization of Sudden Death.* Pittsburgh: University of Pittsburgh Press, 1978.
Bach, George R. and Ronald M. Deutsch. *Stop! You're Driving Me Crazy: How to Keep the People in Your Life from Driving You up the Wall.* New York: Berkley Books, 1979.
Bach, Richard. *The Bridge Across Forever.* New York: Dell Books, 1984.
———. *Jonathan Livingston Seagull.* New York: Macmillan Co., 1970.
Bahadori, Mehdi. *Love to Be Happy: The Secrets of Sustainable Joy.* Nevada City, CA: Blue Dolphin Publishing, 1994.
Bander, Peter. *Voices from the Tapes: Recordings from the Other World.* New York: Drake Publishers, 1973.
Barbanell, Sylvia. *When a Child Dies.* London: Pilgrims Book Services, 1984.
Batmanghelidj, F., M. D. *Your Body's Many Cries for Water.* Falls Church, VA: Global Health Solutions, 1995.
Batzler, Louis Richard. *Some Paranormal Perspectives on Suicide, from the Rising Tide of Suicide; A Guide to Prevention, Intervention and Postvention.* Spiritual Frontiers Quarterly, Summer 1988, Volume XX, Number 3. Philadelphia: Spiritual Frontiers Fellowship, Inc.
Beard, Paul. *Living On: How Consciousness Continues and Evolves After Death.* New York: Continuum Publishing Corp., 1981.
*Beattie, Melody. *Codependent No More: How to Stop Controlling Others and Start Caring for Yourself.* San Francisco: Harper & Row, 1987.
———. *Beyond Codependency: And Getting Better All The Time.* New York: Harper/Hazelden, 1989.
*———. *A Reason to Live.* Wheaton, IL: Tyndale House Publishers, 1991.
*———. *The Language of Letting Go.* New York: Hazelden, HarperCollins, 1990.
———. *The Lessons of Love.* San Francisco: Harper, 1994.
Bender, David L. and Bruno Leone. *Death and Dying: Opposing Viewpoints.* St. Paul: Greenhaven Press, 1987.
Berent, Irving, M.D. *The Algebra of Suicide.* New York: Human Sciences Press, 1981.
Berkus, Rusty. *To Heal Again.* Encino, CA: Red Rose Press, 1986.

*Berman, Alan L. and David A. Jobes. *Adolescent Suicide Assessment and Intervention.* Washington, D.C.: American Psychological Association, 1991.

*Berry, Carmen Renee. *When Helping You Is Hurting Me: Escaping the Messiah Trap.* San Francisco: Harper & Row, 1988.

*Bethards, Betty. *There Is No Death.* Novato, CA: Inner Light Foundation, 1985.

Blaker, Karen, Ph.D. *Born to Please: Compliant Women/Controlling Men.* New York: St. Martin's Press, 1988.

*Bolton, Iris with Curtis Mitchell. *My Son, My Son: A Guide to Healing After a Suicide in the Family.* Atlanta, GA: Bolton Press, 1983. (1325 Belmore Way N.E., Atlanta, GA 30350)

Boritzer, Etan. *What Is God?* Ontario, Canada; Firefly Books Ltd., 1990.

Boss, Judy. *In Silence They Return.* New York: Manor Books, 1972.

———. *A Garden of Joy.* St. Paul, MN: Llewellyn Publications, 1974.

Bozarth-Campbell, Alla, Ph.D., *Life Is Goodbye, Life Is Hello: Grieving Well Through All Kinds of Loss.* Minneapolis: CompCare Publications, 1983.

Bradshaw, John. *Homecoming: Reclaiming & Championing Your Inner Child.* New York: Bantam, 1990.

*———. *Bradshaw on the Family: A Revolutionary Way of Self Discovery.* Deerfield Beach, FL: Health Communications, Inc., 1988.

———. *Healing the Shame that Binds You.* Deerfield Beach, FL: Health Communications, Inc., 1988.

*Brown, Les. *Live Your Dreams.* New York: William Morrow and Co., 1992.

Browne, Joy, Dr. *Nobody's Perfect: How to Stop Blaming and Start Living.* New York: Simon & Schuster, 1988.

*Brzeczek, Richard and Elizabeth Brzeczek, with Sharon DeVita. *Addicted to Adultery.* New York: Bantam, 1989.

Budge, E. A. Wallis. *The Book of the Dead.* New York: Bell Publishing Co., University Books, 1960.

Bundesen, Lynne. *GodDependency.* New York: Crossroad Publishing Co., 1989.

Burnham, Sophy. *Angel Letters.* New York: Ballantine, Random House, 1991.

———. *A Book of Angels.* New York: Ballantine, Random House, 1991.

*Caddy, Eileen. *Opening Doors Within.* Scotland: Findhorn Press, 1988.

Canfield, Jack and Mark Victor Hansen. *Chicken Soup for the Soul.* Deerfield Beach, FL: Health Communications, Inc., 1993.

*Carnes, Patrick. *Out of the Shadows: Understanding Sexual Addiction.* Minneapolis, MN: CompCare Publishers, 1983.

———. *Don't Call it Love: Recovering from Sexual Addiction.* New York: Bantam, 1991.

Casey, Karen and Martha Vanceburg. *The Promise of a New Day.* Minneapolis: Winston Press, 1983.

Chaney, Earlyne. *The Mystery and Meaning of Death and Dying.* York Beach, ME: Samuel Weiser, Inc., 1988.

———. *The Book of Beginning Again.* Upland, CA: Astara, Inc., 1981.

———. *Remembering: A Story of Life After Death.* Upland, CA: Astara's Library of Mystical Classics, 1974.

Choron, Jacques. *Suicide.* New York: Charles Scribner's Sons, 1972.

Coca, Arthur R., M.D. *The Pulse Test: Easy Allergy Detection.* New York: Arco Publishing, Inc., 1982.

Cockell, Jenny. *Across Time and Death.* New York: Fireside, Simon and Schuster, 1993.

Constas, Robert, M.D. *Death Does Not Exist and the Psychology of Becoming Oneself.* Sedona, AZ: Aquarian Educational Group, 1979.

Cornish, John. *About Death and After.* England: New Knowledge Books, 1975.

Course in Miracles. Foundation For Inner Peace, 1975.

Cramer, Kathryn D., Ph.D. *Staying on Top When Your World Turns Upside Down: Turn Your Stress into Strength.* New York: Viking Penguin, 1990.

Currie, Ian. *You Cannot Die: The Incredible Findings of a Century of Research on Death.* New York: Playboy Paperbacks, 1978.

Danto, Bruce L. and Austin H. Kutscher. *Suicide and Bereavement.* New York: ARNO Press, 1977.

Davis, Dorothy W. *Robin's Return and Ray.* New York: Vantage Press, 1986.

*DeAngelis, Barbara, Ph.D. *Secrets About Men Every Woman Should Know.* New York: Dell, Bantam, 1990.

Deats, Sara Munson, Ph.D. and Lagretta Tallent Lenker, M.S. *Youth Suicide Prevention: Lessons From Literature.* New York: Plenum Publishing Corp., 1989.

Delacour, Jean-Baptiste. *Glimpses of the Beyond.* Delacorte, NY: 1973.

Dempsey, David K. *The Way We Die: An Investigation of Death and Dying in America Today.* New York: Macmillan, 1975.

Dobson, James C., Dr. *Love Must Be Tough: New Hope for Families in Crisis.* Dallas: Word Publishing Inc., 1983.

Dorff, Francis. *The Art of Passing Over.* New York: Paulist Press, 1988.

Doss, Richard W. *The Last Enemy: A Christian Understanding of Death.* New York: Harper & Row, 1974.
Dublin, Louis I. *Suicide: A Sociological and Statistical Study.* New York: Ronald Press, 1963.
Dunne, J. W. *Nothing Dies.* London: Faber and Faber, 1951.
Durkheim, Emile. *Suicide: A Study in Sociology.* New York: Free Press Paperback, Macmillan, 1951.
Each Day a New Beginning. New York: Harper & Row, 1982.
Easwaran, Eknath. *Dialogue with Death: The Spiritual Psychology of the Katha Upanishad.* Petaluma, CA: Nilgiri Press, 1981.
Evans-Wentz, W. Y. *The Tibetan Book of the Dead.* London: Oxford University Press, 1957.
Exupery, Antoine de Saint. *The Little Prince.* New York: Harcourt, Brace & World, 1971.
Farnese, A. and Franchezzo. *A Wanderer in the Spirit Lands.* California: Health Research, 1965.
Farthing, Geoffrey. *When We Die.* London: Theosophical Publishing House, 1968.
*Finch, Stuart M., M.D., Elva O. Poznanski, M.D. *Adolescent Suicide.* Springfield, IL: Charles C. Thomas, 1971.
Foos-Graber, Anya. *Deathing: An Intelligent Alternative for the Final Moments of Life.* Reading, MA: Addison-Wesley Publishing Co., 1984.
Ford, Arthur. *The Life Beyond Death.* New York: Berkley, 1971.
Fox, Emmet. *Life after Death.* California: DeVorss & Co., 1966.
Fremou, William J., Maria de Perczel, and Thomas Ellis. *Suicide Risk, Assessment and Response Guidelines.* New York: Pergamon Press, 1990.
Fromm, Erich. *The Anatomy of Human Destructiveness.* Greenwich, CT: Fawcett Crest, 1973.
Fulghum, Robert. *All I Really Need to Know I Learned in Kindergarten.* New York: Ivy Books, Published by Ballantine Books, 1986.
Gerber, Richard, M.D. *Vibrational Medicine: New Choices for Healing Ourselves.* Santa Fe, NM: Bear and Co., 1988.
Gernsbacher, Larry Morton, Ph.D. *The Suicide Syndrome.* New York: Human Sciences Press, 1985.
Gibran, Kahlil. *The Prophet.* New York: Alfred A. Knopf, Inc., 1951.
*Giffin, Mary, M.D. and Carol Felsenthal. *A Cry for Help.* Garden City, New York: Doubleday, 1983.
*Giovacchini, Peter, M.D. *The Urge to Die: Why Young People Commit Suicide.* New York: Macmillan, 1981.
*Gray, John, Ph.D. *Men Are from Mars, Women Are from Venus.* New York: HarperCollins, 1992.
*———. *What You Feel You Can Heal.* Mill Valley, CA: Heart Publishing, 1984.

———. *What Your Mother Couldn't Tell You and Your Father Didn't Know*. New York: Harper, 1994.

*Greaves, Helen. *Testimony of Light*. Suffolk, England: Hillman Printers, 1980.

———. *The Challenging Light*. Suffolk, England: Neville Spearman Ltd., 1984.

Grollman, Earl A. *Suicide: Prevention, Intervention, Postvention*. Boston: Beacon Press, 1988.

Guggenheim, Bill and Judy Guggenheim. *Hello from Heaven!* The ADC Project, P.O. Box 916070, Longwood, FL 32791, 1995.

Hafen, Brent Q., Ph.D. and Kathryn J. Frandsen. *Youth, Suicide, Depression and Loneliness*. Evergreen, CO: Cordillera Press, Inc., 1986.

Hampton, Charles. *The Transition Called Death*. Wheaton, IL: Theosophical Publishing House, 1943.

*Hay, Louise. *You Can Heal Your Life*. New York: Coleman Pub., 1983.

———. *Heal Your Body*. Santa Monica, California: Hay House, 1984.

———. *I Love My Body*. New York: Coleman Publishing, 1985.

Hayes, Patricia and Marshall Smith. *Extension of Life: Arthur Ford Speaks*. Roswell, GA: Dimensional Brotherhood Publishing House, 1986.

*Heller, Rachel F., Dr., and Heller, Richard F., Dr. *Carbohydrate Addicts Diet*. New York: Dutton, 1991.

Hendin, Herbert, M.D. *Suicide in America*. New York: W. W. Norton & Co., 1982.

Hewett, John H. *After Suicide*. Philadelphia: Westminister Press, 1980.

Holzer, Hans. *Life After Death: The Challenge and the Evidence*. Indianapolis: Bobbs-Merrill Co., 1969.

Hodgson, Joan. *Hello Sun: First Steps to Spiritual Understanding*. Hampshire, England: White Eagle Publishing Co., 1972.

Hyde, Margaret O. *Suicide: The Hidden Epidemic*. New York: F. Watts, 1986.

James, John W. and Frank Cherry. *The Grief Recovery Handbook: A Step by Step Program for Moving Beyond Loss*. New York: Harper & Row, 1988.

Jampolsky, Gerald G., M.D. *Goodbye to Guilt*. New York: Bantam, 1985.

———. *Love Is Letting Go of Fear*. Millbrae, CA: Celestial Arts, 1979.

*Janda, Louis H., Dr. and Ellen MacCormack. *The Second Time Around: Why Some Second Marriages Fail While Others Succeed*. New York: Lyle Stuart Books, Published by Carol Publishing Group, 1991.

Joan, Polly. *Preventing Teenage Suicide: The Living Alternative Handbook*. New York: Human Sciences Press, Inc., 1986.
Johnson, Christopher J., Ph.D., and Marsha G. McGee, Ph.D. *Encounters with Eternity: Religious Views of Death and Life After Death*. New York: Philosophical Library, 1986.
Johnson, Debbie. *How to Love Yourself*. Deborah Johnson Publishing, 1988.
———. *How to Make Your Dreams Come True*. Portland: Deborah Johnson Publishing, 1989.
*Johnson, Robert. *We: Understanding the Psychology of Romantic Love*. San Francisco: Harper & Row, 1983.
*Johnston, Jerry. *Why Suicide? What Parents and Teachers Must Know to Save Our Kids*. Nashville: Oliver-Nelson Books, 1987.
Kastenbaum, Robert. *Is There Life After Death?* New York: Prentice Hall, 1984.
Kelsey, Morton T. *Afterlife: The Other Side of Dying*. New York: Paulist Press, 1979.
*Keys, Ken, Jr. *The Hundredth Monkey*. St. Mary, KY: Vision Books, 1982.
*Klagsbrun, Francine. *Too Young to Die, Youth and Suicide*. New York: Pocket Books, 1976.
Kramer, Kenneth. *The Sacred Art of Dying: How World Religions Understand Death*. New York: Paulist Press, 1988.
*Kübler-Ross, Elisabeth. *On Death and Dying*. New York: Macmillan, 1969.
*———. *On Children and Death*. New York: Macmillan, 1983.
*———. *Death: The Final Stage of Growth*. Englewood Cliffs, NJ: Prentice Hall, 1975.
*———. *Questions and Answers On Death and Dying*. New York: Macmillan, 1974.
*———. *Working it Through: Workshop on Life, Death and Transition*. New York: Collier Books, Macmillan, 1982.
*———. *On Life After Death*, Berkeley, CA: Celestial Arts, 1991.
Kung, Hans. *Eternal Life After Death as a Medical, Philosophical and Theological Problem*. New York: Doubleday, 1984.
Kushner, Harold S. *When Bad Things Happen to Good People*. New York: Avon Books, 1981.
Laddon, Judy. *Beyond the Veil*. California: ACS Publications, 1987.
Lake, Dr. Tony. *Living with Grief*. London: Sheldon Press, 1989.
Lamsa, George M. *Holy Bible from the Ancient Eastern Text, George Lamsa's Translation from the Aramaic of the Peshitta*. New York: HarperCollins, 1968.
Leder, Jane Mersky. *Dead Serious*. New York: Atheneum, 1987.
Leogrande, Ernest. *Second Chance to Live: The Suicide Syndrome*. New York: DaCapo Press, 1975.

Lerner, Harriet Goldhor, Ph.D. *The Dance of Anger.* New York: Harper and Row, 1985.

Lester, David, Ph.D. *Why People Kill Themselves: A 1980s Summary of Research Findings on Suicidal Behavior.* Springfield, IL: Charles C. Thomas Publishers.

Lester, David, Ph.D. *Suicide '94: Proceedings 27th Annual Conference, American Association of Suicidology.* Denver, CO, 1994.

Lester, Gene and David Lester. *Suicide: The Gamble with Death.* New Jersey: Prentice Hall, 1971.

Leszcynski, Janna. *A Time To Grieve, A Time To Dance.* Evergreen and Janet A. Leszcynski, Publishers, 1983.

Levine, Stephen. *Meetings at the Edge.* New York: Anchor Press, Doubleday, 1984.

Lewis, C. S. *The Screwtape Letters.* New York: Macmillan, 1961.

*Loehr, Franklin. *Diary After Death.* New York: Pillar Books, 1976.

Lorimer, David. *Survival?* London: Routledge and Kegan, 1984.

Lubetkin, Barry and Elena Oumano. *Bailing Out: The Healthy Way to Get Out of a Bad Relationship and Survive.* New York: Prentice Hall, 1991.

Lukas, Christopher and Henry M. Seiden, Ph.D. *Silent Grief: Living in the Wake of Suicide.* New York: Macmillan, 1987.

Lum, Doman. *Responding to Suicidal Crisis: For Church and Community.* Grand Rapids, MI: William B. Eerdmans Publishing Co., 1974.

Lund, David H. *Death and Consciousness: The Case for Life After Death.* New York: Ballantine Books, 1985.

Lundberg, Jean Pancer and Derek Lloyd Lundberg. *Teenage Suicide in America: A Handbook for Understanding.* Dayton, OH: P.P.I. Publishing, 1985.

*McCoy, Kathleen. *Coping with Teenage Depression.* New York: NAL Penguin Books, 1982.

McCulloch, J. Wallace and Alistair E. Philip. *Suicidal Behaviour.* New York: Pergamon Press, 1972.

McIntosh, John L. *Research on Suicide: A Bibliography.* Westport, CT: Greenwood Press, 1985.

———, ed. *Suicide and Its Aftermath: Understanding and Counseling the Survivors.* New York: Norton, 1987.

Mack, John E., and Holly Hickler. *Vivienne: The Life and Suicide of an Adolescent Girl.* Boston: Little, Brown & Co., 1981.

MacLaine, Shirley. *Out On A Limb.* New York: Bantam, 1983.

Madison, Arnold. *Suicide and Young People.* New York: Clarion Books, 1978.

Mandell, Marshall, M.D. *5-Day Allergy Relief System.* New York: Pocket Books, 1979.

Mandell, Marshall, M.D. and Fran Gare Mandell, M.S. *The Mandells' It's Not Your Fault You're Fat Diet.* New York: Signet Books, 1983.

Mandino, Og. *The Greatest Secret in The World.* New York: Bantam, 1972.

Mannes, Mary. *Last Rights.* New York: William Morrow and Co., 1974.

Maris, Ronald W. *Pathways to Suicide: A Survey of Self-Destructive Behaviors.* Baltimore: Johns Hopkins University Press.

Martin, Joel, and Patricia Romanowski. *We Don't Die: George Anderson's Conversations with the Other Side.* New York: Berkley Books, 1988.

———. *Our Children Forever: George Anderson's Messages from Children on the Other Side.* New York: Berkley Books, 1994.

Meaker, M. J. *Sudden Endings.* New York: Doubleday, 1964.

Meek, George W. *After We Die, What Then?* Columbus, OH: Ariel Press, 1987.

*Mellody, Pia with Andrea Wells Miller, and J. Keith Miller. *Facing Codependence.* New York: Harper & Row, 1989.

*———. *Facing Love Addiction: Giving Yourself the Power to Change the Way You Love.* San Francisco: Harper & Row, 1992.

———. *Breaking Free: A Recovery Workbook for Facing Codependence.* San Francisco: Harper & Row, 1989.

Mitchell, Edgar. *Psychic Exploration.* New York: G. P. Putnam's Sons, 1974.

Miller, Caroline Adams. *Bright Words for Dark Days: Meditations for Women Who Get the Blues.* New York, Bantam, 1994.

Monahan, Evelyn. *The Miracle of Metaphysical Healing.* West Nyack, NY: Parker Publishing Co., 1975.

*Monroe, Robert A. *Journeys Out of the Body.* New York: Anchor Books, 1977.

*Montgomery, Ruth. *A Search for the Truth.* New York: Bantam, 1967.

———. *Here and Hereafter.* New York: Fawcett Crest Books, 1968.

———. *The World Before.* New York: Fawcett Crest Books, 1976.

*———. *A World Beyond.* New York: Fawcett Crest Books, 1971.

*Moody, Raymond A. Jr. M.D. *Life After Life.* New York: Bantam, 1975.

———. *Reflections on Life After Life.* New York: Bantam, 1978.

———. *The Light Beyond.* New York: Bantam, 1988.

*———. *Reunions: Visionary Encounters with Departed Loved Ones.* New York: Ivy Books, Ballantine, 1993.

*Morse, Melvin, M.D. *Closer to the Light: Learning from the Near-Death Experiences of Children.* New York: Villard Books, Divison of Random House, 1990.

Munsch, Robert. *Love You Forever.* Canada: Firefly Books, Ltd., 1986.

Myers, John. *Voices from the Edge of Eternity.* Spire Books Pyramid Publications, 1968.

Norwood, Robin. *Women Who Love Too Much: When You Keep Wishing and Hoping He'll Change.* New York: Pocket Books, 1985.

———. *Letters from Women Who Love Too Much: A Closer Look at Relationship Addiction and Recovery.* New York: Pocket Books, 1988.

O'Connor, Nancy, Ph.D. *Letting Go with Love: The Grieving Process.* Apache Junction, AZ: La Mariposa Press, 1984.

Osis, Karlis Ph.D. and Erlendur Haraldsson, Ph.D. *At the Hour of Death: The Results of Research on Over 1,000 Afterlife Experiences.* New York: Avon Books, 1977.

Pearson, Linnea, with Ruth Purtilo. *Separate Paths: Why People End Their Lives.* San Francisco: Harper & Row, 1977.

Peck, M. Scott. *People of the Lie: The Hope for Healing Human Evil.* New York: Simon & Schuster, 1983.

*———. *The Road Less Traveled.* New York: Touchstone, 1978.

Pederson, Duane and Helen Kooiman. *Going Sideways: Hope, Love, Life versus Suicide.* New York: Hawthorn Books, 1974.

Pelgrin, Mark. *And a Time to Die.* Wheaton, IL: Theosophical Publishing House, 1962.

Pelletier, Kenneth R. *Mind as Healer, Mind as Slayer.* New York: Delta Publishing Co., 1977.

Philpott, William H., M.D. and Dwight K. Kalita, Ph.D. *Brain Allergies: The Psychonutrient Connection.* New Canaan, CT: Keats Pub., Inc., 1980.

Pike, James A. Bishop. *The Other Side.* New York: Doubleday, 1968.

Pincus, Lily. *Death and the Family: The Importance of Mourning.* New York: Pantheon Books, 1974.

Plath, Sylvia. *The Bell Jar.* New York: Bantam, 1972.

Poems That Touch the Heart. Garden City, New York: Doubleday, 1956.

Portwood, Doris. *Common Sense Suicide: The Final Right.* New York: Dodd, Mead & Co., 1978.

*Puryear, Herbert Bruce, Ph.D. *The Edgar Cayce Primer: Discovering the Path to Self-Transformation.* New York: Bantam, 1982.

———. *Sex and the Spiritual Path.* New York: Bantam, 1980.

———. *Reflections on the Path.* New York: Bantam, 1986.

———. *Meditation and the Mind of Man.* Virginia Beach, VA: A.R.E. Press, 1978.

———. *Day by Day: Steps to a New Life.* Virginia Beach, VA: A.R.E. Press, 1981.

*———. *Why Jesus Taught Reincarnation: A Better News Gospel.* Scottsdale, AZ: New Paradigm Press, 1993.

Quinnett, Paul G. *Suicide: The Forever Decision.* New York: Continuum Publishing Co., 1987.

*Rabkin, Brenda. *Growing Up Dead: A Hard Look at Why Adolescents Commit Suicide.* Nashville: Parthenon Press, 1978.

*Rapp, Doris, M.D. *The Impossible Child.* Buffalo, NY: Practical Allergy Research Foundation, PO Box 60, Buffalo, NY 14223-0060, 1989. (800) 787-8780.

*———. *Is This Your Child?* New York: Quill, William Morrow and Co., 1991.

———. *Is Your School Environmentally Sick?* Buffalo, NY: Practical Allergy Research Foundation, 1995.

Rauscher, William V. *The Case Against Suicide.* New York: St. Martin's Press, 1981.

Raudive, Konstantin. *Breakthrough: An Amazing Experiment in Electronic Communication with the Dead.* New York: Lancer Books, Inc., 1971.

Rawlings, Maurice, M.D. *Beyond Death's Door.* Canada: Thomas Nelson, 1978.

Redfield, James. *The Celestine Prophecy.* New York: Warner Books, 1993.

Reynolds, David K. and Norman L. Farberow. *The Family Shadow: Sources of Suicide and Schizophrenia.* Berkeley: University of California Press, 1981.

Richelieu, Peter. *A Soul's Journey.* Wellingbrough, England: Turnstone Press Ltd., 1972.

Ridall, Kathryn, Ph.D. *Channeling: How to Reach Out to Your Spirit Guides.* New York: Bantam, 1988.

Ring, Kenneth, Ph.D. *Life at Death: A Scientific Investigation of the Near-Death Experience.* New York: Quill, 1982.

*Ritchie, George G., Jr. with Elizabeth Sherrill. *Return from Tomorrow.* New York: Fleming H. Revell Company, 1978.

*Robbins, Anthony. *Unlimited Power.* New York: Fawcett Columbine, 1986.

———. *Awaken the Giant Within.* New York: Summit Books, 1991.

Robinson, Rita. *Survivors of Suicide.* California: IBS Press, 1989.

Rosenberg, Jay F. *Thinking Clearly About Death.* New Jersey: Prentice Hall, 1982.

Rosenfeld, Linda and Marilynne Prupas. *Left Alive: After a Suicide Death in the Family.* Springfield, IL: Charles C. Thomas, 1984.

Roy, Alec. *Suicide.* Baltimore: Williams and Wilkins, 1986.

Rudolph, Marguerita. *Should the Children Know? Encounters with Death in the Lives of Children.* New York: Schocken Books, 1978.

*Russell, A. J., ed. *God Calling.* New York: Dodd, Mead and Co., 1978.

———. *God at Eventide.* New York: Dodd, Mead and Co., 1978.

Russell, Robert A. *Dry Those Tears.* Marina del Rey, CA: DeVorss & Co., 1951.

St. Johns, Adela Rogers. *No Goodbyes: My Research into Life Beyond Death.* McGraw-Hill, 1981.

*Sanderfur, Glenn: *Lives of the Master: The Rest of the Jesus Story.* Virginia Beach, VA: A.R.E. Press, 1988.

*Schiff, Harriet Sarnoff. *Living Through Mourning: Finding Comfort and Hope When A Loved One Has Died.* New York: Viking Penguin, 1987.

*———. *The Bereaved Parent.* New York: Crown Publishers, 1977.

*Schneider, Jennifer P., M.D. *Back from Betrayal: Recovering from His Affairs.* San Francisco: Harper/Hazelden, 1988.

Schneider, Jennifer P., M.D. and Burt Schneider. *Sex, Lies and Forgiveness: Couples Speaking Out on Healing from Sex Addiction.* New York: Hazelden Books, 1990.

Scott, Donald, Dr. *Coping with Suicide.* London: Sheldon Press, 1989.

Seigel, Bernie S. *Love, Medicine and Miracles.* New York: Harper & Row, 1986.

*Shamoo, Tonia K. and Philip Patros. *I Want To Kill Myself: Helping Your Child Cope with Depression and Suicidal Thoughts.* Lexington, MA: Lexington Books, 1990.

Sheban, Joseph, (ed.). *Wisdom of Gibran.* New York: Philosophical Library, 1966.

Shneidman, Edwin S., Ph.D., Normal L. Farberow, Ph.D., Robert E. Litman, M.D. *The Psychology of Suicide.* New York: Science House, Inc., 1976.

———. *Essays in Self Destruction.* New York: Science House, Inc., 1967.

Sherman, Harold. *You Live After Death.* Greenwich, CT: Fawcett Gold Medal, 1972.

*———. *The Dead Are Alive: They Can and Do Communicate with You.* Greenwich, CT: Fawcett Gold Medal, 1981.

Sikking, Robert P. *A Matter of Life and Death.* Marina del Rey, CA: DeVorss & Co., 1978.

Silverman, Morton M., M.D. and Ronald W. Maris, Ph.D., Editors. *Suicide and Life-Threatening Behavior.* Volume 25, Number 1, Spring 1995. Official Journal of the American Association of Suicidology, Washington, D.C.,1995.

Sims, Darcie D. *Why Are the Casseroles Always Tuna? A Loving Look at the Lighter Side of Grief.* Albuquerque, NM: Big A & Co., 1992.

Smith, Alson J. *Immortality: The Scientific Evidence.* New Jersey: Prentice Hall, 1954.

*Smith, Judie. *Suicide Prevention: A Crisis Intervention Curriculum for Teenagers and Young Adults.* Holmes Beach, FL: Learning Publications, 1989.

Smith, Lendon. *Food for Healthy Kids.* New York: Berkley Books, 1984.

———. *Improving Your Child's Behavior Chemistry.* New York: Pocket Books, 1976.

———. *Feed Your Kids Right.* New York: Delta Books, 1979.

Smith, Manuel J., Ph.D. *When I Say No, I Feel Guilty.* New York: Bantam, 1975.

Smith, Susy. *Life Is Forever: Evidence for Survival After Death.* New York: G. P. Putnam's Sons, 1974.

———. *How to Develop Your ESP.* New York: G. P. Putnam's Sons, 1972.

———. *Voices of the Dead?* New York: Signet, 1974.

Stark, Harold Richter. *A Doctor Goes to Heaven.* Boerne, TX: Quartus Foundation For Spiritual Research, 1982.

*Stead, Estelle and W. T. Stead. *The Blue Island: Experiences of a New Arrival Beyond the Veil.* Washington, D.C.: ESPress, 1971.

Steadman, Alice. *Who's the Matter with Me?* Marina del Rey, CA: DeVorss & Co., 1981.

Stern, Jess. *Edgar Cayce: The Sleeping Prophet.* New York: Doubleday, 1967.

Steiger, Brad. *You Will Live Again.* New York: Dell Publishing Co., 1978.

*Stevenson, Ian, M.D. *Twenty Cases Suggestive of Reincarnation.* New York: American Society for Psychical Research, 1966.

Storkey, Elaine. *Losing a Child.* Oxford, England: A Lion Book, 1989.

*Sugrue, Thomas. *There Is a River.* New York: Holt, Rinehart and Winston, 1942.

Swain, Jasper. *From My World to Yours.* New York: Walker & Co., 1977.

Thurman, Chris, Dr. *The Lies We Believe: The #1 Cause of Our Unhappiness.* Nashville: Thomas Nelson, 1989.

Veninga, Robert. *A Gift of Hope: How We Survive Our Tragedies.* Boston: Little, Brown and Company, 1985.

Viorst, Judith. *Necessary Losses.* New York: Fawcett Gold Medal, Ballantine, 1986.

Waitley, Denis. *Seeds of Greatness.* New York: Pocket Books, 1984.

———. *The Psychology of Winning: Ten Qualities of a Total Winner.* New York: Berkley Books, 1979.

Walker, Jeanne. *Always Karen.* New York: Hawthorn Books, 1975.

Wambach, Helen, Ph.D. *Life Before Life.* New York: Bantam, 1981.

Weatherhead, Leslie D. *Life Begins at Death.* Nashville: Denholm House Press, Abingdon, Festival Books, 1969.

Wechsler, James A. *In a Darkness.* Miami: Pickering Press, 1988.
Weedn, Flavia. *Softly in Silver Sandals.* Carpinteria, CA: Roserich Designs, Ltd., 1985.
Wekstein, Louis. *Handbook of Suicidology.* New York: Brunner/Mazel, 1979.
Welch, Williams Addams. *Talks with the Dead.* New York: Pinnacle Books, 1975.
Wetzl, Joseph. *The Bridge over the River.* New York: The Anthroposophic Press, 1974.
Whitaker, Terry Cole. *What You Think of Me Is None of My Business.* La Jolla, CA: Oak Tree Publications, Inc., 1979.
White, John. *A Practical Guide to Death and Dying.* Wheaton, IL: Quest, Theosophical Publishing House, 1980.
*White, Stewart Edward. *The Unobstructed Universe: An Unparalleled Detailed Report of Life After Death.* New York: E. P. Dutton and Co., 1940.
———. *The Betty Book: Excursions into the World of Other-Consciousness.* New York: Berkley Publishing Corp., 1937.
*White-Bowden, Susan. *Everything to Live For.* New York: Simon & Schuster, 1985.
———. *From a Healing Heart.* Finksburg, MD: White-Boden Associates, 1993.
*Whitton, Joel, M.D., Ph.D. *Life Between Life.* New York: Warner Books, 1986.
Wickland, Carl A., M.D. *30 Years Among the Dead.* Hollywood, CA: Newcastle Publishing Co., 1974.
Wilkerson, David R. *Suicide.* Old Tappan, New Jersey: Spire Books by World Challenge, Inc. & Fleming H. Revell, 1978.
Wood, Edward Cope. *A Personal Testimony to Life After Death.* Philadelphia: Dorrance & Co., 1963.
Wright, Theon. *The Open Door.* New York: John Day Co., 1970.
Yogananda, Paramahansa. *Autobiography of a Yogi.* Los Angeles: Self-Realization Fellowship Publishers, 1973.
*Youngs, Bettie B. *Stress in Children.* New York: Avon Books, 1985.
Zusman, Jack, M.D. and David L. Davidson, M.D. *Organizing the Community to Prevent Suicide.* Springfield, IL: Charles C. Thomas, 1971.

RECOMMENDED AUDIO AND VIDEO TAPES

DeAngelis, Barbara, Ph.D., *Making Love Work: Your Personal Program for Creating the Relationship you Deserve.* 5 audio, 2 video tapes, guidebook. 12021 Wilshire Boulevard, Suite 607, Los Angeles, CA 90025. 310-820-6600.

Gray, John, Ph.D., *Secrets of Successful Relationships,* 12 audio cassettes; *Healing the Heart,* 12 audio cassettes. John Gray Seminars, 4364 E. Corral Road, Phoenix, AZ 85044. 1-800-821-3033.

Puryear, Anne, *Surviving the Suicide of a Child.* Audio tape. Logos Center, P.O. Box 12880, Scottsdale, AZ 85267-2880. 1-800-737-9620.

Puryear, Anne and Herbert Bruce Puryear, Ph.D., *The Psychic and the Psychologist Present: The Millennium Tapes, A Series of Psychic Answers to Life's Most Often Asked Questions.* 25 audio tapes. Logos Center. 1-800-737-9620.

Rapp, Doris J., M.D., *Allergy Diets; Environmental Aspects of Allergy; Infant Food Allergies.* Audio cassettes. Practical Allergy Research Foundation, P.O. Box 60, Buffalo, NY 14223-0060. 1-800-787-8780.

———. *Environmentally Sick Schools; Allergies Do Alter Activities & Behavior; Why a Clean Classroom?; The Rotation Diet; Environmental Allergy Control.* Videos. Practical Allergy Research Foundation. P.O. Box 60, Buffalo, NY 14223-0060. 1-800-787-8780.

Robbins, Tony, *Personal Power Tapes: A 30-day Program for Unlimited Success.* Audio and video tapes. Robbins Research International, Inc. 9191 Towne Center Drive, Suite 600, San Diego, CA 92122. 1-800-445-8183.

Smalley, Gary. *Hidden Keys to Successful Parenting.* Video seminars. Relationships Today, Inc., Phoenix, AZ 1-800-232-3232.

———. *Hidden Keys to Loving Relationships.* Video seminars. Relationships Today, Inc. Phoenix, AZ 1-800-232-3232.

RECOMMENDED MOVIES (*see first)

**Ghost,* **Always, Permanent Record, Resurrection, Ordinary People, Flatliners, Chances Are, On a Clear Day You Can See Forever,* **Defending Your Life, The Butcher's Wife,* **The Dead Poet's Society, Dead Again,* **Oh God, House of Spirits, Audrey Rose*

Anne Puryear invites you to write and share your stories with her on ways you have handled your grief after the death of a child or loved one, and any experiences of after-death communications you may have had with them since they died.

Anne and her husband, Dr. Herbert Bruce Puryear, are founders and directors of The Logos Center, a nonprofit research, holistic, and educational center with a nondenominational interfaith church. Anne is the president of The Stephen Christopher Foundation, which is being formed to distribute videos and materials about suicide prevention and to provide help for survivors of suicide.

For more information on books, tapes, and videos, to receive the monthly Logos Journal with articles by the Puryears, to be on our free mailing list, or to contact Anne, write or call:

The Logos Center
P.O. Box 12880
Scottsdale, Arizona 85267-2880

Telephone: 602-483-8777
FAX: 602-483-8494

Visit our web site at:
http://www.logoscenter.org
and e-mail us at: email@logoscenter.org

CPSIA information can be obtained
at www.ICGtesting.com
Printed in the USA
LVHW041206261221
707152LV00005B/790

9 780671 536640